Harvard Studies in Business History · 50

Published with the support of the Harvard Business School

Edited by Thomas K. McCraw

Isidor Straus Professor of Business History

Graduate School of Business Administration

George F. Baker Foundation

Harvard University

A Culture of Credit

Embedding Trust and Transparency in American Business

Rowena Olegario

Harvard University Press

Cambridge, Massachusetts, and London, England | 2006

Library of Congress Cataloging-in-Publication Data

Olegario, Rowena.
  A culture of credit : embedding trust and transparency in American
business / Rowena Olegario.
    p. cm. — (Harvard studies in business history ; 50)
  Includes bibliographical references and index.
  ISBN-13: 978-0-674-02340-6
  ISBN-10: 0-674-02340-4
    1. Commercial credit—United States—History—19th century.
  2. Mercantile system—United States—19th century.   3. Corporate
image—United States—History—19th century.   I. Title.   II. Series.

HG3754.5.U6O44 2006
332.7'42097309034—dc22   2006043380

To Charles
with love and gratitude

Acknowledgments

This book owes its origins to William Gienapp, whose chance remark about "some credit-reporting ledgers in Baker Library" led me to the topic of my dissertation. Bill passed away in 2003. He was a wonderful teacher and advisor, and his work stands as a model of clarity and rigor. I am deeply saddened to be unable to share this book with him. Bill was not an effusive man, but I would give much to hear even his reservations and corrections. They were always a spur to do better, and always given with the spirit of helpfulness for which his graduate students esteemed him. I had the good fortune to work for several years as a research associate of Thomas McCraw at the Harvard Business School. Tom was involved with this enterprise at crucial times: in the beginning when I was fumbling to articulate my dissertation's central theses, and at the end, when I needed help refining the book's introductory chapter. Those who have encountered Tom as both editor and friend know that his formidable abilities are exceeded only by his kindness and generosity. Stephan Thernstrom was an early supporter of this project, when it looked nothing like what it eventually became. I am grateful to Stephan for his vote of confidence when I was a fledgling scholar and teacher.

I spent three stimulating years at the University of Michigan Business School as a member of the Society of Scholars. The program no longer exists, but its founders and administrators—Janet Weiss, Gautam Kaul, and James Hines—along with my fellow SOS members—Eric Guthey, Joe Henrich, Joshua Margolis, and Leslie Perlow—created an atmosphere of intellectual fellowship that helped nurture this book. Alexander Dyck recruited me to contribute to the research for the World Bank's *World Development Report, Institutions for Markets* (2002). Shortly thereafter, I was invited by Margaret J. Miller to write a chapter for a book on international credit reporting systems, sponsored by the bank. Along with Roumeen Islam, director of the World Development Report, they pushed me to clarify my ideas so that this history might be useful to policy makers, as well as of interest to my academic colleagues. Their careful reading of my work, and their probing (sometimes skeptical) questions, helped me to place the institution of credit reporting in a more global and interdisciplinary perspective. Robin Schauseil, president of the National Association of Credit Management, gave me unfettered access to the NACM's archives and kindly provided a pleasant space for me to work. Her interest in this book allowed me to extend the narrative into the 1920s.

I benefited from the help of numerous librarians and archivists who oversee the collections that quite literally made this book possible. I especially thank Laura Linard and the staff, past and present, of Baker Library, Harvard Business School; and Travis Blackman, former archivist of Dun and Bradstreet, for his early and open-minded enthusiasm for this project. The comments of anonymous referees of the manuscript and of the article that became the book's fourth chapter were enormously helpful. Walter Friedman and Susan McCraw gave me assistance during a critical phase of the publication process, and I am grateful for their competence and friendship.

Charles Wilson first encouraged me to trade in a career in market analysis and consulting for the more precarious world of academe. His support and enthusiasm for both my career switch and this project have never wavered. With patience, love, generosity, and humor, he made the experiences not only possible but enjoyable. His integrity and open-hearted regard for others, and his ability to combine a ferocious drive to succeed with an almost complete indifference to the trappings of success, are a continuing source of inspiration. For all of those things—and so much else besides—this book is dedicated to him.

Nashville, Tennessee
June 2006

Contents

A Culture of Credit

Introduction

> Much of the business of [the United States] is to-day done on credit
> through what is known as the Open Book Account System . . . Often
> the promise to pay is merely implied. Orders are placed most generally
> without any definite promise to pay. The transaction is largely one of
> faith, supplemented by information the seller has as to the character,
> reputation, financial standing and ability of the buyer to pay.
>
> —CHARLES A. MEYER, *MERCANTILE*
> *CREDITS AND COLLECTIONS*, 1919

This book is a history of how creditworthiness was determined and communicated in the United States from the 1830s to the 1920s: that is, how
what is now called "transparency" in credit transactions became a vital element of American business culture. I am concerned here primarily with
mercantile credit, offered by wholesalers to retailers throughout the country. Mercantile credit was employed to move goods to and between distributors: from manufacturers to wholesale middlemen—importers, jobbers,
factors, commission merchants, and the like—and from these middlemen to retailers. The book is much less concerned with bank or consumer
credit.

I begin with six propositions corresponding roughly with the six chapters of the book:

First, British assumptions and customs crossed the Atlantic and became
embedded in American trade practices. They included a strong willingness
to use mercantile credit as a way to make up for the lack of specie (coined
money) and as a means to attract and keep customers in a competitive
business environment. Mercantile credit tended to bind sellers and buyers
together in a trading relationship characterized by mutual flexibility—an
especially important quality in an unstable and undeveloped economy.

Second, the credit-reporting firm (the best-known being Dun and
Bradstreet) was invented in the United States. It represented a radical
break from traditional closed networks, both in the United States and
other countries. This new institution changed the cultural assumptions
about business transparency.

Third, nineteenth-century creditors used a method for assessing risk that was based on a narrow, specific set of "character" traits, all of which gave an indication of borrowers' ability and willingness to pay their debts in a timely manner. Credit reporters did not tend to scrutinize other traits, such as church attendance, sexual behavior, or membership in organizations, that were purely social or political in nature. Gender was central to credit appraisals; some criteria—most notably the quality known as "energy," or the tendency to be aggressively enterprising—were valued differently in men than in women. For blacks, race was a fundamental criterion, and it was clearly indicated in nearly all the credit reports on black enterprises. But assessments of gender and race were subject to the larger set of traits—honesty, punctuality, sobriety, and thrift being the most important—that were used to assess all businesspeople.

Fourth, ideas about transparency were resisted by many in the business community. A case study of American Jewish merchants reveals how the increasingly powerful credit-reporting agencies declined to grant legitimacy to closed networks and "secretive" business practices.

Fifth, the idea of transparency took several decades to attain maturity and legitimacy. In the 1870s and 1880s, growing numbers of subscribers and increasingly favorable court decisions signaled an important shift in attitudes: the desire among creditors for more transparency had largely overcome their concerns about the strict accuracy of credit reports. In 1896 the establishment of the National Association of Credit Men (NACM) marked the professionalization of the credit-granting function. The new association officially endorsed the move toward greater transparency, and it lobbied for more sharing of debtors' payment records among creditors. After World War I, and despite much internal debate, the association succeeded in establishing a national bureau in Saint Louis for the exchange of domestic credit information and the Foreign Credit Interchange Bureau for suppliers wishing to sell internationally.

Finally—and here I leave the historical account and speculate a bit about the future—the establishment of American-style business credit reporting to developing countries will likely involve a process of legitimization, similar to the one that the United States itself experienced during the nineteenth century.

Throughout this book, I use the word "wholesaler" as a generic term denoting any business that sold to retailers or other distributors rather than to the final consumer. In reality, many different types of middlemen performed that function during the nineteenth century. Importers were the first link in the distribution chain, and they sold goods in bulk. Jobbers bought from the importers and in turn sold to commission merchants, brokers, factors, and—in smaller lots—to retailers. (In 1860 jobbers handled at least 80 percent of all dry goods.) Commission merchants tended to specialize in one of a few lines of goods. They sold either on their own account—that is, they bought the goods outright—or on a commission basis, wherein the original seller retained title to the goods until they were sold. Brokers and factors operated entirely as middlemen and did not sell on their own account. Instead, they dealt in one or more lines of goods and made a commission on the sales.[1]

Most wholesalers based their decisions about offers of credit on written recommendations, applicants' testimonies about the condition of their businesses, and insights that were based on the applicants' appearance and manner. A wholesaler weighed other considerations, too, including the amount of credit he himself had already extended during the buying season. He also relied on whatever crude guesses he could make about what the state of the local, regional, and national economies was likely to be when payments came due in four to eight months' time.

By the 1850s, many New York wholesalers subscribed to the services of the Mercantile Agency, founded in 1841 by abolitionist Lewis Tappan. The Merchantile Agency later evolved into Dun and Bradstreet, the largest institution of its kind in the world. In its early years, the firm provided to subscribers confidential credit reports on what was known as the "country trade"—retail merchants operating in small towns and villages throughout the United States and its territories. No written assessments were provided. Instead, wholesalers dispatched their "confidential clerks" to the offices of the Mercantile Agency, located on the corner of Hanover and Exchange streets in lower Manhattan. Agency clerks read the information contained in large, sheepskin-bound ledgers to the wholesalers' clerks, who scribbled the sometimes patchy bits of data into small notebooks to take back to their employers.[2] As the system grew and became more sophisticated, the credit ratings of individual buyers could be checked by referring to a published volume. The Bradstreet agency, an early competitor of the Mercantile Agency, issued the first such reference book in 1857.

It was not by accident that firms such as the Mercantile Agency first appeared in New York. (Bradstreet moved there from Cincinnati in 1855.) In the 1850s New York City handled five-sixths of the country's textile imports, or about $100 million out of a national total of $120 million. So complete was New York's dominance that even the New England textile manufacturers sent a large portion of their goods there rather than to nearby Boston. Drawn by the unmatched assortment of clothing and textiles, the country merchants took the opportunity to stock up on other items demanded by their customers back home, including dry goods, groceries, hardware, iron and crockery, drugs, hats, shoes, books, millinery, jewelry, saddles, and hides.[3]

Financial information provided by credit applicants was restricted to their "worth," a vague figure based on the "unencumbered" real estate, cash, personal property, and merchandise they owned. Wholesalers in New York and other large cities knew that applicants needed a quick response but verifying an individual's credit history was difficult and time-consuming. Although the telegraph was in wide use by the 1850s, it was neither cheap nor convenient enough to use for routine credit investigations.[4] Nor were there wholesaler associations that shared information on customers' payment histories among members. Even checking references located in the same city as the wholesaler was out of the question. Few wholesalers could spare their own or their clerks' time for such errands, and fellow suppliers were themselves likely to be too busy to cooperate fully. Obviously, checking out-of-town references would take even longer—weeks, perhaps even months.

The question facing any wholesaler was simple but critical: which applicants deserved credit? The answer could be none, some, or all. But any decision involved risk, because almost every potential customer presented at least some cause for concern. Very few applicants could be rated "A-1," a designation reserved for those who had superlative reputations and who already possessed substantial wealth. Yet it was never in the wholesaler's best interest to reject all applicants who failed to conform to an ideal standard of creditworthiness. Doing so would have been tantamount to commercial suicide by the wholesaler. During periods of strong business confidence, an unsuccessful applicant could likely find credit with another of New York's many wholesale houses. A city directory published in 1846 listed 91 wholesalers specializing in dry goods, 86 in flour and other produce, 8 in domestic hardware, and 317 in "general lines." Even taking into account the businesses that appeared in more than one category and were therefore counted twice, these numbers represented an impressive array of suppliers and potential creditors; and, as was true of all city business directories of the period, the lists were by no means exhaustive. Of the hundreds of wholesalers operating in New York City, many could be found who were not meticulous in their investigations or who were more willing to take risks on new applicants. Several even sent "drummers" to the city's hotels to solicit business from visiting country merchants.[5]

Aggressively recruiting new customers could be a useful strategy because, as every wholesaler knew, no customer base was completely stable. Most retail businesses did not last long. They either failed outright, or their owners decided for various personal reasons to close up shop. So, although a wholesaler might have a core group of reliable customers who accounted for a large portion of its sales, it could never take them for granted. "The circumstances of our present business," the *Philadelphia Merchant* observed in 1856, "would absolutely compel wholesale dealers to solicit trade. The supply of goods of every variety is abundant, in our Eastern marts, for the wants of our whole country—the capital invested in trade is immense, and the number of people engaged in business so great that competition in every branch of trade is inevitable. All are anxious to sell, of course—to secure and retain good customers."[6] A wholesaler wishing to prosper, therefore, continually had to replace the customers it lost through attrition and competition and to risk extending credit to individuals who might or might not become repeat customers. Was the risk of not getting paid worth losing a new customer—even one with a flawed credit record?

The decision to extend credit, moreover, had to be revisited throughout the duration of the trading relationship. Because economic and trade conditions changed constantly, so too did the risk. Creditors were obliged to monitor their accounts and take appropriate actions based on the circumstances of specific debtors. Many elements determined whether the wholesaler would prosper: his ability to make quick and accurate decisions about applicants' creditworthiness at the point of sale, his effective monitoring of the riskiness of the accounts throughout the trading relationship, and his collection of payments in a timely manner.

During the spring and fall buying seasons, wholesalers collectively made thousands of decisions involving mercantile credit every day. By the mid-nineteenth century, the American economy spanned the country and encompassed hundreds of new towns and villages. The rapidly expanding population clamored for store-bought goods. Sensing opportunity, numerous individuals set up stores to fill the demand. Some were experienced and able, others considerably less so. But almost all applied to buy goods on credit from wholesalers who were obliged to decide, in the lingo of nineteenth-century commerce, whether or not to "trust" them.

"Trust" and "Transparency"

In the burgeoning American economy of the nineteenth century, "trust" did not refer primarily to the personal ties that gave members of small and tightly knit groups the confidence to trade with one another. Instead, as business writers of the time understood the term, trust denoted the willingness of creditors to risk their capital on potential borrowers who might not be well known to them and who might or might not become repeat customers. Trust was a desirable virtue not only because it cemented the bonds between citizens but also because its existence resulted in higher levels of commerce. The prominent lawyer Daniel Lord expressed this idea in a lecture he gave at the Mercantile Library Association of New York in 1839: "In the operations of a rich and rapid commerce, great confidence must be often reposed in others, without the minute caution necessary to a perfect protection against fraud or unfairness. Commerce . . . is unwilling to linger at every stopping place, to turn from every small obstacle and to distrust every one whom she meets. She fears that were she obliged so to do, one half of her vigor would be lost."[7] In other words, trust was a functional component of the entire national economy.

Information was vital to the establishment and maintenance of trust. Today mechanisms that facilitate the sharing of credit information include credit-reporting agencies, credit information bureaus, and trade associations. In the United States, the credit-reporting agency (or, more correctly, the credit-reporting firm) was the first to appear in the 1830s. Precisely why it was able to take root and flourish on American soil had to do with a combination of historical factors. Most important were the country's high immigration rate, its recent settlement, and the high geographical mobility of its population, all of which discouraged stable information networks from forming.

In Britain, the country whose business assumptions and practices most closely resembled those of the United States, credit reporting was done by trade protection societies. These were closed groups—such as the Society of Guardians for the Protection of Trade against Swindlers and Sharpers, established in London in 1776—whose members agreed to provide information exclusively to other members on a confidential and not-for-profit basis. The United States, by contrast, developed a system of credit reporting in which information on individuals and businesses throughout the country was collected and disseminated by profit-seeking firms. They made their products and services available to any creditor willing to pay for them. Rather than cooperating with one another (as the British societies eventually did), American firms competed for subscribers.

The new organizations relied on existing and widely held business norms for their method of risk assessment. To gauge the trustworthiness of borrowers, the agencies adopted the qualitative standards on which Anglo-American creditors had long depended. These standards were expressed in a language steeped in assumptions about correct moral behavior. Yet, crucially, the criteria the agencies used were not broad and vague but narrow and precise. In addition to considering individuals' capital resources and their business skills and experience ("capacity"), the agencies sought to discover whether individuals were honest or dishonest, punctual or tardy with payments, thrifty or extravagant, energetic or slothful, focused or unfocused. Agencies inquired about a borrower's vices but restricted the inquiry largely to drinking and gambling. Agencies wanted to know, too, about the borrower's age and marital status. All of these traits had one thing in common: they tended to affect borrowers' liquidity and their perceived willingness to pay their debts in a timely manner. Character traits that had little bearing on liquidity—for example, church attendance—were seldom noted. Knowing how to read the specific signs allowed creditors to gauge the risk that particular individuals presented.

The criteria functioned as a set of clear, simple, and consistent rules by which to calculate risk—qualities that were critical to their wide application. The rules became self-reinforcing: the more people relied on them, the more indispensable they were perceived to be. Nor did the method change markedly over the course of the nineteenth century. Analyzing the credit reports and business literature from the 1830s to the end of the century leaves one with a striking impression of continuity: a merchant in 1830 would have had little trouble grasping the method for assessing risk that credit manuals began to formalize and codify only toward the end of the century.

Shared rules and norms arise most easily in homogeneous societies. In countries populated by recent immigrants, the process of achieving a shared culture can involve a high degree of coercion. American creditors and agencies pressured all credit applicants to prove their adherence to certain business norms. In addition to honest behavior and punctual payment of debts, the norms increasingly included the idea that individuals should make their financial statements and record of past behavior available to both current and prospective creditors. Business owners, in other words, were forced to make their situations more transparent. Nineteenth-century businesspeople did not use the term "transparency"; in this work, I use it mainly in the sense provided by one reliable Web-based dictionary: "the full, accurate, and timely disclosure of information."[8] Yet transparency implies something more. As the recent history of markets and public institutions suggests, the term does not refer merely to the availability of more or better information. Rather, transparency is achieved only after prolonged negotiation between those seeking information and those providing it. The former most often employ coercion and persuasion to overcome the resistance of the latter.

Such was the case with mercantile creditors, credit-reporting firms, and business owners in the United States. Whereas ideas about mercantile honesty, punctuality, and thrift were uncontroversial, there arose strong opposition to the idea of making widely available information that traditionally had been private.[9] The resistance was partly sectional in nature, for mercantile creditors and credit-reporting firms were overwhelmingly located in the northeast. Southern newspapers were particularly vehement in denouncing the new credit-reporting agencies as instruments of espionage. In part, too, the reluctance to share information was rooted in a traditional sense of propriety and independence—the idea that individuals' conduct of their business and personal lives should not be subjected to scrutiny by outside parties.

Resistance also had an ethno-religious dimension, especially among immigrant Jewish merchants, the only group that succeeded in establishing its own systems of mercantile distribution. Jewish businessmen tended to balk at answering the prying questions of credit agency correspondents and reporters. Preferring opacity and closed networks, Jewish merchants frequently declined to share information on their finances and operations, and their reputations suffered accordingly. (When Jewish businesspeople did cooperate, the reports on their businesses typically became more positive.)

Ultimately, the powerful entities located in the country's largest commercial centers succeeded in imposing their values and methods on a populace too weak to resist. This historical phenomenon might accurately be labeled hegemonic; yet it is hard to deny that a shared way of doing business can have enormous benefits. Reduced transaction costs are only the most obvious. Equally important, a business culture that relies on widely held norms and rules rather than personal ties and develops a willingness to make information widely available possesses the advantage of scalability: the standards can be used to assess a wide array of trading partners outside of one's own family, religious or ethnic group, or other narrow network.

Theoretically, a market based on a shared set of rules rather than on closed networks should experience increased trade because the number of potential trading partners rises.

The Nature of Mercantile Credit

During the nineteenth century, wholesaling middlemen accounted for the vast majority of mercantile credit. With increased industrialization, wholesalers began to decline in importance, and the credit advanced by and between manufacturers began to account for a larger part.[10]

Mercantile credit was not the loan of money but, rather, the advancement of goods to a buyer in exchange for the promise to pay at some future date. Terms were determined by the custom governing particular lines of trade. The credit could take the form of an informal notation on the seller's books (known as open-account or book credit) or could be formalized as promissory notes, bonds, or bills of exchange.[11] In most cases, the buyer made no down payment, and the goods were not backed by collateral. Mercantile creditors were thus "unsecured," meaning that, legally, their claims ranked behind those of banks and other secured lenders and were among the last to be paid in the event of legal proceedings. Although mercantile creditors could reclaim the unsold merchandise if the buyer defaulted and try to sell the goods themselves, they realized only a small fraction of the goods' value in this kind of sale. Creditors also paid the legal and other costs for collecting bad debts, which further diminished the amount they could recover from a defaulting customer.

Given the risks, why did so many sellers advance credit? The answer is that they had little choice. Sellers might have preferred to operate on a strict cash-and-carry policy but many consumers worked in agriculture, and they needed time to earn money before they could pay retailers for the goods. Credit terms typically ranged from four months to a year or longer, giving farmers time to harvest and market their crops and then pay their own retail creditors, who in turn became able to pay the wholesalers.

The business records of storekeepers in the Old South reveal that between two-thirds and three-quarters of their goods were sold on credit to farmers. The ratio of cash to credit sales could change depending on the season—buying on credit was more dominant during the fall and spring, while cash sales increased during the summer—but credit sales typically prevailed. Attempts to change to a strict cash policy were periodically made, but they invariably did not last, even when retailers offered steep discounts for cash purchases. (Some "cash" customers, moreover, actually paid with produce, goods, or services.)[12]

The idea that credit was an integral part of sales explains why mercantile creditors tended not to charge interest explicitly during the agreed-upon period of the loan. The fact that much lending took the form of book debt, an informal and unstructured arrangement, also discouraged the charging of interest. Instead, sellers implicitly factored the costs of selling on credit into the price of goods and charged interest explicitly only if the debtor missed the payment date.[13] Even then, sellers tended to charge a relatively low rate. When the economy matured and the amount of surplus cash increased, custom and competitive pressures continued to embed mercantile credit into the selling process.

Antebellum Americans fully recognized their peculiarly high dependence on credit: "In every commercial country there is necessarily a system of credit," observed one manual on bankruptcy, published in Boston in 1835, "and in no country has personal enterprise . . . pushed this system to a greater extent, than has been witnessed in the United States."[14] "We all owe each other," stated another observer in the 1850s, "and so far is it possible for us to live on mere credit and nothing else, that when a great merchant fails, nobody is astonished that for years he has been sustaining an establishment, equipage, and what not, on borrowed capital."[15]

Ambivalence about the easy availability of mercantile credit characterized the public discourse on the subject in both Britain and America. Yet almost without exception, those who studied the workings of mercantile credit concluded that it multiplied trade. Daniel Defoe made the observation in *The Complete English Tradesman* (1726), as did John Stuart Mill in *Principles of Political Economy* (1848). Mill denied that mercantile credit was capital conjured up from nothing, as some contemporaries claimed; rather, it allowed existing capital to be more productively employed. An individual who has little capital "but who has qualifications for business which are known and appreciated by some possessors of capital" could obtain goods on credit. In this way, his "industrial capacities" were "made instrumental to the increase of the public wealth." The wide availability of mercantile credit instruments allowed Britain to transact an immense amount of business with only a small amount of precious metals—a striking contrast to countries like France, where the "habit and the disposition to give credit" was not as "generally diffused."[16]

Mercantile credit was further distinguished from bank credit by its flexibility (it could be renegotiated more easily) and decentralized nature, which made organized control and monopoly impossible. To a greater extent than bank credit, mercantile credit in effect bound creditor and debtor together as informal partners. The relationship came to imply mutual responsibility, including the burden on creditors to educate borrowers about good business practices.[17]

Researching Mercantile Credit

The importance of mercantile credit to the American economy is undeniable, yet researching its history poses several problems. The first is the lack of reliable aggregate statistics.[18] Unlike the credit that flows between banks and borrowers, there is something subterranean about the credit that businesses extend to one another. Moreover, the story of business credit has no obvious contours because it lacks a focal point around which to structure a historical analysis and narrative. The phenomenon did not constitute a series of discrete public events; rather, it occurred quietly and for the most part invisibly, on the unremarked level of the day-to-day. The currents of this amorphous, underground spring were driven by millions of individual decisions, for which surviving documentation is sparse and fragmentary.

Confining the analysis to the most prominent innovators is one possible approach, and it leads inevitably to a focus on the Mercantile Agency (later known as the R. G. Dun Company), founded in New York City in 1841, and its competitor, J. M. Bradstreet, founded in Cincinnati in 1849. (The two firms merged in 1933.) In the 1960s, Dun and Bradstreet donated a number of early circulars, as well as over 2,000 of the R. G. Dun ledgers, to Baker Library, at the Harvard Business School. Another collection of circulars and other materials was donated in 2003.[19] I have relied heavily on these rich sources, but this part of my story is tilted toward the Mercantile Agency and R. G. Dun because the early Bradstreet files were less well preserved. The circulars, as well as articles in the business press, hint at the existence of many smaller competitors, the majority of them lasting for only a short period before closing their doors. But they left few documents and are today almost completely forgotten. Attorneys' papers, published manuals, business journals, and the archives of the National Association of Credit Men (now the National Association of Credit Management) help to flesh out the story of business credit granting.

The founding of the Mercantile Agency constituted one obvious watershed in the evolution of business transparency. Another was the Bradstreet agency's publication in 1857 of the first credit-rating volume. Still others were the court decisions affecting the credit agencies, and the formation in 1896 of the National Association of Credit Men. Yet to focus on watersheds would be to miss a significant dimension of this story, which was the fundamental continuity of business assumptions throughout this period. What was considered a bad risk in 1830 was still a bad risk in 1920, and for much the same reasons, regardless of the infrastructural improvements and legal changes that had occurred in the intervening years. However much the meaning of the term "character" may have changed in the larger culture, its business meaning remained constant. Judging from articles in modern trade journals such as *Business Credit*, credit grantors still profess to hold many of the same assumptions about business risk as their nineteenth-century forebearers, despite the availability of ever-more sophisticated tools and models for determining and communicating creditworthiness.

1

Mercantile Credit in Britain and America, 1700–1860

Daniel Defoe—prolific pamphleteer, inventor of the English novel, and a pioneer of modern journalism—was also a sometime merchant and twice a bankrupt. To the end of his life, Defoe was plagued by debt. Yet *The Complete English Tradesman* (a manual he wrote in his sixties, just after the novels—*Robinson Crusoe, Moll Flanders,* and *Roxana*—for which he is remembered), contained one of the first sustained justifications of mercantile credit. In *The Complete English Tradesman,* Defoe outlined the critical role credit played in the economic and moral development of Great Britain.[1]

Writing in the decades after the Glorious Revolution, Defoe witnessed the modernization of England's financial infrastructure and the beginning of its long rise to economic supremacy. An increasingly efficient English state harnessed its citizens' surplus capital for geopolitical ends: it successfully imposed and collected higher taxes and established a large and carefully managed public debt that financed, among other things, England's continuous warfare with France and Spain. Legislators and businessmen created more sophisticated credit instruments, practices, and institutions—including the Bank of England in 1694—that boosted the country's already strong position in overseas trade.[2]

Like many mercantile advice books that preceded it, *The Complete English Tradesman* warned against the dangers of credit, which Defoe likened to a woman, fickle, difficult, and jealous.[3] But to classify this work among advice books would be to misrepresent his larger intent, for *The Complete English Tradesman* was part of a constellation of works, published between 1724 and 1729, that outlined in detail Defoe's grand vision for England. Collectively, they constituted an economic and sociological study of the English and the peculiar characteristics and advantages that would lead to national greatness. Defoe unabashedly called for a form of economic imperialism—the aggressive expansion abroad of English commercial structures and culture even at the expense of natives and other European settlers.[4]

During Defoe's lifetime, England's already considerable dependence on credit intensified, transforming its merchants into the world's most sophisticated users of credit instruments. Unlike nearly all of his contemporaries, Defoe did not consider mercantile credit a necessary evil at best—and at worst the cause of social instability and personal catastrophe. Rather, it was an instrument for achieving individual wealth and, even more important, national commercial glory. By using credit, "the flock of the kingdom in trade is doubled, or trebled, or more," he argued, leading to "infinitely more business carried on." A tradesman who began with only five hundred or one thousand pounds' worth of merchandise was able "to furnish or stock his shop with four times the sum in the value of goods; and as he gives credit again, and trusts other tradesmen under him, so he launches out into a trade of a great magnitude." Credit, Defoe concluded, "is the foundation, on which the trade of *England* is made so considerable." One needed only to observe how "in those nations where they give no credit, or not so much as here, the trade is small in proportion."[5]

Defoe was well aware of the many deceptions that occurred in trade. His manual contained numerous warnings against dishonesties of all kinds, including a chapter titled "On the customary Frauds of Trade, which honest Men allow themselves to practice, and pretend to justify." Yet he also insisted that honesty and mutual trust were ultimately what made mercantile credit so widespread in England. English merchants "are rather honester and fairer in their Dealings here, than other Nations, I mean than other trading Nations." Empirical proof of their honesty lay in the volume of trade extended on nothing more than personal reputation. England was a country where "a Man sells his Goods upon Trust . . . with the greatest Tranquility and Ease of Mind in the World, and has as punctual and honest Dealing, as if he had a Bond and Security for Payment." Defoe traced the webs of credit relationships tying the substantial manufacturers and London wholesalers to the households that bought their goods. He estimated that some two-thirds to four-fifths of all English trade was made possible by credit.[6]

Defoe's own experiences should perhaps have led him to different conclusions entirely. As a younger man, he had been involved in a number of dubious transactions, borrowing money to invest in unworkable schemes that included harvesting the musk of civet cats to sell to Dutch merchants.

Trying to extricate himself from the failed enterprises, Defoe misled his friends and long-suffering mother-in-law, in a pattern of deceit that worsened the more the investments turned sour and the deeper he descended into financial ruin.[7] Defoe's novels also complicate his later pleas for honesty and fair representation in trade: both Moll Flanders and Roxana prosper not through honest dealings but through misrepresentation and illicit bargains. Yet, his own experiences and that of his novels' heroines notwithstanding, Defoe insisted that the high levels of trust underlying England's widespread use of credit was proof of the country's advanced status as a civilization. In linking capitalist values with moral development, Defoe foreshadowed the arguments that reemerged a century later in the United States, in the writings of Daniel Webster, political economists Henry Carey and Calvin Colton, and numerous lesser proponents of liberal credit and currency.[8]

British Practices

Daniel Defoe's coupling of mercantile credit with economic and cultural advancement may have been novel, but the use of credit instruments in long-distance trade was already, by his lifetime, a centuries-old practice.[9] Credit instruments, used primarily to transfer funds, were in wide circulation by the early Middle Ages. Jewish and Islamic traders, for example, used letters of credit (*suftaja*) to transact business over long distances. Large interregional trade fairs held in the Champagne region of France during the twelfth century used a payments system centered on *lettres de faire*, which allowed merchants to settle their debits and credits at a later fair. Soon after, there appeared what many historians consider the most important financial innovation of the late Middle Ages—the bill of exchange, of which the earliest version was probably invented in Genoa late in the twelfth century.[10]

By the fourteenth and fifteenth centuries, the practice of assigning (transferring) debts rather than coin for the settlement of other debts was already common in overseas trade. Various instruments—including, for example, the Italian *tratta*—were not fully negotiable because medieval law imposed restrictions; nor did they have the legal protections that bills of exchange would be accorded in England beginning in the seventeenth century. Nevertheless, M. M. Postan's work on medieval trade and finance definitively demonstrates the ubiquity of mercantile credit in England, particularly in the wool trade. Merchants who dealt in highly exportable commodities such as wool, cloth, and wine used credit at every stage of distribution, for up to 75 percent of their transactions.[11]

The total amount of credit extended fluctuated according to economic conditions and the supply of bullion brought in through overseas trade.[12] Most economists do not view these early credit instruments as having increased the money supply. But by minimizing the use of specie, such instruments facilitated the movement of funds among trading partners and increased the efficiency of existing money.[13] By making goods available for productive use even before the money to pay for them had been earned, mercantile credit helped realize what John Stuart Mill later called the "industrial capacity" of entrepreneurs and workers.

Mercantile credit, in turn, made possible the retail credit extended by traders and shopkeepers to final consumers. Recent research has established the popularity of retail credit in England and the resulting high level of household indebtedness beginning in the first half of the sixteenth century. Retailers' account books reveal that many debts were tiny; the running accounts were regularly and partially paid off, frequently in kind rather than coin. Wealthy customers were allowed to run substantial debts before paying them off because tradesmen wanted to defer to wealthy clients' privileged social positions and retain their business. Such credit arrangements could work fairly well, so long as the accounts were competently managed and the economy remained stable. The opposite was often the case, however, and English society struggled to adapt to the pressures imposed by the new credit economy. In the seventeenth century, the number of legal disputes among retailers and households exploded. It reached a high point around 1700 before falling again during the course of the eighteenth century.[14]

Of course, lending of all kinds was also on the rise. Large-scale lending to the crown and investments in joint stock companies led to the emergence of a money market during the late sixteenth century. A century later, bonds and bank loans increased substantially, propelled by the London goldsmiths and scrivener bankers who brought borrowers and lenders together and paid interest on deposits.[15] Even so, mercantile credit constituted the largest source of trade financing. Eighteenth-century English ledgers and account books indicate that the major portion of merchants' assets consisted of accounts receivable, in the form of promissory notes, bills of exchange, and book credit.[16] Banking facilities, in fact, evolved largely in order to provide discounting services, allowing merchants to use credit instruments as money for paying their own bills.

Merchants themselves provided capital to one another by taking advantage of banking facilities to make bills of exchange more negotiable (that is, more widely accepted as payment) and by extending credit liberally, on longer terms.[17] In short, British merchants opted to take on the attendant risks of using mercantile credit rather than forgo opportunities. Historians have acknowledged the mostly beneficial effects of this choice, which allowed surplus capital to be used more productively and stimulated enterprise and change.[18]

During the eighteenth century, British merchants came to rely on long credits to a greater extent than the French or even the Dutch. In Holland, almost all goods were sold on six weeks' credit, with buyers responsible for their own financing. Although instances of long credits occurred in France, most mercantile lending there was probably confined to between three to six months.[19] The British, in contrast, extended long credits to help solve the problem of an inadequate money supply. Interest rates in Britain indicate that money was scarce relative to the growth of trade. From the late seventeenth to the mid-eighteenth centuries, rates were close to twice those charged in Holland: 5 to 6 percent versus 3 to 3.5 percent. Specie, especially small-denominated coins, was hard to come by, leading one writer to comment that "from a Deficiency of Money in our Nation have proceeded the general Use and Length of Credit, which is such, that we deal by Ink altogether, as if Money was a useless unfashionable Thing."[20]

Money and credit became much more available after 1730, as demonstrated by the secular decrease in interest rates: the government borrowed at 6 percent in 1700, but by the middle of the century rates fell to 3 or 4 percent.[21] Yet periodic shortages still occurred, making long credits vital to overseas trade. During the panic of 1772, according to the British-Dutch banker John Hope, no British merchant could "borrow money under five *per cent.* and no American or West Indian merchant can fulfill all the orders of his correspondence, without asking credit of his [suppliers] till there is time to expect his returns." The result, he observed, was that credit terms lengthened to between nine months and two years.[22]

Terms were generous not only because of custom or as a response to the periodic shortage of money but also because credit had become a device for attracting business and maintaining trade relationships.[23] Guilds and networks kept new entrants out of some markets but generally trade became more open and competitive. In 1673, for example, the Eastland Company lost its exclusive privileges in the wool export trade, as did the Merchant Adventurers in 1689. Predictably, numerous new firms rushed into the market. Smaller and weaker than their more established rivals, the new firms clamored for at least twelve months' credit from their suppliers. Apparently, these suppliers of goods were only too ready to comply. During the 1690s, claims arose that the large factors were monopolizing trade by granting long credits. They may not have had a choice; those who could or would not offer long terms risked losing customers to competitors who would.[24] In retail, too, the custom of extending credit became so pervasive that tradesmen who refused to do so found themselves unable to compete.[25]

Overseas trade gradually became more concentrated in the hands of a few large firms, but the total amount of trade grew, with the North American and West Indian markets presenting particularly good opportunities. In 1750, English exports to North America accounted for nearly 11 percent of total exports. By the end of the century, British exports to North America totaled £5,700,000, or just over 31 percent of exports. North America was an especially important market for British cotton and woolen textiles.[26] The American War of Independence (1775–1783) and the Napoleonic Wars (1803–1815) may have disrupted commerce, but they also opened up opportunities for new firms.[27] Credit became an even more important weapon in the competition for customers. A few mercantile creditors, such as the second- and third-generation English Quaker firms, remained conservative in granting credit, but their newer Scottish, English, and (later) American rivals used it more aggressively to court customers.[28]

Reliance on bills of exchange increased markedly. Merchants in Antwerp had enhanced the negotiability of foreign bills beginning in the 1500s; soon, clearinghouses were established in the great trading fairs of Europe to handle the instrument. By the seventeenth century, bills of exchange were widely used to transfer funds, primarily via Amsterdam, the world's most developed capital market.[29] Dutch methods may have migrated to England with William of Orange; at any rate, bills of exchange soon flourished in the hands of English merchants, who made the instruments even more negotiable, subject to a complicated system of endorsements. (In contrast, the French and Dutch continued to use bills of exchange more conservatively.)[30] Key to the bills' effectiveness was the general belief that they would be paid when they came due, unlike informal book debts, which were more subject to negotiation between creditor and lender. Defoe estimated that only about 5 percent of book debts were promptly paid. In contrast, the terms governing bills of exchange were "sacred in trade," their repayment more strictly observed even than that of bonds.[31]

The rigid repayment schedules accorded to overseas bills gradually transferred to domestic ones. These "inland" bills were not widely used before 1650, and even afterward, their use was confined to larger merchants or members of the gentry.[32] But at the beginning of the eighteenth century the legal protection accorded to inland bills worth more than twenty pounds rose to the level of foreign bills.[33] As a result, bills of exchange became more popular than promissory or bank notes in England's domestic trade. Even modest shopkeepers came to rely heavily on them, and the wide use of bills of exchange helped knit together the country's regional economies. The bills' circulation was aided by the discounting facilities provided by the Bank of England and the more traditional goldsmith-bankers.[34] Jacob Price estimates that by the early 1780s the bank was discounting monthly some ten thousand overseas and domestic bills, worth about 1 million pounds. (The actual number of bills in circulation was much higher, because most bills never reached the bank.) Bills of exchange helped launch the proliferation of country banks, established during the late eighteenth century partly to help the existing system of mercantile credit function more efficiently. When these banks began appearing, much of their business consisted of discounting bills.[35]

This is not to imply that bills of exchange were perfectly safe or optimally efficient. The system of endorsement and acceptance, wherein merchants vouched for each others' capital strength, was not a foolproof safeguard against default. Correspondence of the period indicates that while astute individuals could master the system's intricacies, many others found it complex, even bewildering. Moreover, the bills increased merchants' interdependency, making the entire structure of credit more vulnerable to economic shocks. Yet neither the complications nor the imperfect legal system seriously hindered the bills' effectiveness. Moreover, their extended use enhanced London's financial role because all bills payable in Britain were required to go through the Bank of England or one of the many merchant houses in the capital. Thanks largely to this requirement, London came to surpass Amsterdam in the eighteenth century as the center for European trade finance.[36]

Large merchants, rather than manufacturers or bankers, were key to the functioning of this structure.[37] They mobilized the surplus capital accrued in the course of business or through inheritance and marriage, and the collective decisions they made had a profound effect on the availability of mercantile credit.[38] Long credits were inherently risky, but these large creditors helped stabilize the economy by refraining from a too-strict insistence on payments when unexpected downturns occurred.[39] Not all large creditors practiced restraint, but those who did were motivated less by altruism than self-interest, as happened during the panic of 1772, when some 25 percent of bills in the Chesapeake tobacco trade were protested. (Protested, or "dishonored" bills triggered serious penalties: in addition to the face amount, the drawer was liable for interest from the date of protest as well as the costs of protest. Penalties for foreign bills were even harsher. In addition to interest and costs, a charge of up to 20 percent of the principal was imposed.)[40] Most creditors demanded immediate payment of their outstanding debts, but a number of the largest, and therefore the best equipped to practice restraint, relaxed their payment schedules until debtors could stabilize their own financial positions and eventually pay up. Terms were extended by a further three months to up to one year, depending on the line of goods, subject to a 5 percent per annum rate of interest. Conversely, early payments were entitled to a discount.

The collective restraint averted panic and minimized the number of failures among the large suppliers and their customers. Joshua Johnson, an American merchant who had moved to London to buy more advantageously for his firm, arranged with his largest creditors to extend his twelve-month obligations to fifteen or eighteen months and was charged only 5 percent per annum for the extra time. Johnson's large creditors even allowed him to pay off some of his smaller and weaker suppliers first to avoid being thrown into prison by these more desperate creditors.[41]

Underlying and making possible the wide use of credit were the shared assumptions governing credit practices, or what can be referred to as a credit culture. As one historian has observed, weights and measures may have varied across sixteenth-century England, but "the social mores of credit and reputation were as common in London parishes as in rural Derbyshire or the north Norfolk coast." Local courts drew on a consistent body of common law from an early date.[42] By the mid-eighteenth century, bankruptcy laws and court procedures—the critical mechanisms for dealing with increased debt and bankruptcy—were firmly in place.

As Britain moved to the forefront of the world's trading nations, there arose a long public debate about the impact of government, mercantile, and consumer credit on public morals. Public censure was heaped on the new financial middlemen, who exploited the government's growing need to borrow to fund its wars. Unlike the highly taxed landowners, these "parasites" did not pay their fair share of taxes, nor did they assume the traditional social responsibilities of the landed aristocracy.[43] By contrast, the credit used to fund mercantile activities was considered more legitimate; but even so, contemporaries worried about the temptations that easy credit offered to young or foolhardy traders, and they were especially troubled by the propensity of British merchants to be dazzled by the American market. A young man, groused one writer, who "chose to apply for credit in England, upon the faith of having opened a connection in America . . . could get ten times more credit than a sober, industrious man, who confined his trade to his own country." Contemporaries also feared credit's ability to sabotage social hierarchy by creating the illusion of wealth and respectability.[44]

As the use of mercantile credit burgeoned, reputation came to assume an even stronger cultural force. Even "safe" instruments such as bills of exchange ultimately depended on the reputation of the issuer, and merchants' letters from the period demonstrate that reputation remained the key determinant in obtaining credit.[45] The mere whiff of trouble—any rumor that a tradesman was struggling to meet financial obligations—could bring creditors to his door, demanding that he pay his debts immediately. A merchant's reputation was, therefore, literally his stock-in-trade, an asset to be protected at all cost. That being the case, Defoe maintained that whoever "wounds a tradesman's credit, without cause, is as much a murtherer [murderer] in trade, as he that kills a man in the dark is a murtherer in matters of blood."[46]

In the seventeenth and eighteenth centuries, credit granting and all of the skills associated with it became among the most critical determinants of success for British merchants and traders. Many transactions could be entrusted to correspondents abroad or specialist brokers at home. But the one thing a merchant "could not delegate," according to a historian of British trade during this period, "was the giving of credit and maintenance of his financial liquidity."[47]

American Practices

For most of the eighteenth century, the North American and West Indian colonies comprised the most dynamic sector of Britain's overseas trade. During the last three decades in particular, and despite the disruptions caused by the American War of Independence, British and American merchants continued to form tighter business networks. Increasingly, they visited or resided in each others' countries to learn more about available goods and the specific demands of consumers.[48] The transmission of mercantile practices from Britain to America was aided by links of language, culture, and kinship, a legacy that Price calls part of the "infrastructure" that helped foster commerce in colonial and post-Revolutionary America. Among its most important but historically elusive components were the accumulated knowledge, customs, and expectations that evolved to meet particular problems and that became deeply ingrained through repeated experience.[49] Solutions were similar because the problems and opportunities were similar. These included a chronic lack of money, combined with growing markets and ever-increasing competition.

British trade credit provided the basis for American practices and attitudes in at least two areas. First, the British model of strong merchants (rather than banks) as the most important source of trade financing was replicated in American trade. Wholesalers based in the country's commercial centers—men such as the Tappan brothers of New York, discussed in the next chapter—supplied the bulk of the capital that sustained the mercantile credit system. Second, American merchants, like their British counterparts, extended long credits over great distances to compensate for the shortage of money. The availability of credit encouraged new entrants, whose existence stimulated greater competition that, in turn, led to the use of credit as a tool for attracting and keeping customers.

British exporters to America bought their goods on twelve months' credit, primarily from suppliers and factors in London, Bristol, Manchester, Liverpool, and Glasgow.[50] Because British exporters received long terms from their own suppliers, they were willing to extend the same to their American buyers. In the late 1770s, it took about two months for goods shipped from Britain to reach the American mainland; the credit clock began ticking not when the order was placed but when the goods were shipped. Interest was not explicitly charged unless the debtor failed to pay by the end of the agreed-upon time. The cost of carrying the buyer during the period of the loan was folded into the price of the merchandise; thus, cash sales received a "discount." British merchants retained American lawyers to collect bad debts. In Virginia, lawyers charged 5 percent for the service.[51]

Wholesalers in the northern colonies obtained mercantile credit from their British suppliers. Chesapeake planters, by contrast, depended on retail credit, primarily from storekeepers sent over by Glasgow and, later, London firms. These suppliers advanced tools, furniture, and a host of European and East Indian goods on credit, which their American debtors later paid for in tobacco. Along with other southern staple crops such as indigo and rice, tobacco was in regular demand in Europe, greatly facilitating the remittance of payments. To simplify exchanges, some merchants arranged what in effect were barter agreements: for example, tobacco and linen were frequently exchanged in a number of international ports.[52] Creditors would no doubt have preferred speedy repayment, but it sometimes took as long as four years before credit sales were paid off.[53]

Precisely why creditors were so willing to extend credit for such long periods was explained by Glasgow merchant Archibald Henderson. Scottish storekeepers, he wrote, "do not always depend for payment on the real ability of the people to whom they sell them, but often trust to the labor and industry of many, who are in the Possession of little or no real property." He speculated that the reasons had to do with the opportunities open to the region's young men: "In a young country where land may be got at a low rent, and where a valuable staple is raised, young men soon leave their Parents, and marrying, settle plantations for themselves." To do this, they needed "household furniture and working tools," furnished "upon Credit, by some Factor or Storekeeper." Labor and honesty, not real property, provided the basis for credit, which accounted for its wide diffusion and the relatively small sums that were owed. Competition among the Scottish factors, Henderson believed, also played a role.[54]

The large amount of mercantile credit available from British suppliers functioned as start-up capital for ambitious Americans and British immigrants, many of them young and inexperienced. British suppliers, according to one official view, were uniquely inclined "to run the risk, and to give the credit, which are essential to the support of a commercial connection with all newly established countries."[55] During the Revolutionary era, obtaining credit from roughly twenty large English houses was the most common route for breaking into Philadelphia's wholesaling sector. Established importers in Philadelphia saw a host of new competitors appear, funded by the generosity of British suppliers. American importers, too, extended large amounts of credit. They purchased merchandise from British suppliers on twelve months' time and then sold the goods to Philadelphia shopkeepers on terms of around six to eight months. Mercantile credit was widely available as a form of venture capital, and this may well have accounted for the dynamism and periodic gluts in the Philadelphia market.[56]

Deftness in handling credit became an important skill. Joshua Johnson, the Maryland merchant who set up in London, studied the difference in credit terms among types of goods. In letters home to his American partners during the early 1770s, he reported that chinaware could be bought on six months' credit; grocery and lead shot on nine; linen, woolens, and ironmongery on twelve; and silks on fifteen. In contrast, sugar and to-bacco had to be paid for in cash or a sixty-day bill or note, and tea was best bought for cash at the East India Company's auctions.[57]

The American Revolution further stimulated market participation and activity. Petty entrepreneurship, Gordon Wood has shown, became seen as deserving of respect, even encouragement, and writers on political econ-omy began tying commerce to the greater good. Demand for money was one indication of the spread and growth of commercial activity. Charleston merchant Henry Laurens wrote during the Revolutionary War that de-mand was no longer "confined to the capital towns and cities within a small circle of trading merchants, but spread over a surface of 1,600 miles in length, and 300 broad." After the war, demand increased for publicly created and backed paper money to make up for the shortage of specie.[58] Ordinary Americans, in other words, desired the kind of liberal credit fa-cilities that merchants and tradesmen had for so many decades extended to one another. Instead of commercial paper, however, credit would take the form of paper money issued by banks, whether government owned or pri-vate. To Americans of the early national and Jacksonian periods, the "credit question" consisted of whether banks should be liberal or conser-vative in issuing paper money.[59]

Trade between America and Great Britain proved so attractive to both sides that not even the Revolution could permanently alter it.[60] Accord-ing to the minutes of parliamentary hearings on the state of British trade, merchants in Great Britain continued to extend long credits to American customers. The testimony of a Mr. Wood, a merchant from Manchester, reveals that six months' credit was considered short in the American trade; the nominal credit was twelve months. He estimated that for the export trade to the United States as a whole, the average was at least fifteen months, with interest charged only when the time expired. Wood reported that his own firm did not receive payments from American buyers sooner than eighteen months, and he complained that the Americans frequently chose to pay the interest charge rather than settle their bills in full. In America, the debtor did "not consider it any great reflection on his char-acter for punctuality if he is occasionally a few months in arrears for his payments." (This suggests that the charging of interest, far from encour-aging immediate payment, may instead have relieved debtors of the psy-chological pressure to do so.) Other testimony mentioned that Americans sometimes paid cash to take advantage of discounts, but this appears to have occurred only in a minority of cases.[61]

British merchants knew that extending large credits to American traders was not profitable in and of itself; rather, it was "a matter of necessity," according to the *Edinburgh Review*. Granting credit was forced upon merchants "by the competition of other capitalists." The French statesman Charles Maurice de Talleyrand confirmed that British credit was so plentiful that American merchants extended little of their own capital: "C'est donc reéllement l'Angleterre," he wrote, "qui fait le commerce de consommation de l'Amérique."[62] Generous amounts of British credit help account for the continued American dependence on that country for the bulk of its imported manufactured goods. European suppliers, by contrast, were more inclined to demand cash on delivery. Moreover, language problems greatly complicated the ordering of goods for which color, style, and materials were paramount.

As America expanded west, new settlements were served almost immediately by retail establishments. Drawn by the promise of high returns, entrepreneurs eagerly set up stores in remote areas. Storekeeping, wrote one Springfield, Illinois, man in 1828, was "the best [business] that can now be engaged in, in this part of the State."[63] Elaborate advertisements for consumer goods confirm that the American habit of consumption, first encouraged by British mercantilist policies during the colonial period, never slackened. The British practice of "dumping" its surplus goods in the United States after the War of 1812 may have been politically unpopular, but the greater availability of cheap merchandise had a profound effect on American popular tastes.[64] Even places far removed from established commercial centers were well supplied with consumer goods, whose availability was made possible by credit from British and, increasingly, American suppliers. Storekeepers, in turn, gave out large amounts of retail credit so that consumers could afford their wares. One western merchant estimated that he was owed some $150,000 by his customers, a full three times the value of the stock he had on hand at any one time.[65]

After 1830 British merchants established branches and agents in the United States, easing the transfer of payments across the Atlantic.[66] Competition was robust among the leading Anglo-American merchant houses—Barings, Brown, Shipley and Company, Wiggins, Wilson's and Wilde's—as well as European firms like Rothschilds, Huths, and Souchays. Large American importers now absorbed as much as 80 percent of Britain's exports to the United States, and the British merchant houses financed a substantial portion of the purchases.[67]

American importers, jobbers, commission merchants, factors, brokers, and auctioneers sprang up to service the growing inland trade. They brought together sellers and buyers, sorted goods into lots that were economical for both, arranged for the transportation and storing of goods, facilitated payments—and advanced credit.[68] The services they provided remained critical until the later nineteenth century, when manufacturers developed the ability to reach retailers and consumers directly through advertising and the establishment of their own selling departments.[69]

Inland trade conformed to what was by then a familiar pattern. Jobbers bought from importers on six to eight months' credit and extended roughly the same amount of time to the country merchants.[70] Six months' credit without interest, followed by 6 to 10 percent for an additional six months, was typical.[71] Among country merchants, credit became by far the preferred method of payment, even though cash earned discounts of up to 10 percent.[72] Wholesalers in the major northeastern commercial ports increasingly could rely on banks for working-capital loans, which allowed them to buy for cash.[73] In a few exceptional cases, the sheer size of their businesses generated enough cash to fund operations. A. T. Stewart, the nation's largest importer, bought exclusively for cash, earning a discount of at least 2 percent—a substantial savings, given the scale of his purchases.[74] Most merchants, however, bought on some combination of cash and credit.

Reliable statistics on the scale of mercantile credit extended throughout the United States do not exist for this period. In a circular dated 1858, the Mercantile Agency (a credit-reporting firm whose evolution is covered in the next chapter) estimated that 157,394 village and country stores owed an average of $14,500 each to city jobbers, an aggregate value of nearly $2.3 billion. The amount of trade done on credit could be several times the capital resources of a business. Some jobbers advanced to country stores goods worth "three or four or even five times the amount of his [the jobber's] capital," the agency reported. They did not consider themselves at risk until they sold "ten, twelve, or fifteen times the amount of their capital" on credit—a ratio prudent business writers considered much too high.[75]

Until traveling salesmen became more numerous after the Civil War, storekeeping in the West and South involved traveling twice a year to the eastern cities to purchase supplies.[76] One travel writer found it strange that merchants in large southern towns should travel to Boston and New York to buy British and German goods when they might instead have bought directly.[77] He failed to consider the liberality with which northeastern suppliers extended credit. So generous were the amounts that one *Hunt's Merchants' Magazine* writer acidly referred to it as a "gratuitous contribution for building up and improving Southern small towns and neighborhoods."[78] In the mid- to late 1850s, in particular, northeastern wholesalers extended large amounts of credit to southern storekeepers based on the region's booming economy. The *New York Tribune* termed it a common practice to sell large orders to southern firms of no known capital, "nominally on twelve months time but really on fourteen or fifteen months, as the goods are sold and delivered in February and the notes at twelve months dated the first of April ensuing."[79]

The West was no less dependent on credit. "In this country," according to one western merchant, "a universal credit system is pursued."[80] Between one-third to three-quarters of the region's storekeepers bought their supplies in eastern cities, despite the considerable costs involved and the necessity of entrusting their businesses to junior partners or clerks during their absence. Even when western commercial centers began offering more credit facilities, many traders continued to head east, lured by greater assortments, more fashionable merchandise—and, of course, attractive credit terms.[81]

As in Britain, long-term credit from large merchants provided the start-up capital for smaller establishments, as well as a good deal of their working capital. One trader who had operated on the eve of the Civil War later recalled how "the domestic goods commission houses were practically supplying capital for the jobbers, who, in turn, were to a great extent carrying the retailers."[82] In most of the South and West, mercantile credit accounted for more business capital than did banks. Although banks in commercially advanced areas such as Philadelphia and New York City provided both discounting facilities and overdrafts, those in newer regions did not advance short-term loans to storekeepers.[83] Note brokers were another source of quick capital that could only be found in the large commercial cities; in New York, they charged between 12 and 30 percent.[84] Because these sources of capital were largely absent in the newer areas of the country, mercantile credit filled the gap, allowing owners of thinly capitalized village and country stores to grasp opportunities whenever and wherever they happened to arise.

Again like the British, American merchants learned to use credit as a competitive weapon. In the mid-nineteenth century, large merchants and smaller storekeepers alike faced shrinking profit margins brought on by the beginnings of mass production and standardization. Most found themselves unable to match the profit margins of the previous generation. In 1817 travel writer Elias Pym Fordham reported that western merchants "considered 75 per cent to 100 per cent to be a fair mark-up, 50 per cent barely acceptable, and 25 per cent as insufficient to keep a man in business, since other enterprises in the West offered better opportunities."[85] John Williams, an entrepreneur in Springfield, Illinois, reportedly achieved profit margins of 100 percent during the 1820s, a figure that "was not considered too big a profit in those days," the *Illinois Daily Journal* recalled in 1854.[86] By midcentury, however, falling profit margins forced merchants to court trade more aggressively and turn over their merchandise at a faster pace.

Competition among commercial centers also intensified, as new ones sprang up in the interior regions and vied with one another to become gateways to the west. Beginning in the 1830s, these new centers—Saint Louis, Cincinnati, Chicago, and a host of smaller cities—enabled storekeepers in the interior regions to meet the demands of their markets more efficiently by making several buying trips a year and purchasing smaller lots.[87] Storekeepers could now buy most of their merchandise during an annual or semiannual trip east and then augment those purchases throughout the year with trips to towns and cities located nearby.[88] Boosters encouraged the practice by playing up the advantages of buying closer to home. Charles Cist, publisher of *Cist's Cincinnati Advertiser* and one of that city's most prominent boosters, wrote that going east added at least five percent to a merchant's purchasing costs. He argued that "by purchasing in Cincinnati, at a distance so short and a point of such easy access from home, the western merchant is enabled to buy in three or four days what will require as many weeks in a trip east."[89] Many merchants agreed. Although dealers of fashionable goods continued to buy considerable amounts directly from eastern markets, others transferred their business to the newer inland centers. Through savvy self-promotion by the city's boosters, the wholesale trade of Chicago eventually eclipsed its midwestern rivals', reaching an estimated $15 million in 1860 and $33 million in 1869.[90]

Ambitious small towns, too, promoted themselves as secondary wholesale centers for the even smaller towns that surrounded them.[91] Like a number of its central Illinois neighbors, Springfield in the 1840s began trying to attract the area's wholesale trade. In a typical notice, clothing dealer E. R. Wiley invited "country merchants and retail dealers in Ready Made Clothing" to call at his store. "I can make it in their interest to buy of me rather than in the St. Louis or eastern markets," he promised.[92] Local newspapers praised resident merchants for "abandoning the contracted sphere to which their predecessors confined themselves." Progressive merchants, declared the *Illinois Daily Journal*, "have extended their operations far and wide, annihilating distance, surmounting difficulties, and defying competition."[93]

In this competitive atmosphere, suppliers extended credit to encourage larger purchases and cultivate what they hoped would become a lasting relationship. Northeastern suppliers felt the competition from new inland rivals so keenly that many relaxed their standards and began extending larger amounts of credit, prompting boosters of the newer areas to make disparaging remarks about eastern commercial standards. Cincinnati's William Smith observed that "many merchants doing business in various towns in the Western States" could "buy as much Dry Goods in Eastern Cities as they please," even though their "credit at home is, in many instances, second class and in not a few absolutely worthless."[94]

Dangers of the Credit System

The fact that nearly all merchants bought and sold on credit made them vulnerable to swings in the business cycle; even the safest, most reputable merchants were occasionally "embarrassed." Those with strong capital resources could afford a margin of error, but there were few such merchants in the newer regions. One contemporary noted that some merchants in smaller western towns were "utterly inexperienced in business." They were "led into serious errors in buying, and in selling on [credit with] insufficient security."[95]

The overriding problem for merchants who relied on large amounts of credit was liquidity, the ability to pay bills when they came due. It was not enough simply to have assets; merchants had to have cash, notes, and bills of exchange readily at hand. Some merchants found themselves in the paradoxical position of having a substantial net worth, primarily in real estate and payments due to them from customers, but with no cash or negotiable paper to meet their own bills. Conversely, traders who had a negative net worth but who managed to obtain cash to meet their immediate debts could continue operating for long periods; such was the case for some retailers who bought on credit but sold for cash.[96]

Success in collecting payments determined how well merchants could discharge their own obligations. Unfortunately for mercantile creditors, a number of obstacles impeded the smooth settlement of debts. Inadequate currency in the countryside meant that storekeepers often conducted barter with their customers, while paying their own debts to suppliers in negotiable drafts.[97] One retailer who worked in a country store in the first half of the nineteenth century recalled that the business sometimes went a whole week without seeing more than five dollars in cash.[98] Instead, country stores accepted produce and homemade commodities as payment.[99] Butter, made primarily by women and girls, was a popular item for barter. (In 1850 the women of Sugar Creek in Sangamon County, Illinois, produced over 26,000 pounds of butter, an average of nearly 180 pounds per household.)[100] Storekeepers sold the items locally or shipped them to a distant port to obtain cash (or cash equivalents) with which to pay their own creditors. They could not, however, predict with absolute accuracy what the produce would be worth when it was finally put on the market.[101]

An informal honor system dictated that farmers settle up their store accounts once a year, usually in early spring.[102] Yet they did not always comply with the custom, and storekeepers were often forced to threaten legal action. Notices such as the one run by David and Isaac Spear of Springfield, Illinois, could be found in nearly every small-town newspaper. The Spears stated that to meet their own engagements, they "would be compelled to place the notes and unsettled accounts of those indebted to us in the hands of an officer for collection. Many of the debts are of long standing and payment has been frequently requested."[103] The social ties and obligations that arose among people residing in the same community complicated the collection of debt. No doubt many a storekeeper found pleas for extensions from long-time customers difficult to resist.

Out-of-state creditors faced the greatest obstacles in collecting. Typically, they hired a local attorney to institute court proceedings, for which the creditor paid a fee of around 10 percent of whatever could be collected, plus a variety of other costs.[104] Historian Edward Balleisen has outlined the complex and time-consuming procedure:

> In the most common action, a creditor would file papers with a local court . . . If the creditor proved the existence and legality of the debt, he received a judgment . . . After judgment, he had the common-law right to an "execution" on the debtor's property. This process called for a sheriff to take possession of as much of a debtor's goods and real estate as necessary in order to satisfy the creditor's claim, to sell that property, and to transfer the resulting proceeds to the creditor, up to the amount owed plus court costs. In many states, the holder of an obligation . . . could also ask a court to attach the property of a

debtor in anticipation of a future legal judgment; usually such attachments required an affidavit that the debtor was either concealing himself to avoid the normal process of law or about to leave the state.

Creditors were fortunate to recover anything at all. The estates of most individuals who filed under the 1841 bankruptcy law, for example, yielded little or nothing for their creditors.[105]

Other difficulties can be gleaned from an advertisement run by one "Edwin A. Davis, Attorney-at-Law and General Collecting Agent" in the *Ohio Gazeteer and Business Directory for 1860–61*. Davis, who was based in Indianapolis, urged out-of-state creditors to bring suit in the U.S. Circuit Court for the District of Indiana rather than in the county courts, because the latter gave debtors greater opportunity to employ delaying tactics. In the U.S. Circuit Court, by contrast, "collections are speedily made by the U.S. Marshal, who, unlike the County Sheriff, elected by the people of the county, grants no favors, by way of lenity, to debtors against whom he has executions." In addition, "judgments in this Court operate as a lien on all the Real Estate of the defendant, throughout the State, while in the County Courts this lien only extends to the county."[106] Davis's arguments were of course an attempt to drum up business for himself. Still, his advertisement points to potential loopholes and delay tactics available to debtors, including prevailing on elected county sheriffs to hold up collection.

Distant creditors were dependent on local attorneys such as Davis to represent their interests. Ideally, the local attorney monitored collections and kept creditors informed of all developments. While some may have been conscientious in performing these duties, others were much less so. One handbook claimed that attorneys often "neglect to hand over what they collect. They take more interest in their neighbor who is sued, than in the creditor who lives a hundred miles away."[107]

Actions by state governments, especially during financial crises, also worked against out-of-state creditors. Many states enacted stay laws that imposed a lengthy waiting period between the granting of a judgment and the auctioning off of a debtors' assets. Appraisal laws, another delaying mechanism, prohibited the forced sale of debtors' real estate unless they achieved a minimum price determined by a local assessor.[108] State exemption laws were another problem. During the eighteenth century, colonial exemption laws typically amounted to a small amount of clothing, some necessary household items (such as bedding), farm implements, and tools of a trade. In the plantation colonies, land could not be attached at all, while in the northern colonies, it could be attached only under certain conditions (outside of a mortgage foreclosure).[109] During the nineteenth century exemption laws became even more generous, especially in the newer western states. Reference books detailing the exemption and collection laws in each state and territory began to be published as an aid to creditors. However, the state laws changed frequently, which limited the books' usefulness.[110]

Compared to Europe, debtors in the United States were in a relatively strong position versus creditors. States had the power to establish insolvency courts that could discharge debtors from their legal obligations to creditors living in the same state. Assignment—legal instruments that transferred an insolvent debtor's assets to a trustee charged with liquidating the property and distributing the money to creditors—also worked in favor of debtors. "Except in a few states," explains Balleisen, "failed debtors could make a creditor's access to dividends from such trusts dependent on a legal release from any obligation to pay the outstanding part of the claim. In a number of jurisdictions, makers of assignments could even designate different classes of creditors, specifying that members of a preferred class would receive full payment before other creditors received a cent."[111] Because of these obstacles, creditors often preferred to work out a payment arrangement directly with the debtor rather than rely on third parties to collect the debts, even if this meant extending the payment schedule to months or even years. Some creditors who were owed relatively small amounts did not find it cost effective to try to recover at all. The R. G. Dun credit-reporting agency argued that debtors should be obliged to deposit notes that would come due at a bank (somewhat like a modern postdated check): "This will prevent the debtor from being tempted to use money which, in fact, is not his own, but *belongs to his creditors.*"[112] The suggestion was sensible, but it did not catch on.

The Importance of Information

Mercantile credit was a remedy for imperfect and inadequate flows of money. To be used effectively, however, it required the unimpeded flow of another commodity: information. From the earliest days of commerce, personal knowledge and network connections had made up the primary system of information gathering and transmittal.[113] In overseas trade, where personal knowledge of buyers was frequently not possible, kinship and religious ties—among Quakers, Huguenots, and Jews, for example— helped to surmount the obstacles. Informal gatherings in taverns, inns, and coffeehouses provided an opportunity to exchange trade gossip. In England and Europe, guilds were another important venue for transmitting information.

In the late eighteenth century, attempts to improve the flow of information led English mercantile and retail creditors to band together into trade protection societies. Based loosely on the guilds, the societies were established in London and other commercial centers to protect members against "swindlers and sharpers" by formalizing the transmittal of trade gossip. The societies were local in scope and made no distinction between mercantile and consumer creditors. Because of their private nature, most left little or no historical documentation, and some have passed out of memory altogether.

One early group, the Society of Guardians for the Protection of Trade against Swindlers and Sharpers, was established in London in 1776. A surviving list of members for the year 1812 indicates that the society at that time had approximately 550 members, nearly all in London. Members operated in a wide variety of trades, both wholesale and retail, and included carpet manufacturers, druggists, stationers, flour factors, lead merchants, watch manufacturers, and woolen drapers, among many others.[114]

It is unclear how long this group remained in operation, but another, the Society of Mutual Communication for the Protection of Trade (later the Mutual Communication Society), proved longer lasting. Modeled on the Master Tailors guild, the society was founded in 1801 at the British Coffee House in London's Charing Cross. The society's constitution expounded two principles that lay at the heart of all trade protection societies: "Every Member is bound to communicate to the Society without delay, the Name and Description of any Person who may be unfit to trust, for the security and satisfaction of the other Members; and shall, on all occasions, impart, without reserve, any information that may be solicited by any of the Members." The second principle decreed that the society was run not for profit but solely as a service to its members; all expenses were to be paid from a common fund. Three further regulations governed the society: first, that the information would not be divulged outside of the membership; second, that members' decisions about whom to trust for credit would not be constrained in any way by the society; and finally, that no member would give false or malicious information or combine with others to deny credit to any individual. Tickets were issued and a strict procedure implemented so that only members had access to the society's records.[115]

In 1823 John Smith, owner of the *Liverpool Mercury,* called a meeting of that city's businessmen at a local hotel, where they agreed to set up the Liverpool Society of Guardians. The yearly membership fee was seven shillings. Smith appears to have adopted the trade protection cause as his own, for three years later he convinced traders in Manchester to establish a society there. Similar groups were soon operating in Bath, the Yorkshire/Lincolnshire area (centered in Hull), Leeds, Leicester, Glasgow, and Aberdeen. In 1839 steps were taken to form the London Association for the Protection of Trade, and the society was officially established in that city's West End in 1842.[116] Membership requirements in all of the societies were strict, to ensure that information was trustworthy. The Liverpool society bylaws, for example, specified that businesses who wished to join had to be recommended by two existing members. Their acceptance was voted on by the entire membership during the quarterly general meetings. Withholding information, sharing information with nonmembers, and going bankrupt were cause for expulsion, and the secretary kept a list of persons who were deemed inadmissible into the society.[117]

From the beginning, the Liverpool society bylaws recommended that "correspondence be established with similar Societies throughout the Kingdom," indicating that national coverage was an early goal.[118] Some sharing of information appears to have occurred in the 1830s, when a number of the association heads (or "secretaries") began meeting informally. The meeting became a conference of secretaries in 1848, and in 1865 the National Association of Trade Protection Societies was established. Its constitution required all member societies "to reciprocate with all and each of the other Societies, in procuring and giving information in answer to enquiries without undue delay" and to exchange circulars with one another. By 1868, according to its annual report, the confederation had "solicitors, agents, or correspondents in 2,500 towns and places" throughout the United Kingdom. By the end of the nineteenth century, the national association had seventy-six member organizations totaling some forty thousand individual members.[119]

These trade protection societies have not been well researched, so it is not possible to say if they actually achieved good national coverage. Cooperation certainly was not guaranteed. In 1849, for example, a group seceded with great acrimony from the City of London Trade Protection Society to form the Metropolitan Institute. It is doubtful that these two groups shared any information at all, which would have compromised the effectiveness of both.[120]

* * *

The practices and attitudes of British merchants became embedded in the credit culture of America, Britain's largest customer and trading partner. The two countries came to share certain characteristics, including the willingness to extend long credit on generous terms, despite considerable risks. In both, large merchants became critical as sources of credit and as promoters of stability, and merchants and shopkeepers alike responded to competition by using credit to court and retain customers. British and American merchants walked a fine line between prudence and risk taking. Although mercantile advice manuals strongly urged that credit be reserved only for customers whose character and past behaviors were known, in reality sellers often chose to take risks on individuals who were new and untested. Their behavior was prompted by the highly volatile nature of the customer base: sellers were forced to turn to unknown or newly established tradesmen and shopkeepers to replace customers who failed or who chose to close up shop for personal reasons.

Mercantile credit was critical both to the expansion of British trade and the settlement of the American continent. Widely used by everyone from small storekeepers to large suppliers, mercantile credit made possible the plentiful consumer credit upon which American rural families came to depend. Yet even with its many advantages, the liberal system of mercantile credit was accompanied by numerous risks that contributed to economic instability. As more and more people became drawn into the credit-based economy, tension grew between the desire to enlarge entrepreneurial opportunities and the equally strong wish for economic stability.

Creditors, especially in large commercial centers like New York City, understood that good information on buyers was the key to reducing risk. In England, trade protection societies were established for this purpose beginning in the 1770s. Members of these societies agreed to share exclusively with one another on a not-for-profit basis information on "swindlers and sharpers." In the United States a radically different model for information sharing was invented in the 1830s. Despite the shared assumptions and practices of British and American merchants, the two countries eventually diverged with regard to the institutions they employed to share credit information. American entrepreneurs developed the "mercantile agency," the forerunner of the modern business credit-reporting firm. Its founding shaped American ideas about financial transparency and helped embed a set of norms into the credit-granting practices of the country's businesses.

2

A "System of Espionage": The Origins of the Credit-Reporting Firm

In 1852, the *London Times* took note of a "novel system of protection" that had appeared in the United States. The system, said the *Times,* was the result of "the peculiar position of the traders in the Union, their go-ahead spirit of speculation, and the wide extent of their commercial trans-actions." Even the name of the new organizations, "mercantile agency," had a peculiarly American ring; to English ears the term referred not to a credit-reporting agency, which was unknown in England, but to a mer-chandise broker or factor.[1] "The importance of such a system in an exten-sive country," the article continued, "where commercial transactions must be carried on to a great extent upon the credit and character of the parties concerned, is manifest, and is another remarkable proof of the smartness of Brother Jonathan in accommodating himself to all the exigencies of his situation."[2] The *Times* discerned three important characteristics of the new institution. First, it was an American invention, used exclusively by mer-chants in the United States. Second, the agencies were a response to the country's geographical extensiveness. And third, American merchants tended to extend credit on the basis of "character" instead of (for example) social standing or membership in networks.

The credit-reporting, or "mercantile," agencies that so intrigued the *Times* writer were a response to a general perception, widespread in both England and America, that the extensive use of mercantile credit resulted in substantial losses and failure. Poor statistical information prevents us from achieving a strict accounting of failure rates during this period, but from about the 1840s onward, the mercantile literature in the United States disseminated the widely accepted fact that only between 3 and 10 percent of all businesses managed to avoid liquidity problems. Period-icals offered a stream of anecdotal evidence similar to the one that ap-peared in *Cist's Cincinnati Advertiser* in 1847: "It is the experience and observation of intelligent persons in our Eastern cities, that there is hardly a firm in existence now, which did business twenty years ago; and that nine out of ten in mercantile life, in the long run, amidst the fluctuations of its pursuits, are broke."[3] The conventional wisdom found its way into *Walden* (1854) when, criticizing the heavy mortgages under which most farmers labored, Thoreau declared that "what has been said of the merchants, that a very large majority, even ninety-seven in a hundred, are sure to fail, is equally true of the farmers."[4]

How accurate the "ninety-seven in a hundred" statistic was is open to question; Samuel Terry, author of a remarkably modern and detailed handbook on how to run a store (published in 1869 but based on his experiences in earlier decades), gave what was probably a truer picture. Terry estimated that only about 15 percent of retailers were able to make enough to quit business by the time they were fifty years old. An additional 25 percent continued making a living and always paid their debts. The remaining 60 percent "either entirely fail, and go out of business, or make some compromise with their creditors and continue on with varying success afterwards."[5] Terry's estimate was less bleak than the 90 to 97 percent failure rate offered by contemporaries. For creditors, however, it was hardly cause for celebration.

Wholesalers and other suppliers knew that good information on customers could mitigate the high risks involved in trade. Obtaining it, however, was expensive. One way to overcome the problem was for suppliers to band together into trade protection societies, where members agreed to alert one another regularly about bad debtors. The arrangement had emerged in Great Britain beginning in the late eighteenth century (see Chapter 1). Another way to obtain information on potential buyers was to hire an agent to procure it. In 1841 New York City wholesalers organized under the name of the Merchants Vigilance Association and hired Sheldon P. Church to produce reports on current and potential customers. The association lasted only three years.[6] Precisely why the association did not continue longer is unknown, but it is likely that the cost of procuring the information became prohibitive.

Few organizations could afford to carry out their own investigations. Among those who could were the large British mercantile houses that dominated Anglo-American trade. From 1829 to 1853, Baring Brothers employed retired Boston merchant Thomas Wren Ward to review and transact a large portion of its American business. During his first three years as Barings' agent, he was said to have reviewed some $50 million of commercial credit on behalf of his employer. (Ward's relationship with Barings was long-lived. His son, S. G. Ward, continued to work for the firm into at least the 1850s, and the system was continued until 1871.)[7] Both Church and Ward were "agents" in the accepted sense of the term; that is, they conducted work on behalf of their principals, the Merchants Vigilance Association and Barings, respectively. Neither Church nor Ward owned the information they procured, so they could not sell it to other prospective buyers.[8] The distinction was not remarked upon at the time, but it became an important legal one later, when the mercantile agencies' methods were questioned in the courts.

Mutual protection societies and hired agents were the exceptions. The vast majority of credit assessments depended almost exclusively on oral or written recommendations by people who could vouch for potential borrowers. Recommenders could be local or distant suppliers with whom the buyer had previously done business, or respectable acquaintances such as lawyers, bankers, and even ministers in the community. A note written by a mercantile house vouching for New York City wholesalers P. G. Berry and Company was typical of this kind of personal recommendation. The note, handwritten on one of P. G. Berry's own circulars, reads, "Dear Sir: We have sold our business to the firm that heads this circular and shall leave the city in a few days. We cheerfully recommend them as honorable and responsible men and any product you may wish to send to this market will secure as much care and attention as if sold by ourselves."[9]

Because such letters were key to initiating transactions, nearly every merchant could expect to be asked to write them, sometimes on behalf of relative strangers. One southern retailer recalled that during a trip through the North Carolina backcountry in 1819, he was continually asked for his written recommendation by storekeepers whom he did not know well. He obliged but stated frankly in his letters that he was unable to judge the capital strength of many of these supplicants.[10] Aware of the critical importance of introductory letters, merchants were understandably reluctant to refuse requests. As Defoe had written a century earlier, "to refuse giving a character [reference] is giving a bad character, and is generally so taken, whatever caution or arguments you use to the contrary."[11] One author of a handbook for jobbers, writing just after the Civil War, remarked that "there are very few men, in certain sections of the country, who will absolutely refuse to give a letter of introduction to a neighbor . . . Men dread the ill-will of their neighbor, and particularly the ill-will of an unscrupulous neighbor: so, when such a neighbor asks a letter, they give it."[12]

Aided by such letters, personal acquaintance, or word-of-mouth information, wholesalers made decisions about whether or not to extend credit, often while the buyer was on the premises. Transactions were settled immediately by signing a note or draft that was payable on an agreed-upon date in the future.[13] Large wholesalers made many on-the-spot decisions; the New York silk-importing business of Arthur Tappan (discussed below) routinely filled up to thirty ledger pages worth of transactions every day during the fall and spring buying season.[14] Because of the number and speed of the transactions, wholesalers were sometimes forced to assess a buyer based purely on the buyer's own testimony, supported by his physical appearance. Judging a man by his looks was deemed a talent that could be learned; the "sciences" of phrenology and physiognomy—assessing individuals by the size, shape, and characteristics of their heads and faces—continued to have adherents until the early twentieth century.[15] Most merchants probably did not subscribe to these ideas. Even so, many believed that face-to-face contact was the best method for determining trustworthiness: "The main source of information," wrote Edwin T. Freedley in *A Practical Treatise on Business*, "is to see the man and hear his statements. This, like other means of information, will sometimes fail, but generally the appearance and manners of a man will show his character . . . In nine cases out of ten the first impression will be found to be correct."[16]

Personal recommendations made up what modern scholars call "reputation collateral." Such a system can work well—as in modern academe, for example. Yet the system had a serious drawback, in that it limited transactions to a fairly small circle. *Hunt's Merchants' Magazine* noted in 1851 that the merchant was "confined in his purchases to a few houses, where he might have formed an acquaintance. If wholly unacquainted, he was obliged to take letters from responsible parties at home, and was limited in his business relations to the few to whom those letters were addressed."[17] Hiring agents to investigate potential customers and trading partners also contained this problem, as Barings' experience confirms. The firm's reliance on Thomas Ward confined its business correspondence largely to New England firms at a time when New York was becoming a more important center for commerce. In 1853 a partner in a new Boston firm dismissed Ward, and presumably the system he represented, as "antidiluvian."[18]

Letters of recommendation became inadequate as the volume of trade expanded and the number of people entering the distribution sector increased. During boom periods, many suppliers preferred to risk advancing goods to marginal or unknown traders rather than lose potential profits.[19]

Some enterprising wholesalers actively searched for new customers and solicited trade by writing to new storekeepers in their trading area or offering to act as financial intermediaries for their customers by paying small bills to other wholesalers in the same city.[20]

As with their British and colonial predecessors, antebellum suppliers were at times more eager than careful. "It is not unfrequent," one writer commented in 1839, "that simple orders on our Northern merchants, from persons at the West, for goods on long credit, are duly honored, and this without the sellers having any security whatever of the ability and good faith of the purchasers." The decision to extend credit to such buyers was not necessarily rash, for the willingness to take risks was a necessary trait in a quickly expanding market. "Caution too often grows into cowardice," the same writer continued. "I have seen retailers refused credit by wholesale merchants, because they possessed but little capital . . . This fault is to be deprecated as much as the other."[21]

By the 1830s, the idea of establishing an alternative mechanism for providing credit information was already very much in the air, greatly aided by an expansive postal system that covered even the newly settled areas of the country.[22] No one knows precisely who invented the new model, but it differed markedly from older information-sharing arrangements such as trade protection societies. Instead of a closed network, the new credit-reporting system consisted of a third party that collected information on a wide array of potential buyer-borrowers; the information was then offered to the business world at large, for a subscription fee. At least one firm, Griffin, Cleaveland, and Campbell of New York City, had already begun operating such a scheme by 1835.[23] It did not last, but in 1841, the abolitionist merchant Lewis Tappan established a similar firm, which he called the Mercantile Agency, a term that became generic for the industry. Tappan bought the defunct Griffin, Cleaveland, and Campbell's subscriber base the following year. As the first lasting organization of its kind, the Mercantile Agency would make history as the predecessor of Dun and Bradstreet.

Lewis Tappan, Organization Builder

Lewis Tappan (1788–1873) is remembered today as one of America's most prominent abolitionists. In the 1990s he achieved recognition in the Hollywood film *Amistad* for his part in freeing a group of mutinous slaves. Yet these activities have not managed to soften his historical image, for Tappan stretches the biographer's natural inclination to be indulgent. "It must be sadly admitted," writes Bertram Wyatt-Brown, author of the classic work on Tappan's life, that he "scored all too well on the familiar checklist of the Yankee do-gooder's grave defects: moral arrogance, obstinacy, cliquish conformity, provincial bigotry, and abrasive manners—with a streak of unpleasant opportunism when circumstances allowed." Tappan's piety grated even on his family and close friends. Theodore Weld once remarked that Tappan's intense zeal led to "a habit of coming to unfavorable conclusions about men on too *slight* grounds." Lewis's older brother Benjamin, who rose to prominence as a Democratic senator from Ohio, chided him: "You are a man of impulse & I suppose will ever be. I do not dislike you for this but I marvel you do not tire in trying to proselyte me." Lewis Tappan even managed to exasperate an ally, the fiery evangelical preacher, Charles Gradison Finney. When Tappan tried to impose his ideas about "forbidden marriage" between Catholics and Protestants by expelling such "mixed" couples from a poor congregation in New York's Chatham Street (which Tappan had helped to found), Finney called him a "pious fraud." Tappan himself seemed aware of his shortcomings, admitting in a letter to English abolitionist Sophia Sturges, "I have been zealous for the truth, anxious for the conversion of man, liberal in supporting the institutions of religion, but have not to the extent I should have done, had that love for fellow-Christians, and that compassion for sinners that Jesus inculcated."[24]

Tappan's most impressive trait, however, was his genuine belief in equality for black people, a conviction that alienated him from most white Americans of his day, including many of his fellow evangelicals. Tappan declined to vote for Lincoln in 1860, thinking the Republican candidate insufficiently radical on the slavery issue. (He voted for Lincoln in 1864, after the war had radicalized the President into issuing the Emancipation Proclamation.) Tappan urged ending the "absurdity of excluding people from [railroad] cars on account of their complexion" and was an early and radical believer in black suffrage, writing to his friend Charles Sumner that black men would never have their rights until they had "a musket in one hand and a ballot in the other." When Lincoln issued the Emancipation Proclamation, the seventy-five-year-old Tappan attended a celebration at the Cooper Union in New York, where he joked to a crowd of supporters that "a white man was as good as a black man, if he behaved himself." There are strong indications that he would have sanctioned mixed-race marriages more readily than the intermarriage of Protestants and Catholics, a prospect that horrified him.[25]

Four of the six Tappan brothers—John, Charles, Arthur, and Lewis—became reformers and philanthropists. Lewis was emotionally closest to Arthur, two years his senior and (for a time) financially the most successful of the clan. Called "St. Arthur de Fanaticus" by his enemies, Arthur gave a substantial portion of his fortune away to religious and antislavery causes. Even more severe than Lewis in outlook and disposition (and, perhaps as a consequence, the victim of severe headaches that periodically debilitated him throughout his life), Arthur ran his silk-importing business according to strict rules of conduct. He required his employees to be temperate, keep away from theaters, and attend service twice on the Sabbath. On Monday his employees were obliged to report which church they had attended on the previous day. To guard against dishonesty, they were asked the name of the clergyman and the text that was read.[26] Although Arthur made his fortune in the New York wholesaling district, "Babylon" eventually grew too much for him, and he moved his family to New Haven, where Yale had long been a citadel of Calvinist orthodoxy. From there, he continued to commute to his Pearl Street store in lower Manhattan.

The Tappans' unyielding piety and arrogance were in many ways their salvation. Had they been more anxious about obtaining other people's favor, more sensitive to criticism, Arthur and Lewis Tappan could never have become abolitionists, a calling that during the 1830s literally became a life-threatening activity.[27] A crowd of rioters attended the initial meeting of the New York Anti-Slavery Society in 1833, at which Arthur Tappan was elected president; the brothers escaped through the building's back door. In 1834 Lewis's house was ransacked by a mob, which threatened to do the same to Arthur's store. Arthur was spared only because the mayor and a body of troops arrived in time to stop the destruction. The harassment did not stop. In 1836 Lewis received a package containing a black ear, with a note recommending that it be added to his "collection of natural curiosities." An overwrought Lydia Maria Child wrote "assassins are lurking at the corners of streets to stab Arthur Tappan . . . 'Tis like the times of the French Revolution, when no man dared trust his neighbor." Her fears were fanned by southern newspapers and individuals who reportedly offered extravagant rewards, one as high as $100,000, for Arthur's delivery. (In a rare show of levity, he quipped that "if that sum is placed in a New York bank, I may possibly think of giving myself up.")[28]

The brothers' radical abolitionism might have been considered as simply eccentric by their fellow New York merchants were it not for the fact that southern customers threatened to take their business away from the city. The editor of the *Petersburg (Virginia) Constellation* urged: "Strike at the root of the evil, fellow citizens of the South! It is *you* who have enriched these miscreants . . . We ought to wear nothing bought of the Tappans or suffer it to be worn in our families." New York merchants deeply resented the brothers' effect on trade, and a few were rumored to have egged on a crowd of ruffians who trashed Lewis Tappan's home.[29]

Lewis Tappan earned his place in history through his abolitionist activities, yet he came to the cause relatively late in life. Like others of his generation who later became philanthropists, Tappan spent most of his early manhood in trade. Beginning at the age of fifteen as an apprentice to a dry goods dealer in Boston, Tappan engaged in a succession of commercial ventures that took him to Philadelphia, England, and eastern Canada by the time he was twenty-five. The peripatetic life was no doubt difficult, but it paid off: by his late twenties, Tappan had amassed a fortune amounting to some $60,000 to $70,000 (about $1.2 to $1.5 million in 2003 dollars).[30] As Tappan's early experience illustrates, mercantile success during the early nineteenth century required a willingness to be highly mobile, and family ties frequently were stretched to the breaking point in the pursuit of monetary reward. But those ties, especially among male relatives and in-laws, were important for obtaining venture capital and mitigating the consequences of failure.

Family connections were invaluable because Arthur and Lewis Tappan were not mere storekeepers but substantial New York wholesalers, members of a fraternity adept at risking large amounts of money in the hope of turning a substantial profit. Importing and wholesaling were not the sort of businesses engaged in by men content to make small and steady increases; these were serious speculative ventures, and only the most steady-nerved succeeded. While running his silk-importing business, Arthur encountered liquidity problems involving dizzying amounts of money. (His brush with bankruptcy in the 1830s apparently failed to instill caution. As an old man, Arthur used his remaining resources to speculate on West Virginia real estate but died before he could witness the market's subsequent collapse.)[31] Like his brother, Lewis Tappan saw his fortune fluctuate along with the markets; but unlike Arthur, he showed more skill at holding on to his money.

Even so, in the late 1820s, when he was nearly forty years old, Lewis experienced the severity of the business cycle firsthand. He suffered serious financial difficulties when the New England mills and factories in which he had invested were hit with grave losses. The difficulties forced him to borrow large amounts from his brothers Arthur and John to pay off creditors. Lewis moved his family to New York, where in 1828 he became a partner in Arthur's silk-importing business. The move was made to help pay off Lewis's debts to his brothers, a process that took several years. Located on the Pearl Street side of Hanover Square in lower Manhattan, Arthur Tappan and Company was one of the largest wholesaling businesses in its line. Lewis managed the firm's daily operations until he withdrew as an active partner in 1837, although he continued to help run the business for several years thereafter. In the early 1830s, the firm had revenues of over $1 million a year, with Arthur himself earning perhaps $30,000 annually.[32]

Less than ten years after Lewis's difficulties, the business cycle dipped again. The panic of 1837 hit the Tappan brothers severely. Arthur originally operated under a policy of selling only for cash or short-term credit (it was said that he had refused to bend this rule even for the great New York department store owner A. T. Stewart). But when Arthur's radical abolitionism alienated his southern customers, he extended large long-term credits to attract new business without raising his prices to compensate for the additional risk. Meanwhile he paid increasingly higher rates to borrow in a money market made tighter by the British curtailment of credit. By 1836 Arthur was already severely extended, and on May 1, 1837, he was forced to suspend payments to his creditors, to whom he owed the colossal sum of $1.1 million. Arthur's notoriety prompted one New York merchant to remark that the suspension would "produce a deeper sensation all over the country than would have remitted from the failure of any other firm." Luckily for Arthur, his reputation for strictly observing the terms of his contracts was well known. Elizur Wright once grumbled to a mutual acquaintance, "our friend A. T. should be disabused of the idea that if he . . . should fail to pay [his] notes at *three o'clock* someday, the cause of God's oppressed would fall through." Arthur's creditors, trusting that he would make a good-faith effort to repay them, allowed him to continue operating his business, and Arthur spent the next eighteen months making good his debts. Lewis never forgot his brother's extraordinary efforts to clear his name. Many years later, Lewis marveled to a friend, "Think of a man owing upwards of a million dollars divided among a hundred creditors, and paying off every cent while money was worth from 9 to 15 per cent a year."[33]

The precise reason Lewis Tappan entered the field of credit reporting is not clear. A combination of reasons probably led to his decision. The difficult years of the late 1830s had strained the brothers' relationship, and

Lewis resolved to leave the firm—a wise decision, in retrospect, as Arthur filed for bankruptcy some years later. No doubt the fifty-three-year-old Lewis's brushes with bankruptcy also led to a desire for a more secure source of retirement income. Weary of the unstable nature of the whole-sale trade, Lewis Tappan came to see the credit-reporting business as potentially immune from the vagaries of the business cycle. He later wrote to a nephew, "In prosperous times [subscribers] will feel able to pay for the information and in bad times they feel they must have it."[34] The observation was shrewd. Tappan was right to believe that suppliers would always look for buyers and that his service would allow them to make the most reasonable choices no matter what the current state of the economy happened to be. Tappan's credit-reporting agency was unique in another sense: from the beginning, it was a for-profit organization, distinctly different from the British trade protection societies run primarily as a service to members rather than to make money.[35]

Lewis Tappan's experience and temperament well suited him to the venture. Credit reporting took advantage of the brothers' wide connections among the dry goods trade and the substantial amount of information they had amassed on buyers from around the country. Lewis was indefatigable and, by all accounts, a gifted organizer who relished the chance to impose order upon chaos. A clerk described him as "a *hard task* master. He has wonderful endurance himself & drives others as if made of the same stuff."[36] In some respects, Tappan's talent for dealing with boring details was surprising, given that his friends and relatives frequently described him as "impulsive."

Yet establishing organizations to reform undesirable behavior—whether it be drinking, owning slaves, or speculating on credit—came naturally to Tappan, who during his lifetime funded or helped to found some of the country's most important reform organizations, including Lane Seminary, Oberlin College, the American Anti-Slavery Society, the American Missionary Association, and numerous publications. In the months immediately before setting up the Mercantile Agency, Tappan was helping to keep Arthur Tappan and Company afloat, wrapping up the *Amistad* affair, and founding new antislavery organizations and Negro Sunday schools. His eldest daughter, eighteen-year-old Eliza, died of tuberculosis in May 1841, an event that characteristically threw the grieving Tappan into a renewed frenzy of activity.[37]

The idea of establishing a credit-reporting agency clearly appealed to Tappan's evangelical sensibilities. In 1843 he wrote to a relative that the

Mercantile Agency "checks knavery and purifies the mercantile air."[38] Yet the man who dealt extensively on credit and who sought to impose order on the practice was himself of two minds on the subject. Equally committed to both his business and reform activities, he embodied the ambivalence that many Americans felt about the widespread and extensive use of credit, a sentiment that also fueled the decades-long controversy about banks.[39] In 1861, twenty years after he had established the Mercantile Agency and thirteen years after he had resigned as its proprietor, Tappan wrote, "The supposed gains, under this [credit] system, are very fallacious, while the net gains in the long run, under the *cash system*, would be much more lucrative to the individual and more beneficial to the community." His objections were founded on his conviction that if "the cash system were generally adopted, more money would be paid into the Lord's treasury, and it would be a great restraint upon the feverish and almost insane spirit of speculation . . . that harass business men, lead to bankruptcy, to neglect of families, to neglect of their own souls and the souls of others."[40] Tappan outdid many Jacksonians in his stated dislike of credit, yet he aggressively catered to the needs of creditors and, as a successful merchant himself, tacitly accepted the need to take speculative gambles.

Early Organizational Problems

"Most showed considerable apathy," Tappan wrote glumly in his diary on July 7, 1841, his first day of trying to drum up subscriptions. Only eleven firms (ten, if Arthur Tappan and Company is excluded) subscribed during the Mercantile Agency's first five months. One merchant advised him to hire someone else to do the selling because Tappan himself was so much the object of suspicion among his fellow New Yorkers. The enterprise lost money the first year, unable to cover almost $18,000 in operating costs plus an additional $3,500 for the Tappan family's expenses.[41]

In hindsight, Tappan's initial difficulties are not surprising. Anyone attempting to create a new market for information has to contend with several unavoidable problems. For one, the buyer cannot properly appraise the value of the information until he has paid for it; since it is an unreturnable commodity, the buyer takes on the bulk of the risk.[42] Moreover, information is notoriously difficult to control, and subscribers can, sometimes unwittingly, transmit it to others who have not paid for it. (Tappan discovered that a few nonsubscribers were paying subscribers' clerks to obtain information for them.) If the information proves valuable to customers, ex-employees can become competitors, who model their services on the successful first-mover. Barriers to entry tend to be low; in the case of credit reporting, no firm owned any patents on the process, so rivals freely copied one another's methods and attempted to poach customers and correspondents.

If the information vendor manages to surmount all of these difficulties, it faces yet another set of problems. As its subscriber base and the amount of information it collects expand, and as the speed of circulation accelerates, both the physical and procedural means of dealing with the mounting information become outdated: ledgers and cabinets overfill, bits of information are cross-indexed to the point of chaos, pricing systems that previously made sense no longer appear logical and fair. Yet equipment and procedures tend to become entrenched, and replacing them can be frustrating, not to mention time consuming and expensive, for both the firm and its subscribers. Tappan faced all of these difficulties in the course of his tenure. His success at overcoming them is a tribute to his doggedness, organizational talents, and ability to select competent partners. Nearly all of his competitors were apparently less adept at doing so and did not survive.

In January 1842, Tappan implemented changes. He lowered his subscription rate and acquired the files of Griffin, Cleaveland, and Campbell, an organization that had engaged in credit reporting during the 1830s but had closed its doors prior to the Mercantile Agency's founding. These moves gained him thirty-three new subscribers.[43] The fact that the information's real value was unproven made it somewhat difficult to come up with a fair pricing scheme. Tappan opted for a sliding scale: $50 per year for firms that reported up to $50,000 in revenues, with a maximum of $300 per year for firms with revenues of more than $400,000. Renewal was automatic; subscribers not wishing to renew were to notify the firm three months before their subscription lapsed. Basing the price on customers' revenues rather than actual use had at least two benefits: it simplified administration and made the agency's own revenue stream more predictable.

Tappan did not have the promising new field to himself. Six months after the Mercantile Agency was established, a firm calling itself "The Commercial Agency" was set up by two entrepreneurs named William A. Woodward and William Coxe Dusenberry. Unlike Tappan, they claimed to cover the entire country.[44] In 1844 another rival firm appeared in the very same building that Tappan occupied, founded by none other than a former employee, Warren A. Cleveland. The following year Tappan complained to a friend that "rival agencies have sprung up & unless we went ahead we should go astern."[45] Burdened by numerous outside obligations, Tappan was unable to devote the time to growing his agency, and it was left to his partners to accelerate the firm's expansion. Edward Dunbar, who had operated the agency's first franchise office in Boston under his own name, later reported that he had great hopes for broadening the agency's services to include purchasing notes and other types of banking business. "With a complete record of the traders and merchants in the country and in the cities, our advantages for this kind of business would be greater than those of any private or public institution in the country. I thought that in time, an advantageous correspondence with merchants, manufacturers, and bankers in England might be carried on."[46]

Tappan structured the agency on the lines of a modern-day franchise, referring to it as an "association." Offices located outside of New York were partly or wholly owned by other parties who contributed a share of their profits to Tappan in return for access to the network's growing scale advantages. All of the offices agreed to share information with one another without charge. Reports were sent to New York first, where they were copied into large, bound volumes before being sent on to other branches.[47]

In setting up his agency, Tappan may have drawn on his experiences with the American Anti-Slavery Society, a national movement headquartered in New York but composed of active local branches. Ironically, these same abolitionist activities seriously stymied the agency's attempt at increased scale because many southern businesses refused to have any dealings with the Tappan brothers. The dilemma appeared so great that his senior partners, Edward Dunbar and William Goodrich, persuaded Tappan to withdraw his name from the proposed Philadelphia office. Tappan did so for a sizeable cash settlement. Information would continue to move between the New York head office and its partner offices and the charges would be prorated, but Tappan would not technically be a member of the partnership. When Dunbar and Goodrich proposed a similar arrangement for a Baltimore branch, Tappan again demanded a large cash settlement, but this time his demand was not accepted. The Baltimore branch was not established until 1846, by which time Dunbar had left the firm.[48]

Lack of southern coverage made the Mercantile Agency vulnerable to competitors. W. A. Cleveland, the Mercantile Agency employee-turned-competitor, took advantage of Tappan's awkward situation by issuing a circular to promote his own firm, urging the need "for an agency that shall embrace the whole United States, so that merchants who do business with the North and South can have access to information from *all sections* of the country."[49] By 1844, Tappan acknowledged that the lack of southern coverage would prove fatal, and he appointed Dunbar and four others to canvass the region for correspondents. Tappan attempted to bypass southern hostility by suggesting that correspondents from that region address their reports to Edward E. Dunbar and Company, but Dunbar refused to participate in the subterfuge, and Tappan himself came to regret the deception.

Further problems arose between Dunbar and Tappan over the rights to the southern reports, which Dunbar believed he owned, having been largely responsible for obtaining them; he had even run the southern department of the New York office in his own name. The case went to the chancery court in Albany, which in 1846 decided in Tappan's favor. Dunbar left the firm for California, but not before publishing a pamphlet detailing his side of the dispute.[50] The Mercantile Agency eventually expanded its southern coverage, but only after Tappan left the firm in 1849.

The firm relied on a network of "correspondents," including sheriffs, merchants, postmasters, and bank cashiers for its information. Attorneys, however, made up the bulk of correspondents, a strategy that grew out of existing practices. Attorneys' papers, scattered in numerous historical collections throughout the United States, testify to attorneys' central position in the commercial life of towns and localities. Those living in small towns, in particular, functioned as a nexus between outsiders and locals. For outsiders, local attorneys were the first and most logical source of entry into a town's business life. They were approached by outside companies for help in selling stock, and wholesalers and jobbers relied on them to collect information on, and overdue payments from, local businesses. Lewis Atherton has documented a number of instances where southern attorneys provided information and debt collection services to northeastern wholesalers. In what was probably a typical arrangement, one law firm in North Carolina charged a 5 percent commission on regular collections and a higher rate for more complicated cases.[51]

Griffin, Cleaveland, and Campbell, the defunct firm whose books Tappan bought, relied on attorneys. A circular to its correspondents explained that "whenever any of our subscribers wish to travel in the country, they will be furnished with letters of introduction to all our correspondents, so that you may thus become personally acquainted. This will be for the interest and satisfaction of both." The circular went on to explain that the corresponding attorneys were allowed to keep all of the fees generated by these introductions but in return were expected to provide information at the request of the agency or its subscribers. Subscribers, for their part, were expected to pay "postage, and such reasonable charges as our correspondent shall make."[52] Tappan implemented a similar system, dependent primarily on local attorneys. (There is no indication how other correspondents such as postmasters and sheriffs were compensated; most likely, they were paid a flat fee.)[53]

From the viewpoint of modern-day attorneys, writing reports for agencies whose value was not yet established, in exchange for possible collection business, may not seem an effective use of time. In the antebellum period, however, the legal profession began attracting new kinds of men—entrepreneurial, self-made, and interested in law primary for the chance it afforded to make a good living. Law was one of the institutions democratized during the Jacksonian period, a phenomenon driven partly by the need for lawyers in the new western areas. Western lawyers tended to be jacks-of-all-trades, attracting a diverse set of clients ranging from railroad companies to outside creditors to their fellow townspeople.

In 1849 a lawyer referral service, the American Legal Association, was established to take advantage of the growing need for legal services and the desire of lawyers to attract clients. The association's aim was "to furnish professional and business men with the name of at least one prompt, efficient and trustworthy Lawyer in every shire-town and in each of the principal cities and villages in the Union, who will transact with dispatch and for a reasonable compensation, such professional business as may be entrusted to him." For five dollars, any attorney could become a member of the society, which published the *United States Lawyer's Directory and Official Bulletin*. The directory was revised annually until the association collapsed in 1854. (New editions came out sporadically until 1868.)[54] These circumstances explain why the Mercantile Agency and its competitors managed to recruit enough correspondents to make the credit-reporting system function. Critics of the agencies frequently alleged that young, inexperienced lawyers were most attracted to this sort of work. However, the example of Abraham Lincoln, who worked for the Mercantile Agency in the 1850s when his practice was already well established in Springfield, is evidence that experienced lawyers also participated.[55]

At the end of the nineteenth century, the newly professionalized "credit men" pushed for greater sharing among creditors of ledger information—the payment records of their customers, which modern scholars now cite as the single most important indicator of the likelihood that a business will pay its debts (see Chapter 6). For most of the century, however, there was no notion that ledger information should be made generally available. Because this valuable information was inaccessible, the new credit-reporting agencies focused on borrowers, and specifically on their financial circumstances and past behavior.

Local knowledge was the most reliable source for this information. Tappan wrote to his subscribers that the firm's "resident agents," or correspondents, "have greater facilities, by long and personal acquaintance and observation, for acquiring the information and furnishing statements which can be relied upon." The local correspondent, "having his eye upon every trader of importance in his county, and noting down, as it occurs, every circumstance affecting his credit, favorably or unfavorably, becomes better acquainted with his actual condition than any stranger can be."[56] The point was affirmed by an article favorable to the Mercantile Agency published in *Hunt's Merchants' Magazine:* "Information of this character can, in general, be satisfactorily obtained only at the *home* of the trader." *Hunt's* was emphatic on this point: "*Hence, the main object, with the agency is, to furnish THE HOME STANDING of the merchant, obtained from intelligent and reliable sources, THERE* . . . There, and there only, can [a creditor] learn whether [a potential borrower] owns property, and is a man of good character—whether he does a legitimate or a speculative business—and whether he is competent, steady, and attentive, or otherwise."[57]

The phrasing of credit reports leaves no doubt that the local standing of individuals was the key to their trustworthiness. The credit-reporting book kept by an anonymous merchant in Jackson, Michigan, in 1861–1862 stated that Lattimer and Stanton, the owners of a local drug store, "have the confidence of the community."[58] Locals' lack of confidence in individuals also was reported.[59] The importance of local knowledge tended to work against traders who had recently moved into the community. The Jackson, Michigan credit-reporting book reported that one of the town's merchants kept "a very good stock" but that he was "a stranger, not extensively known."[60] Reliance on community standing hurt the creditworthiness of many Jewish merchants, because their business strategies often involved migration to progressively larger towns, which prevented them from establishing strong connections to particular communities (see Chapter 4).

Tappan hoped that the prospect of obtaining collecting work would encourage corresponding attorneys to report bad news to subscribers as quickly as possible. The Mercantile Agency's circulars, such as this one sent to Jacksonville, Illinois, attorney David A. Smith in 1846, explained the incentives:

> Dear Sir,
> We have recommended *Mess. Addicks Van Dusen & Smith* to employ you in securing or collecting any claim they may have against persons in your district, assuring them that we believe you are entirely responsible and will execute any business they may entrust to you with promptness and fidelity—*and requesting them to inform us whether the business is done satisfactorily, so that we can use the fact as an encouragement to other merchants to send their claims to you for collection.* Respectfully Yours, Wm Goodrich & Co.[61]

Tappan and his partners encouraged subscribers to assess the attorneys' performance, a feedback mechanism that allowed the attorneys to build their own reputation collateral. To his subscribers, Tappan explained that a local attorney had compelling reasons to perform his duties honestly and competently, for "being entrusted with the business of a large number of subscribers, his reputation, in the transaction of business for one, is at stake with all." Therefore, "any negligence of his in doing business for one, would prejudice all the others against him."[62]

Surviving attorneys' papers suggest that the arrangement worked. One subscriber who had engaged a local attorney to collect payments from an overdue account wrote the attorney, "We have advised our friends & neighbors . . . to send you also their claim . . . & we want you to serve us both alike & hope you will do as well for one as the other."[63] Similarly, wholesalers Dorr and Chandler of New York retained Montgomery, Alabama, attorney Charles Crommelin on the basis of his work for the Mercantile Agency, which was "too correct" to doubt. Like merchants, therefore, attorneys had good reason to build reputation collateral. The need was particularly acute because there was as yet no national association to censure unethical practices or to disbar unqualified or dishonest attorneys. Many small-town lawyers clearly welcomed the chance to attract business from outsiders. The papers of one Louisiana attorney reveals that he requested the privilege of reporting on several parishes in that state, but Tappan could only promise him three for the time being.[64]

For Tappan, the advantages of using local correspondents were obvious. It reduced his initial cash outlay to little or nothing, aside from the cost of producing and mailing recruitment circulars, allowing him to offer the service at a more reasonable rate. Had the agents been paid in cash, Tappan estimated that "the amount of their compensation would greatly exceed the income of the Agency, which, in that case, could not be prosecuted unless the subscribers paid about treble what they now do."[65] Tappan resorted to other clever methods to save money, such as sending his correspondents copies of newspapers—in his case the *New York Tribune*—to acknowledge receipt of their reports. (Until the rates for letters were drastically reduced in 1845 and 1851, the U.S. Post Office charged substantially less to deliver newspapers than first-class letters.)[66]

Attorneys working for the agencies formed their own information networks with counterparts in other towns. In 1845, for example, Calvin DeWolf of Chicago contacted Springfield, Illinois, attorney Mason Brayman on behalf of the Mercantile Agency:

> Dear Sir,
> I am requested by Messrs Lewis Tappan & Co. of N.Y. to write to you when it is necessary to get information or have legal business transacted at your place . . . I have a suit in our County Court in progress in favor of Henry M. Holbrook of Boston against L. P. Langer & Co. . . . on a note given in 1843 for $3,000. David Langer informs me that there are judgments against them for large amounts in the U.S. Court. Will you inform me whether this is so? Who are the parties? (plffs [plaintiffs] & Dfts [defendants]) and the amounts of the Judgts & when rendered. There are two other $3,000 notes still in Boston, *and any information you can give in relation to the condition of the affairs of the Langers may result in sending one or more of them to you for suit in U.S. Courts.*[67]

DeWolf went on to say that he might send other business to Brayman, obviously offering an incentive for the Springfield attorney to cooperate.

Implementing a system wherein correspondents, agency managers, and subscribers cooperated for mutual gain required the agencies to continually educate the parties about what each needed from the others. A steady stream of circulars issued from the agency offices, containing instructions and suggestions, much of it seemingly mundane and based on common sense but apparently not intuitively obvious. The following, for example, appeared in small print at the bottom of a circular sent to subscribers by the Mercantile Agency's Philadelphia office, instructing them about what the attorneys needed to prosecute a case effectively:

> We suggest to the merchant who sends this letter to pay the postage, and to send *his name at length, and that of his partners,* if he has any,

to the attorney. By attending strictly to this, much time may often be saved, as the attorney cannot commence suit without the full names of the parties. It is best, also, to give the attorney *positive instructions* as to the course you wish him to pursue.[68]

The attorney, meanwhile, was instructed to acknowledge receipt of correspondence from subscribers

by the first mail, and to keep his client advised from time to time of the progress made in securing or collecting the claim. Merchants always wish to have their letters acknowledged promptly, and do not regard the postage. They also wish to be advised after every term of court of the progress of their suits.[69]

Self-correction was inherent in the credit-reporting system. Circulars invited subscribers to inform the agencies of errors. Testimony in the *Ormsby v. Douglass* case (discussed below) confirms that the Mercantile Agency consulted with the subjects of reports to clear up discrepancies.[70]

The agency's network of correspondents widened as Tappan asked current ones to recommend others in their locality. By 1846 the agency had 679 correspondents located throughout the country.[71] Tappan tried to recruit individuals who were sympathetic to his abolitionist activities, including the Boston lawyer and antislavery advocate Ellis Gray Loring; the Connecticut lawyer Roger Sherman Baldwin, who subsequently became senator and then governor of the state; and Michigan's James G. Birney, the presidential candidate for the Liberty Party in 1840 and 1844. Securing competent correspondents was a constant problem, and some of Tappan's tactics for recruiting or mollifying them were inadequate, even insulting. For example, he sent them free issues of *Columbian Lady's and Gentleman's Magazine* and *The Christian Parlor Magazine,* periodicals that were not of high quality or that were of little interest.[72]

At first glance, the use of attorneys for both information gathering and debt collection appears to hold the potential for conflict of interest. One attorney from western New York voiced what must have been a general concern: "I think the tendency of yr agency is greatly to diminish bus[iness] in the county. If yr cor[responden]ts make correct reports yr subs[cribers] will have but little trouble in collecting their debts and seldom need an attorney."[73] But this proved too optimistic. Even good borrowers found themselves occasionally at the mercy of the business cycle, and creditors continued to need the help of local attorneys to collect debts.

More vexing for Tappan was the problem of compelling subscribers to use the agency's corresponding attorneys for all of their debt collections. In 1843 he tried imposing a penalty, stating in a circular that any subscriber acting on information provided by the agency but engaging the services of a nonagency attorney was "to give immediate notice thereof to said TAP-PAN, and pay him, in every such case, for the attorney who collects the information for the Agency in that county, the sum of Five Dollars, and also one half of one per cent. of every such claim up to One Thousand Dollars, and one fourth of one per cent. of any excess, on the amount collected."[74] But the agency could not enforce the policy, and Tappan soon gave up trying to penalize subscribers. Attorneys, meanwhile, complained that they were not receiving the business that Tappan had promised them. Yet, apparently, enough of them received additional business from their association with the credit-reporting agencies to allow the system to function.

The growing network of correspondents increased the agency's coverage, but Tappan and his partners continued to be anxious about the quality of the reports. Lack of control over the competence of their correspondents remained, for decades, the agencies' biggest stumbling block. Circulars urged correspondents to be thorough and punctual. Subscribers, stated a typical circular, "will inevitably get into habits of delinquency if they find my correspondents are remiss in bringing up their part of the system. It is for mutual interest that each party should faithfully perform what he has undertaken."[75] To ensure the accuracy of the reports, Tappan planned to implement a kind of audit system, using special "traveling agents." The information they obtained was to be "compared with that furnished by local correspondents, in order that any inaccuracies in the reports of either may be detected."[76] It is unclear how thoroughly Tappan was able to audit his correspondents' reports. He probably used the traveling agents primarily to recruit and appoint new correspondents, especially in the South in 1845.[77]

Beyond Tappan's many organizational and managerial problems lay the need to secure legitimacy both for the Mercantile Agency and the entire infant industry. Even more than banks, credit-reporting agencies were unregulated organizations created by entrepreneurs to meet new business needs. Because they were less visible to ordinary citizens than banks, the agencies escaped the intense political debate that surrounded those financial institutions. Nevertheless, the agencies provoked the same mixture of deep suspicion and cautious approval among those who had an opportunity to observe their operations.

In 1836 North Carolina attorney James W. Bryan wrote to Griffin, Cleaveland, and Campbell that "an excitement of no ordinary character has been created among the merchants of Newbern, N.C., in consequence of a belief on their part, that an undue representation of their standing, and ability as merchants has been made through the agency of your firm to their New York creditors." Bryan had been charged with being a correspondent of Griffin, Cleaveland, and Campbell, and he requested that the firm state in a letter that he was not connected with them. Griffin, Cleaveland, and Campbell wrote back that southern merchants had viewed the plan in "so objectionable a light" that the firm had decided not to pursue it in the South: "If you have been the subject of suspicion we sincerely regret it, as you are not our correspondent or agent & are in no way connected with us in this plan."[78]

Compared to other regions, the South remained much less kindly disposed to credit-reporting firms, almost all of which were located in the northeast. But no part of the country was devoid of hostility against the agencies. Edward Dunbar, Tappan's former partner, claimed that in setting up the Boston branch in 1843, "I had neither the countenance of my friends nor the confidence of merchants, in my novel, or as many regarded it, mysterious undertaking." Tappan himself felt compelled to reassure potential correspondents that the service was not "a system of espionage."[79]

Correspondents had good reason to be worried about how their fellow townspeople would perceive their activities. Being scrutinized, even for the purpose of determining a person's creditworthiness, was seen as humiliating. Referring to the practice in general (rather than to credit-reporting specifically) one writer argued that being assessed

> subjects [merchants] to doubts and inquiries which are injurious and unpleasant; it causes their private life, their business speculations, and their personal and family expenditure to be looked into and watched by others; in short, they are put under *surveillance,* and the babbling of lying mischief, or the tongue of malignant slander, may, in a few sneaking, skulking words, blast their credit, and bring their creditors down upon them, when they are unprepared, and not expecting them . . . An independent man hates this.[80]

Even articles favorable to the agencies, such as the one that appeared in the *Cyclopedia of Commerce,* acknowledged that "to the casual observer [the mercantile agency] partakes of the nature of a system of espionage, seemingly at variance with that candor and love of open dealing so characteristic of our commercial usages."[81]

Surviving circulars record the new credit-reporting firms' continuous efforts to justify their methods to a skeptical public. The Mercantile Agency's most cogent arguments revolved around the increased efficiency that its unprecedented scale made possible. Merchants, Tappan argued, gained significant cost savings, "it being much less expensive for a large number to unite in procuring information from the same source than for each to send out special agents."[82] Moreover, the use of local correspondents was superior to the older method, whereby New York wholesalers sent their own agents to report on distant buyers. Being part of their local communities, correspondents would naturally be more discreet and sensitive, performing their duties "without being inquisitorial and without doing injustice either to the country or city merchant."[83] Yet arguments for the Mercantile Agency's efficiency and discretion were apparently not enough. In his early letters and circulars, Tappan also felt pressured to deny that the agency was doing anything new or revolutionary. He could rightly claim that he did not himself invent the idea of the agency, having borrowed many of his tactics from Griffin, Cleaveland, and Campbell. Instead, Tappan emphasized that he merely did for merchants what they would have done for themselves in the normal course of business.

Correspondents, too, needed convincing of the legitimacy and legality of their activities. In a handwritten letter addressed to William G. Brown of Virginia (presumably a potential correspondent), W. A. Cleveland quoted "an eminent law firm in the South," which wrote, "We have no feelings of delicacy about this matter [of providing reports on local merchants], believing that there is nothing in it dishonorable or unjust to anybody. We are the Agents of our Clients already and for the same objects. This is only an enlargement of that."[84] In 1842 Tappan wrote to his correspondents that the information they provided "is the same, only on an extended scale, that you would give to a merchant [in New York], who should write to you for information as to the responsibility, &c. of a single merchant in your place." The correspondent, Tappan explained, would provide the information to the agency "as you would to [the subscriber himself], as information which it is proper for an attorney to give to a CLIENT, not holding himself legally responsible from any error in judgment."[85]

Tappan no doubt wished to reassure correspondents made uneasy by criticisms such as those in the *New York Herald*, whose editor referred to Tappan as a man who kept "an office for looking after everybody's business but his own." A Norfolk, Virginia, attorney declared in one of the town's newspapers that "to act as a spy" on one's neighbors, as the agencies did, was an act that even a slave would disdain. James Webb, editor of the *Morning Courier* (later the *Courier and Enquirer*) and an old enemy, wrote that the agency was "a new clap-trap for notoriety . . . carrying on the business of a secret inquiry into the private affairs and personal standing of every body buying goods in New York."[86]

Public suspicion was hardly mollified by the high level of secrecy that Tappan felt was necessary to protect the value of the agency's main, and highly vulnerable, commodity: the information it collected on individuals. Until the publication of its first reference book in 1859, no written reports were issued; instead, subscribers were obliged to collect the information in person or to send a "confidential clerk." The agency's clerks transmitted the information orally to subscribers or their representatives. Subscribers who testified in *Beardsley v. Tappan* in 1851 described the process of retrieving information from the agency: "The book [of reports] is kept on the inside of a raised desk on which it stands," explained one subscriber, "and the person on the outside is not in a position where he can read from it." Another subscriber reported that the agency clerk "had a large book before him like a large ledger; he opened it, and appeared to read from the book, or from a paper in the book; as he read, I wrote down on a slip of paper what he read . . . I took the pencil memorandum to my store; the clerk read very slowly and distinctly, and I wrote it down carefully with a pencil; I afterwards copied this pencil memorandum in ink."[87] Contracts specified that subscribers were not to share with others the information they received, and they were forbidden from revealing to the subjects of the reports what the correspondents had written about them. At one point, Tappan even asked subscribers not to reveal that they used the firm's services.[88] The agency offices, with their forbidding counters separating clerks from subscribers and where communications were whispered, reinforced the cloak-and-dagger nature of the business.

The Tappan brothers' reputation for meddling and spying only made things worse. As part of their reform activities during the early 1830s, Arthur and Lewis had organized spy cells to monitor tavern keepers and report any infractions of the law to the authorities. According to his biographer, Lewis Tappan "once threatened a tailor who refused to sign a petition to stop the Sunday mails: 'I shall report you to my brother and his connexions, and you shall have no more of our custom!'" Even Benjamin Tappan called his younger brothers' activities "sickening."[89]

Yet Tappan's disclaimers notwithstanding, the new organization and its competitors did not merely constitute a more efficient prosecution of existing methods. Instead, they represented a radically new model for the collection and transmission of credit information. Attaining legitimacy was contingent on increased familiarity: as credit reports became more widely used, they became perceived as essential to the responsible management of risk. But until that happened, agencies labored under a cloud of skepticism or outright hostility, forcing proprietors such as Tappan continually to defend their methods.

Douglass and Dun

Lewis Tappan stamped his forceful personality upon the agency he founded. Ironically his successors, Benjamin Douglass (coproprietor from 1847 to 1859) and Robert G. Dun (sole proprietor from 1859 to 1900), did not share many of Tappan's fundamental beliefs. In 1846, attempting to reassure correspondents that his abolitionism did not interfere with the agency's activities, Tappan wrote that "sagacious merchants" considered "the capacity and general character of those whose agency they desire in the management of their business rather than . . . their opinions on other subjects." In his early relationship with Benjamin Douglass, he was as good as his word. Tappan was willing to overlook the younger man's strong proslavery sentiments because he admired Douglass's propensity for hard work.[90]

Benjamin Douglass (1816–1900) was only thirty-one years old when, as the agency's head clerk, he purchased a one-third proprietary interest in 1847. Born in Maryland, Douglass was the son of a Scottish-Presbyterian merchant who established a West Indian trade based in Baltimore and New York. Young Benjamin worked as a merchant in Charleston and as a cotton factor and commission merchant based in New Orleans. Unlike Tappan, who never visited the South, Douglass felt at home there; during the Civil War, he would write letters and pamphlets defending his native region. Also unlike Tappan, Douglass found time for cultural and intellectual pursuits, even employing a Jewish rabbi to instruct him in Hebrew and Arabic.[91]

Douglass's patience was tested in his dealings with the Tappan brothers. Arthur never fully recovered from the Panic of 1837. Although he managed to pay off all his debts after the suspension, the business continued on a precarious course until he finally filed for bankruptcy some years later. In 1848 the once-prominent Arthur Tappan was reduced to being a junior partner in a nephew's dry goods firm. The devoted Lewis devised a way to provide his brother with a sinecure and restore his sense of dignity. In 1849 Lewis sold one-half of the Mercantile Agency to Arthur for $25,000 and the remaining one-sixth to Douglass (who already owned one-third) for $12,500, making Arthur Tappan and Benjamin Douglass equal partners. Douglass was to manage the firm and at the end of five years acquire the right to purchase Arthur Tappan's shares for $18,000. The arrangement would have proceeded smoothly had Arthur not invested his profits from the Mercantile Agency in a New Jersey machine-making plant in 1854. It turned out to be heavily in debt, forcing Arthur to put the concern up for bankruptcy sale. When Douglass exercised his option to purchase Arthur's shares, he argued that Arthur had already drawn out a substantial portion of the profits; the $18,000 that had originally been agreed was therefore too high. Lewis responded by suing Douglass, whom he now called "an Old School Presbyterian—a pro Slavery man—and a Buchananite." Ultimately, Arthur obtained a $12,000 settlement, even though he had never played a major role in the firm.[92]

Benjamin Douglass's successor, Robert G. Dun, joined the firm in 1846. Four years later, he and his brother, James, became the agency's resident reporters in Milwaukee. Born in Scotland, Robert Dun was, like Douglass, a Scottish Presbyterian. His parents emigrated to Chillicothe, Ohio, the poor relations of one of southern Ohio's wealthiest families. When his father died, Robert Dun, his brother, and three sisters were supported by their uncles. Although not wealthy, the Dun siblings were raised among people of means and discernment, and Robert remained close to them throughout his life. Benjamin Douglass and Robert Dun were tied together by more than just their business interests. They were also double brothers-in-law: Douglass married Dun's sister, Elizabeth, in 1842; in 1856 Dun married Douglass's sister, also named Elizabeth. Like the Tappans, the Douglass-Duns were a close-knit clan. When Dun's wife died, he did not venture far in search of a replacement; he married his late wife's niece, Mary (Minnie) Bradford.[93]

Robert Dun was as sympathetic to slaveholders as was Benjamin Douglass, and Dun steadfastly opposed the Civil War on political and practical grounds. (There is no record of what Tappan felt about this irony.) "I am a firm believer in States rights," Dun wrote to a cousin. "I think the Gov't at Washington has no right to declare war against any State or States." Subduing the South, Dun believed, would require far more treasure and manpower than the North could realistically provide. He claimed that the agency lost some $100,000 in 1860–1861 because of the conflict, a fact that added to his disgust at the Lincoln administration. Nor was Dun's loathing of the war confined to the issue of states' rights. To his brother he wrote in April 1863, "It is plain that God intended the Negro to be the servant & slave of the superior race. This is as plain to me [as] that it is natural for the parent to govern the child; for the mind of the Negro is as that of a child when compared with the Caucasian."[94]

Dun's lavish spending habits would also likely have offended Tappan. In 1870 Dun bought a house on New York's stylish Madison Avenue, two blocks from J. P. Morgan. Dun had fourteen servants, an art collection that at his death was valued at $250,000, a private carriage drawn by a team of horses, a summer home (Dunmeres, at Narragansett Pier, Rhode Island), and a fine wine and liquor cellar. Dun once spent $1,500 on wines during a trip to France, and he eventually developed cirrhosis.[95] None of these habits prevented him from successfully running his agency. But it is a striking irony that Robert Dun's way of life so often veered from the set of business values and habits that reformer Lewis Tappan had prescribed, and which the credit-reporting agencies upheld.

Although Lewis Tappan faced resistance from the southern trade, his successors eventually built a network of agencies located in all of the country's principal trading centers. The numerous clerks, reporters, and correspondents on its payroll made the agency among the largest private employers in the country. It was run as both a decentralized association of offices, each with its own manager, and as a centralized firm whose strategy and policies were dictated by the New York head office. Administrative talent counted for a great deal, given the agency's unusual size and structure; like Tappan, both Douglass and Dun were gifted managers who responded imaginatively to the opportunities presented by the growing scale of American commerce. Their combined tenures spanned fifty years, during which the United States evolved from an underdeveloped economy to the world's largest agricultural and manufacturing power.

Douglass was much more expansion minded than was Lewis Tappan, who because of advanced age and numerous outside interests did not strenuously pursue subscribers other than large eastern wholesalers, primarily in New York.[96] More exclusively focused on the agency, Douglass could afford to have grander ambitions for it. In addition to promoting growth aggressively in the West and South, he sought to diversify the firm's client base to include not only wholesalers and jobbers but also banks, fire insurance companies, manufacturers, and commission houses. Douglass broadened the agency's services beginning in 1855, when he established a claims department to help clients collect overdue payments from customers. (By 1900 profits from this business accounted for one-quarter of overall profits.) He also attempted to take advantage of the agency's subscriber lists by offering a direct-mail service: companies wishing to solicit new business could hire the agency to mail advertisements and circulars to its vast subscriber base. It was not a resounding success, and Douglass later abandoned the idea.[97]

Dun continued Douglass's focus on expansion by continually searching for new customers and sources of revenue. As the pioneering organization of its type, the agency experimented with different policies and forms of operation, sometimes to the frustration of its correspondents and subscribers, but often for the overall improvement of its service. With few precedents to guide him, some of Dun's ideas proved to be inappropriate. For example, in 1864 he tried to convince the newly established Internal Revenue Department to buy the agency's reference books as a basis for assessing tax liability. A few years later, he offered to market $5 million worth of stock for the National Telephone Company—in hindsight a clear conflict of interest because the agency was also reporting on the firm's creditworthiness. (Nothing came of either idea.) In 1867 Dun published the *Mercantile Agency United States Business Directory*, which contained the names and addresses of firms that were reported on. The volume was clearly meant to have been published annually, but it proved unprofitable.

Both Douglass and Dun positioned the agency as the provider of timely information on a broad range of business topics. Beginning in 1857, the agency used its formidable information-gathering abilities to publish annual statistics on the number of business failures around the country and the aggregate liabilities and losses they represented, which it sent as a circular to subscribers. Additional circulars issued by the various offices featured information on local economic conditions. A number of journals, including the *New York Independent, DeBow's Review,* and *Hunt's Merchants' Magazine,* began regularly to reprint the Mercantile Agency's failure statistics and economic analyses. In 1861 the Mercantile Agency used its resources to estimate the extent of southern indebtedness to northern suppliers, which the firm placed at over $300 million.[98]

Both men tightened the agency's organizational structure. Douglass centralized control by buying a share in most of the network's independent firms. By 1857 only the E. Russell and Company branch in Boston and the J. D. Pratt branches in Baltimore and Richmond remained completely independent. (It was not until 1897 that Robert Dun acquired the last of the independent U.S. offices from Edward Russell, who for several decades had owned and run the Massachusetts and Maine offices in Boston, Worcester, Lynn, Portland, and Bangor.) Douglass improved the internal communication within the firm by requiring branch offices to exchange information with each other rather than exclusively with New York; he even sued William Goodrich, the Philadelphia office manager, for refusing to comply. Yet despite all of the changes, the accounting system that Tappan had established remained essentially intact. The agency remained an association of independent units but one that required free interchange of information among them. Later in the century, this posed a hardship in the West for smaller offices, which had fewer staff and larger territories to cover.[99]

In the mid-1850s, Douglass began adding more paid, full-time reporters, which generally improved the quality and reliability of the information the agency provided to subscribers. But maintaining the quality and timeliness of the information continued to be difficult; like Tappan, Douglass exhorted correspondents and branch managers to be more thorough. "Many of our correspondents," stated a typical circular, "would they extend their inquiries a little further . . . would often find that many new traders have commenced business since the dates of their last reports."[100] Another declared, "The effect upon our merchants of giving [subscribers] a *ready reply* about a *new concern* is wonderfully favorable. It compels the inference that our advisers are prompt, watchful, and energetic men, and that subscribers' interests are in safe and worthy hands."[101] The papers of Elijah Morgan, an attorney in Ann Arbor, Michigan, reveal that other collection agencies and credit-reporting firms sent similar letters. In 1858 the American Collection Agency reminded Morgan of his failure to answer four previous letters. Tappan and McKillop also wrote to Morgan, stating that a subscriber who had sent him a mortgage for foreclosure had not yet received a reply. "Your silence places us in a very awkward position," the agency admonished, "& unless this communication receives immediate attention, the parties intimate that the matter will be taken out of your hands." Several more such letters followed, indicating that even conscientious attorneys often failed to deliver the prompt attention and service that the agencies promised to their subscribers.[102]

Competition from other agencies intensified the pressure on correspondents to reply quickly and accurately to requests for information. The numerous small start-ups were a particular source of anxiety. A Mercantile Agency circular warned that "by a lively system of correspondence with

such agents as they can get, these little establishments are enabled to pro-
long their existence, and even in some instances to gather items of importance *before they reach us.*[103] In 1852 the agency alerted its correspondents
that a new concern, Potter and Russell, "will send a traveling agent through
your state, who may endeavor to induce you to enter into correspondence
with them."[104] A few years later the Mercantile Agency fumed that "the
provoking pertinacity with which the little rival offices here continue their
efforts to open a correspondence with our friends, is a subject of much annoyance to us." The agency reminded its correspondents of the benefits
provided by its network, the industry's largest: "Our patronage and resources so far exceed all others combined, that a connection with other
agencies must be, comparatively, profitless." It also insisted on "the right
to the exclusive advices of our correspondents, as regards other agencies."[105] Because several credit-reporting firms were competing for the
same information, it was tempting for correspondents to offer their
services to more than one company. Alonzo Snyder of Louisiana worked
simultaneously for the Mercantile Agency and the W. A. Cleveland agency,
presumably without their knowledge.[106] Elijah Morgan, the Ann Arbor
attorney, also corresponded with a number of collection and credit-reporting
firms.[107]

The Effects of Competition

In the United States, the evolution of credit-reporting firms was driven
not by government regulations and initiatives but by competition. The
constant appearance of new rivals forced the Mercantile Agency continually to increase the scope of its coverage. Industry pioneers Griffin, Cleaveland, and Campbell had instructed its correspondents not to bother
reporting on the "many merchants who are too small to come here to
make their purchases." Instead, correspondents were simply to "give the
names of such merchants, stating the fact, that, in your opinion, they
ought not to come to this city."[108]

Tappan, however, instructed his correspondents to "record all facts that
come to your knowledge, of persons changing their business, failing, moving away, new partnerships, &c., &c . . . The name of *every* trader in your
district should be reported, with all necessary particulars, whether they
have ever purchased in this city or not."[109] The Mercantile Agency's
ledgers eventually contained tens of thousands of entries on business establishments that were modest in size. Some were minuscule, with total

capitalization of only a few hundred dollars. Yet from the beginning the Mercantile Agency invested money and considerable effort to gain information even on the smallest of these, on the theory that they would be of interest to jobbers and wholesalers intent on gaining new business or anxious to replace the large number of customers who closed their doors every year.

The Bradstreet agency, soon to become the Mercantile Agency's most serious rival, also realized the value of expanded coverage. It advertised in 1864 that "special attention has been given to the Reports of the smallest Dealers in Country Villages, Hamlets and Cross Roads . . . Some 5000 (small) places not previously in our 'Book of Reports,' have now been fully reported and added to its pages, together with a large number of new Firms and omitted names in the places previously reported, being in the aggregate over 30,000 additional . . . names."[110] The need to demonstrate better coverage than rival firms resulted in greater inclusivity. As a result, numerous small establishments owned by women, blacks, and recent immigrants found themselves placed under the scrutiny of the Mercantile Agency, the Bradstreet agency, and their competitors.

Competition between the Mercantile Agency and Bradstreet was especially fierce. Like Tappan, John Bradstreet was descended from old New England stock (he counted Puritan poet Anne Bradstreet as one of his forebears). In 1848 the Cincinnati lawyer was made assignee of a large, insolvent estate. The position allowed Bradstreet to acquire a considerable amount of valuable information on the debtors and creditors of the estate, which he soon realized would be of interest to several New York suppliers. Bradstreet proceeded to sell them the information, thus establishing a profitable new business for himself.[111] With sons Milton and Henry, Bradstreet moved his headquarters in 1855 to New York City, where they set up the John M. Bradstreet and Sons Improved Mercantile and Law Agency for Cities. The name was chosen to distinguish Bradstreet from the Mercantile Agency, which was more oriented toward the country trade.[112]

One of the Mercantile Agency's most strategically important moves occurred in response to a product first offered by the Bradstreet agency. In 1857 Bradstreet began publishing a bound reference book that contained information, presented in the form of rating keys, on the creditworthiness of some twenty thousand businesses scattered throughout the country, primarily in the large cities. (Bradstreet provided a loose-leaf version from 1852–1858, which relied on a coded system, but which did not use a rating system.)[113]

The initial (1857) volume, called *Bradstreet's Improved Commercial Agency Reports,* had 110 pages containing ratings for 17,100 mostly large establishments in nine locations. No copies of this volume appear to have survived, but the one published in 1860 contained the following rating system, which included information on character and past behavior, as well as Bradstreet's estimation of the subject's creditworthiness.

KEY to Bradstreet Reference Book, 1860.

1. Making money
3. Losing money
5. Expenses large
6. Economical
7. Business too much extended
8. Business not too much extended
9. Temperate
10. Not temperate
11. Attends closely to business.
12. Does not attend very closely to business.
13. Pays large interest.
14. Does not pay large interest.
15. Often hard run for money.
16. Often pays before maturity.
17. Good moral character.
18. Not very good private character.
19. Sometimes suffers notes to be protested.
20. Does not always pay accounts at maturity.
21. Credits prudently.
22. Takes large risks in crediting.
23. Does not value prompt payments sufficiently.
24. Sued.
25. Not sued.
29. Pays promptly.
30. Rather slow pay.
31. Honest.
32. Honesty not fully endorsed.
33. Good business qualifications.
34. Medium business qualifications.

35. Endorses too much.
36. Does not endorse.

Aa Good for any amount required.
A Best of credit.
B Very good credit.
C Good credit.
D Good for smaller lines.
E Fair for small lines.

Source: *Bradstreet Commercial Reports,* . . . vol. 7, 2nd ed., July 31, 1860, p. 8. Earlier looseleaf versions contained the following numbers: 2 (Making money rapidly), 4 (Losing money rapidly), 26 (Purchases east), 27 (Purchases in Cincinnati), 28 (Purchases in East and West). Bradstreet apparently decided that these markings were superfluous, and he eliminated them.

Bradstreet's was not the first such published volume. Washington Hite, an attorney in Bardstown, Kentucky, had produced a sixty-four-page volume in 1846, which provided eastern suppliers with terse information on local merchants. The following year Sheldon Church published a larger volume, 434 pages long, covering merchants in the West, South, and Southwest. These volumes, however, provided impressionistic descriptions only; neither used rating keys, and each was a one-off rather than a serial publication.[114] By publishing its information, Bradstreet's service became much more convenient than the Mercantile Agency's because it put information directly into the hands of subscribers, whose clerks were no longer obliged to spend such onerous amounts of time at the agencies' offices. Moreover, the rating keys allowed subscribers to compare potential borrowers more easily. Although Bradstreet, like the Mercantile Agency, continued to urge subscribers to buy the full reports, the reference book became Bradstreet's biggest competitive advantage, and its publication seriously affected the Mercantile Agency's business. The latter's profits dropped alarmingly, from $48,269 in 1857 to $14,302 in 1858, and the agency lost over two hundred subscribers.[115]

Both Douglass and Dun recognized that they had to counter the threat. However, Douglass's experience with a libel suit in 1851 (*Beardsley v. Tappan,* discussed below), when he spent twenty days in jail rather than reveal the name of a correspondent, appears to have made him reluctant to endorse the reference book. The published volume allowed easy access to sensitive information by individuals who had no direct interest in it, circumstances that went against the spirit of recent court decisions, especially *Taylor v. Church*. Sheldon Church was sued for libel by two firms in Columbus, Mississippi; on appeal, each received $5,000. "The peculiar features" of the case, a Mercantile Agency circular explained, "and those which operated against him [Church] in the ruling of the Court, were that he *printed* his reports, and *sold them* in book form to eastern merchants; thus giving information (libelous or otherwise) to the purchasers of the book about men in whom they *had no interest*."[116] In addition to the obstacles posed by the recent court decisions, Douglass had always believed that publishing the agency's valuable information made the firm the target of pilferage by smaller competitors.

Pressure to respond to Bradstreet's challenge proved too great. Upon Douglass's retirement in 1859 the Mercantile Agency issued its own reference book, a 519-page volume containing over twenty thousand firms in the United States and Canada. Only larger firms were included because Douglass and Dun believed that small establishments could be rated only by thoroughly evaluating their financial circumstances, including their bank records. The book was issued with a lock and key to emphasize the confidential nature of its information, and the contract specified that outdated volumes had to be returned to the agency. (When rivals began publishing reference books, the requirement became standard throughout the industry.) Compiling and updating such a massive reference work taxed the firm's resources and strained the relationships between Dun and his top managers. But it paid off. The Mercantile Agency's more extensive network of correspondents resulted in wider coverage, which allowed its reference book eventually to surpass Bradstreet's.[117] The New York office alone sold $24,000 worth of books in the first five months. When the reference book began to be issued semiannually in 1873, the Mercantile Agency found itself in the publishing business. Printers could not keep up with the new publication schedule, so Dun invested $15,000 on type and equipment for the New York office. Even here, the Mercantile Agency was a step behind Bradstreet, which had done its own typesetting beginning in 1862.[118]

Bradstreet's book, including periodic notification sheets, was priced at $50 for nationwide coverage ($25 for New York City alone), with unlimited full reports. Dun priced the Mercantile Agency's competing product at $200 a year, with only one annual edition plus a notification service. The notification system worked in the following way: a subscriber who took both the book and the reports checked the newspapers daily for coded references to individuals for whom the firm had additional information. If any were of interest, the subscriber had the option of going to the agency's office to retrieve the new items. It was a less convenient method than Bradstreet's sheets, but the scope of coverage was superior. Dun experimented with different ways to convey the information; some of his innovations were later rescinded. For example, the 1860 edition divided merchants into six categories, but the classification proved difficult to maintain. During the Civil War, Dun decided to include estimates of capital worth, an innovation that definitively distinguished the product from Bradstreet's. Collecting the data for 150,000 firms delayed issuance of the new reference book, but its publication significantly lifted the firm's profits, which had declined substantially during the war.[119] Despite the improved coverage, the published volumes did not make the more-detailed reports obsolete. To the contrary, circulars continued to urge subscribers to come into the agency offices to obtain full information, especially on customers whose creditworthiness was in question.

The Continuing Quest for Legitimacy

The effectiveness of credit-reporting agencies improved, but serious problems remained, which put the agencies on the defensive and compromised their legitimacy in the eyes of some merchants and the larger public. Despite a rapidly improving transportation and communications infrastructure, information was still updated only two to four times a year, supplemented by notification services. Although the telegraph came into wider use, news still moved too slowly to prevent some suppliers from shipping goods to buyers who were on the brink of insolvency. The problem was particularly acute for out-of-state creditors because most state laws favored those who were the first to arrive on the scene. By the time a distant lender heard about a borrower's difficulties, the assets of the business had probably already been picked over by local creditors.

Checking the Mercantile Agency reports against other contemporary sources reveals that the agency's coverage was seldom comprehensive. A significant portion of merchants in Springfield, Illinois—almost 25 percent of dry goods, 20 percent of clothing, and 15 percent of millinery establishments—were insufficiently known to the Dun agency reporters to make an accurate assessment possible. Phrases such as "don't know much about them," "they keep to themselves," "not known here," or the equally eloquent evidence of terse entries and blank lines in the agency's ledgers testify to the difficulties that correspondents faced in obtaining complete information. Nor did the agency cover all businesses. Comparisons with the Springfield city directories of 1850, 1860, 1870 and 1880 (which themselves were not comprehensive) indicate that a significant number of businesses did not appear in the agency's ledgers at all. A study done of Poughkeepsie businesses found that the Mercantile Agency assessed only 37 percent of that city's grocery establishments in the 1850s. Some twenty years later, the figure was still only 80 percent.[120] Because of these shortcomings, many creditors, particularly in the South, preferred to obtain their information through more traditional methods: letters of recommendation, direct communication with locals (including local attorneys), and mutual acquaintances.[121]

Journals such as *Hunt's Merchants' Magazine* and *DeBow's Review* began to portray the agencies in a positive light during the 1850s. Even so, potential subscribers such as Barings and Brown Brothers continued to use their own sources of credit information.[122] Meanwhile, the press denounced the agencies' activities as intrusive. "No home will be secure, no privacy will be sacred from these harpian visitors," complained a Louisiana newspaper in 1854. "Neighbor will doubt neighbor & fear will check social intercourse."[123] "One's personal habits," charged another critic, "can be discovered; whether he was happy in his family, whether his family was a large or a small one, and whether he supported a mistress in addition to his family expenses."[124] Business writer Edwin Freedley acknowledged that as "an additional means of information either for confirming previous reports or for suggesting further inquiry, it is no doubt worth to subscribers more than the amount of subscription money." But he expressed grave doubts about the reports' accuracy. Moreover, the system had the potential of placing power in the hands of a few: "In its infancy it may be harmless . . . but, should it grow to maturity, and be generally relied upon, the credit of the mercantile community . . . would be in the hands of a few men, self-constituted umpires, and their unknown and irresponsible agents, subject to the errors of ignorance and mistakes of carelessness, with no guaranteed exemption from the influence of private malice, favoritism, bribery, or corruption."[125]

Compelled to respond to these criticisms, agency proprietors emphasized that their firms simply did what wholesalers would have done for themselves but more efficiently and at lower cost. Using an older term with which its readers would have been familiar, a Mercantile Agency circular stated that the firm was "a grand Mutual Benefit Association, the wholesale and jobbing merchants clubbing together, and, through its medium, employing the Attorneys retained by the Agency, and thereby amassing an amount of information which largely encourages and facilitates trade."[126] In 1852, one year after *Beardsley v. Tappan* placed serious potential impediments to the agencies' work, the Mercantile Agency issued a circular defending the legitimacy of its procedures:

> The public are ready to recognize the unquestionable truth which lies at the foundation of the business, viz.: that every man who gives credit to another is, of right, entitled to know his *prospect* of payment. The necessity for this knowledge originated, justifies, and maintains the Mercantile Agency. If it be right to *obtain* this information, it is equally so to *give* it. The propriety of our correspondents giving us *full* and *elaborate* reports of all parties likely to ask credit away from home, is, therefore, fully established. True, *we* are not directly interested in the solvency or insolvency of the traders: but we are employed by those who are; and if it be right for them to obtain the information at all, it matters not whether they do so directly or by proxy.[127]

The agency suggested that agreeing to be scrutinized was a sign of creditworthiness, for it indicated that an individual had nothing to hide: "It is becoming a well recognized principle, that the *man who asks others to trust him,* has no right to object to the most searching scrutiny of his position and character, and no honest and well disposed trader will object."[128]

Yet pressure to make known one's financial standing, what a later generation would approvingly term "transparency," was resented by many traders until at least the end of the nineteenth century. (Indeed, there was something perverse in the Mercantile Agency's insistence that other businesses ought to be more transparent while conducting its own affairs with secrecy.) Business writers and the credit-reporting agencies struggled to change the public's attitude. In his handbook for retailers, Samuel Terry argued that there "is nothing necessarily mean, cringing or contemptible in any retailer making known to the wholesale dealer, the amount of his capital, his former career, and the circumstances which tend to show his industrious habits, his prudence and economy, and his opportunities for obtaining a thorough knowledge of the business he proposes to engage in."[129]

More serious even than the grousing in the press were the legal chal-

lenges.[130] The agencies' unprecedented methods of collecting and transmitting sensitive information, some of it erroneous or outdated, made
them the targets of numerous lawsuits. In the early 1850s, two important
cases, *Taylor v. Church* and *Beardsley v. Tappan,* came before the courts.
Both revolved around the issue of privileged communication. A related issue was whether the new firms were "agents" in the accepted sense, that
is, an individual or group of individuals performing work for, and being
under the control of, another. Thomas Ward, the agent for Barings, was an
example of the conventional definition: he did not try to sell the information gathered for Barings to other parties, nor did he print and circulate it.
The new credit-reporting firms brought into question the legal definitions
of "agent" and "principal": for whom, exactly, were the firms acting as
"agents"? Could the firm's subscribers be regarded as "principals"? Not
surprisingly, the novel relationships introduced by the new institutions
stretched the conventional legal definitions, with important implications
for the notion of privileged communication.

American credit-reporting firms were not the first to confront this problem. At around the time Ward had begun doing his work for Barings, the
trade protection societies in England faced the issue of privileged communication in *Goldstein v. Foss, et al.* (1826). Foss, secretary of The Society
for the Protection of Trade against Swindlers and Sharpers, had sent
members printed reports listing the names of persons alleged to have engaged in fraudulent trades. Goldstein's name appeared on one of the circulars, and he sued the society, charging that the printed lists constituted
libel. The court agreed with him, stating that such lists were not protected
as privileged communication. Another case more favorable to the trade
protection societies, *Fleming v. Newton,* came before the House of Lords
in 1848. The defendant, the Scottish Mercantile Society, circulated "The
Scottish Mercantile Society's Record" among its members. Among the
pieces of information included was a list of protested notes, which was part
of the public record. One Newton family member, who had dishonored
two promissory notes, applied for an interdict to prevent the publication
of his name in the register. Upon appeal, the Lord Chancellor stated that
the society was merely copying information available in the public record
and that the act was not done out of malice.[131]

In the United States, the question of whether credit reports were protected as privileged information first emerged in *Taylor v. Church* (1851).
The defendant in that case had gathered information on the plaintiff,
wholesaler Taylor, Hale, and Murdock, and had subsequently printed and

circulated the information as part of a credit-reporting service. The Mississippi wholesalers sued for libel, charging that Church had circulated the information to merchants who had no immediate interest in them but only wanted the information for future reference. The judge's opinion expressed the difficulty in ruling on an institution that was "of recent date, novel in its character." Recognizing that "the questions which have been presented to us in this argument are important, not only to the parties immediately concerned, but to the mercantile community," the court "felt the importance of these considerations, both in regard to those who need the information, and also in reference to a continuance of such agencies, in the investigation of the questions before us." The court sided with the plaintiff, stating that because the information was circulated to parties who had no immediate interest in it, the information could not be considered privileged. An appeals court upheld the decision in 1853.[132]

Beardsley v. Tappan was the more notorious suit. Two Ohio merchants sued the Mercantile Agency for inaccurately stating that their firm was about to fail. (Although Tappan was named as the defendant and attended the trials, the agency had assumed all liabilities when he left the firm in 1849.) Again, the case revolved around the issue of privileged communication. Counsel for the Mercantile Agency argued that the reports constituted privileged communication between principals (subscribers) and their agents (the credit-reporting firms) and therefore did not constitute libel.

However, the judges who heard the case in both the circuit and district courts interpreted the question narrowly, reasoning that because the information was available to such a large number of partners and clerks and potentially to any subscriber who requested it, credit reports did not enjoy protection as "privileged communication." Benjamin Douglass was declared in contempt of court for refusing to reveal the name of the correspondent who had filed the report. He served twenty days in jail, a decision that earned him a tribute from the *New York Tribune* editor, Horace Greeley. In 1864 a motion for a new trial was denied. Judge C. J. Nelson summed up the conflicting positions in the case, noting that "to legalize these establishments in the manner and to the extent used by the defendant, is placing one portion of the mercantile community under an organized system of espionage and inquisition for the benefit of the other; exposed, from the very nature of the organization, to perversion and abuse." However, he acknowledged that "to refuse to legalize them may be restricting injuriously the right of inquiring into the character and standing of the customer asking for credit in his business transactions."

The case eventually reached the U.S. Supreme Court, where the judgment was finally reversed in 1870 on narrow technical grounds that did not involve the issue of privileged communication.[133]

These cases did not put the agencies out of business; however, they became a nagging worry when the firms began to publish reference books beginning in 1857. Douglass, perhaps because of his jail experience, never overcame his anxiety about these new products and even went so far as to issue the books with a lock and key to minimize the transmission of information to nonsubscribers.[134]

The two cases encouraged supporters of the agencies to come to their defense. To the charge that the agencies were intrusive, a writer in *Hunt's* responded that the information they collected "is not made public. It is not communicated, even to subscribers, except when the trade, by soliciting credit, renders inquiry into his circumstances necessary." (The article was written prior to the introduction of published reference volumes.) Neither was the system at all new. The principle of inquiring about a borrower's character, the writer maintained, "is universal. It belongs to the retail credit business, as well as to the wholesale . . . The whole business of banking, marine, fire and life insurances, &c., &c., is conducted in the same way." Moreover, the system was self-regulating because the "entire success of the system depends upon the general truthfulness and justice of their records."[135]

Another early defender of the new organizations wrote in 1856 that the mercantile agencies "possess advantages superior to any other system yet introduced":

> They frequently warn the city creditor of danger to his interests in some distant part of the country, and furnish him with facilities for protection.
>
> They warn against irresponsible and fraudulent traders, often tracing them from State to State, and recording their movements in each locality.
>
> They aid the solvent country merchant in giving him a credit, and the city merchant in selecting his customers, thus acting as a valuable means of introducing buyers and sellers to each other.
>
> They are disinterested *references* for the country merchant, for it is impossible to find any business in which *honesty* and *interest* are more thoroughly blended.
>
> They throw difficulties in the way of rash speculation and overtrading.

They tend to keep down the cost of goods to the consumer, as without their advantages a larger percentage would necessarily be laid upon goods to leave a margin for bad debts, delays, and extraordinary expense in making collections.

They reduce the *cost* as well as the *risk* of doing business with distant parts of the country, as information they furnish would cost probably ten times as much as if sought through any other channel.

They tend to produce greater solvency and prosperity among city merchants and business men generally.

They aid sound country merchants, for they throw obstacles in the way of the irresponsible and dishonest who attempt to buy goods with no reasonable expectation or intention of paying for them—thus protecting honorable dealers from unfair competition.[136]

The Mercantile Agency achieved further credibility when *A Cyclopedia of Commerce and Commercial Navigation* (1859) included a favorable entry on the firm and made its name synonymous with the entire credit-reporting industry:

The valuable services it has rendered to the domestic trade of the country, as a check upon our credit system, are acknowledged by the mercantile community . . . It is obvious that the gigantic labor of reporting the business men of Canada and the United States could not be performed by any one office, nor could the expense be borne by the merchants of any one city . . . Reports obtained with the care thus exhibited, and from such a variety of sources, must certainly approach as near perfection as is practicable under any circumstances.

The article addressed the objection that the agency "is *secret* in its operations":

It is necessarily of a confidential, and, to a certain extent, of a secret nature, because such communications must always be so. What merchant, banker, or president of an insurance company, who asked for and received such information as that kept by the Agency, from a business correspondent, would think of using it in any other way than as confidential, and to be kept strictly secret? Who would give such information, however pure the inquirer's motive might be, unless he were assured that he could implicitly rely upon this?

The entry concluded that "these agencies are now considered a conservative check upon undue credit, and as highly conducive to sustaining the credit of substantial and legitimate parties—they aid the credit of the sound man, while they promptly reveal the weakness, and fraud, and cases of distrust among those not fully entitled to credit."[137]

Ultimately, the growth and staying power of the Mercantile Agency and the Bradstreet agency testified to their perceived effectiveness. A growing body of subscribers was willing to pay for the service. Some made full use of their subscriptions; New York dry goods wholesaler A. T. Stewart reportedly kept a "confidential clerk" at the Mercantile Agency nearly the entire day to check references.[138] Smaller businesses also subscribed in large numbers. For them, the credit-reporting agencies provided the primary and sometimes the sole means of obtaining information on potential customers.

Credit reporting firms and other information-sharing mechanisms help solve the problem of "asymmetrical information." The problem occurs because borrowers possess more information about their own willingness and ability to pay than do lenders. The term also refers to circumstances in which some lenders possess more or better information about borrowers than do other lenders. Information asymmetry can result in creditors making wrong choices: desirable borrowers, those who would have paid their debts in full and on time, may not get the credit they need, while undesirable ones succeed in obtaining loans. The concept of asymmetrical information corrects a flaw in classical economic theory, which assumes that information is always perfect, always "symmetrical," and that all borrowers and lenders exist on a level playing field. Experience and common sense suggest that this is almost never the case in the real world.[139]

Solutions to market coordination problems, provided they are found at all, are the result of human trial and error. Credit reporting was one such solution. The institution has today become ubiquitous, making it difficult to recapture the moments of experimentation when the institution was new and some of its methods (by modern standards) slightly dubious—and when entrepreneurs sought not only to exploit opportunities but to distinguish their products and services from one another. In the process, they were forced to convince a skeptical mercantile population of the superiority of their service over older alternatives.

A number of alternatives did exist. For example, each supplier-creditor might have gathered data on its own, in the manner of Barings. Banks, too, might conceivably have provided credit information services. They were in an unparalleled position to obtain information on individuals' assets, and much incidental information on character and business ability came their way in the course of doing business. Older information-sharing arrangements, such as trade-protection societies, also were available for emulation.[140] In the United Kingdom, a network of local trade-protection societies was established by the 1860s. They alerted one another about the "swindlers and sharpers" who were the bane of a credit-fueled economy.

None of these alternative models, however, presented a viable solution within the American context. Hiring special agents as Barings did was too expensive for nearly all American firms. Banks were of limited use because banking in the United States was highly fragmented during the nineteenth century (and for much of the twentieth.) Branch banking was largely prohibited, which limited their potential for transmitting information across large distances. Conflicts of interest, such as the need to preserve client confidentiality, further diminished the willingness of banks to function as credit-reporting institutions.

Trade protection societies based on the British model also did not become the norm in the United States, even in places such as New York City, where one might have expected to find them. A few attempts to establish such groups were made, but the arrangements did not last. The less-established nature of trade in the United States, the high mobility of its population within a vast geographic territory, the high churn among businesses, and competition among sellers militated against the formation of stable networks.[141] It is possible, too, that the early appearance of credit-reporting firms may have delayed the establishment of national trade-protection societies devoted to the interchange of credit information. At any rate, when manufacturers' and wholesalers' trade associations began appearing in the 1870s, their primary goal was to maintain prices rather than share credit information. Groups whose members exchanged information on debtors began forming only in the following decade, a full century after such arrangements had become the norm in Great Britain.

American entrepreneurs created the credit-reporting firm to exploit this gap in the market. Although Lewis Tappan, John Bradstreet, and their many rivals did not consciously set out to invent a radically new model, the institution they created differed substantially from older arrangements. Most fundamentally, the credit-reporting firm divorced the information about a borrower from the transaction itself and made the information a commodity that could be bought and sold to any interested party willing and able to pay the costs.[142] Moreover, credit-reporting firms were for-profit ventures; in contrast to the trade protection societies, they sought the largest possible market for the information they gathered. (Credit-reporting firms did not appear to have the "natural limit" problem of the network model. The firms benefited from ever-increasing scale, whereas networks could not continue to add members indefinitely without compromising their effectiveness and increasing their overall costs.) In the course of enlarging their potential subscriber base, the firms' proprietors were forced to confront deep cultural resistance to the idea of making one's financial circumstances and personal habits open to widespread scrutiny.

Because they were for-profit ventures, credit-reporting agencies competed with one another, whereas trade protection societies were run on a cooperative basis. Barriers to entry in the new industry were fairly low; firms could not patent their processes, so rivals felt free to copy each others' methods. Competitive pressures led credit-reporting firms to attempt the broadest coverage possible. Both the Mercantile Agency and Bradstreet gathered information on a wide array of businesses, not just those that were of interest to particular subscribers. They instructed correspondents to report on even the smallest businesses in their locality, and their advertising circulars highlighted the extensiveness of their coverage compared to that of rivals. In this way, peripheral establishments were brought under the purview of the credit-reporting firms. They covered a large variety of businesses, including ones owned by women, ethnic minorities, and African-Americans, regardless of whether the businesses had actually applied for credit. Competition among the agencies helped to transmit the idea that all businesses, regardless of size or credit needs, should be appraised—a vital step to embedding the preference for transparency in American business culture.

Finally, credit-reporting firms provided both positive and negative information on individuals and businesses, whereas networks restricted information to negative items only. The main function of the British trade protection societies was to alert members about debtors who had not paid their bills or had engaged in fraudulent behavior; they did not make all of their customer information available to other members.[143] Sharing information on good borrowers tends not to occur in network arrangements because members fear losing their good customers and borrowers to competitors.

The following table summarizes the key differences between the two models of information transmission:

Networks vs. Credit-Reporting Agencies

Within networks, information is . . .	While information from credit-reporting agencies is . . .
an intrinsic part of the transaction	separated from the transaction and made into a commodity
not sold for profit	sold for profit
circulated only to members	available to anyone willing to pay
concerned only with those in the network or its immediate periphery	highly inclusive, providing broad coverage
restricted to the negative	more likely to include positive as well as negative items

Like banking and other modern financial institutions, the legitimacy of credit reporting was challenged by the mercantile community and the general public. Caught up in the demands of their businesses, entrepreneurs seldom reflect on the historical and cultural implications of their activities. Credit-reporting agencies were an exception; their novelty and the sensitive nature of their product and practices compelled an early and constant dialogue among the agencies, their correspondents, subscribers, and the larger society.

3

Character, Capacity, Capital: How to Be Creditworthy

As capitalist values spread in the United States and more people became drawn into the credit economy, outward appearance, or "reputation," took on extraordinary significance. So, too, did the anxiety that appearances could be manipulated: "Reputation, rather than character—to *seem*, rather than *to be*," fumed the *Daily Illinois State Journal* in 1856, "has become the ultimate aim of too many in all departments of business and professional life."[1] Americans sensed that the need to cultivate a good business reputation led to new levels of hypocrisy, making it difficult to distinguish "seeming" from "being." Business writers, however, continued to insist that character assessment was an integral part of determining creditworthiness.

In the late twentieth century, credit scholars and practitioners came to agree that an individual's payment history was the single most important item for predicting the probability of default. Consumer credit reports, in particular, relied almost exclusively on payment records to determine individuals' credit scores, known as FICO (after Fair, Isaac Company, the firm that originated the model). During the nineteenth century, however, there was no generally held notion that creditors should share this information with one another. Lewis Tappan instructed his correspondents to report the names of their subjects' New York suppliers so that he could contact them for payment information, but his motive probably had more to do with soliciting subscriptions than obtaining payment records.[2]

Outside of trade protection societies (which were rare in the United States), creditors were reluctant to share information about their accounts, and the information that did circulate was almost exclusively negative. There was no incentive to share positive information and every reason not to, including the fear that competitors would steal one's good customers.

Because reliable payment information was nearly impossible to obtain, the new credit-reporting agencies focused on the financial situation of individuals, including his or her "worth." Yet here, too, accurate financial information was elusive, due to widespread ignorance about and neglect of good bookkeeping practices. Cultural norms, moreover, held that being asked to provide a written statement of one's financial situation was a slight to one's honor. At any rate, because credit terms were lengthy (ranging from six to twelve months or longer), a borrower's current liquidity was not as helpful to creditors as records of past behavior.

Lacking good information on individuals' payments to other creditors and frequently unable to access their financial standing, merchants accepted "character"—the visible indicators of past behavior—as a proxy for credit-worthiness. *Hunt's Merchants' Magazine,* founded in 1839 as one of the country's first national business journals, frequently reprinted lectures delivered at mercantile library associations, establishments that served young, middle-class men in the country's commercial centers.[3] In a typical lecture, one Judge James Hall told his audience at the Young Men's Mercantile Association in Cincinnati that "the credit of a merchant depends mainly on his character for integrity, capacity, and industry."[4] Character, wrote Richard Smith, editor of the *Cincinnati Price Current,* "to a man of business, and indeed to every person, is as dear as life itself . . . Such respect as is awarded to the possessor of an unspotted character is not purchasable, nor does it require a pecuniary effort to command it."[5] Business manuals, periodicals, and lecturers exhorted traders to meet their payments on time, to be energetic but careful, to be thrifty, and to refrain from drinking and gambling, all for the supreme purpose of safeguarding their creditworthiness. The *New York Evening Gazette* in 1845 summed up the business wisdom that underlay the expanding, credit-dependent economy: "Risk anything before you risk your reputation."[6]

The role of "character" in the formation of social identity and status has been examined at length by historians of the American middle class.[7] Karen Haltunnen and Judith Hilkey focused on advice manuals to trace cultural anxiety about social relations that accompanied the transition of the United States from a rural to an urban nation, from a society characterized by the independent proprietor to one in which the corporate order reigned supreme. Like the writer in the *Daily Illinois State Journal,* the authors of many of these manuals dwelt on the theme of sincerity and hypocrisy. Other historians have examined the gender, racial, and ethnic dimensions of character, as well as the deepening sectional tensions that shaped it during the 1850s.[8]

From the point of view of business history and economics, however, the significance of character lies in its link to the problem of information asymmetry, the age-old dilemma faced by creditors, who have less information than do borrowers themselves on the latter's ability and willingness to repay debts. Scarcity of information shaped a number of institutional practices and innovations in the United States, including the phenomenon of "insider lending" in early American banks. These institutions, Naomi Lamoreaux has shown, functioned as investment clubs because they were well positioned to gather information on the businesses in which they invested.[9] Likewise, the focus on character traits by American trade creditors was driven by information scarcity, the result of practical and cultural obstacles that hindered the procurement of individuals' payment records and accurate financial statements.

The paucity of this information did not keep creditors from attempting to calculate creditworthiness in a systematic way. By the 1830s and 1840s, a shared set of criteria for doing so had emerged within the business community. In addition to capital and "capacity" (business ability), the criteria for determining creditworthiness included the so-called character traits of honesty, punctuality, thrift, sobriety, energy, and focus. Experience, marital status, and age were also deemed important. The list is significant as much for what it generally did not include—membership in churches or social and political clubs, to take only the most obvious examples. To be sure, these items were mentioned (and, not surprisingly, historians have tended to make much of these instances), but not as frequently as might be expected, given the centrality of social and political organizations in American life. Sex and race were central to the construction of creditworthiness, but they did not constitute the sole basis for judgment. Other considerations, including past behavior and experience, were also taken into account.

By the last decades of the twentieth century, this way of assessing creditworthiness had come to seem hopelessly unsophisticated, and many components of it had become illegal. In the information-scarce environment of the nineteenth-century United States, however, such an approach helped to mitigate the ambiguities inherent in long-distance trade. Provided with a clear set of rules, mercantile creditors became more willing to sell goods on credit to merchants who were unknown to them and who may or may not have become repeat customers.

Obstacles to Obtaining Information

Nineteenth-century creditors faced a scarcity of information on borrowers that their modern descendants would find hard to fathom. Reliable income statements and balance sheets, the basic indicators of a business's financial condition, were difficult to procure. There were exceptions: some insurance companies, for example, made their financial statements public as early as the 1830s. (*Hazard's* published the financial returns of Massachusetts's insurance offices in its inaugural volume in 1839.)[10] Some railroads not only published their financial statements but also engaged in sophisticated reporting and analysis. During the late 1820s pioneering corporations such as the Baltimore & Ohio (B&O) began issuing thick annual reports packed with tables and exhibits. B&O engineers developed formulas for calculating "proportions" (the ratio of revenues to expenses), which allowed them to understand fixed versus variable cost patterns.[11] Other instances of regular, even sophisticated, accounting methods could be found as early as the Revolutionary period, when nearly all counting houses used double-entry bookkeeping methods. In the early nineteenth century, a few firms in the ice trade and the logging, paper, and textiles industries, as well as the government's armories, used some form of cost accounting. Specialized manuals such as *The Steamboat Clerk* (1839) appeared, part of a wave of accounting textbooks that journals such as *Hunt's* regularly reviewed beginning in the late 1830s. The journal also featured articles on accounting issues and problems.[12]

Yet financial information on the great majority of businesses remained unavailable to outsiders. Records were used internally, for the purposes of administration only; in the era before income taxes and regulatory commissions, they were not intended to be shared with outsiders.[13] No generally accepted accounting principles (GAAP) existed. (The American Institute of Accountants issued the first such auditing standards only in 1939.) Instead, writers of antebellum accounting textbooks competed to have their systems accepted as the best for American business.

Perhaps most startling for modern-day analysts, accounting practices did not place much emphasis on profitability or cash flow, and some businesses did not even bother to balance their books on an annual basis. Family accounts were mixed in with business accounts; personal expenses were paid for with earnings, and business costs were lumped in with family expenses.[14] Lack of interest in income reporting was not peculiar to the United States; in England, too, the practice was not well established. There, even the passage of the Joint Stock Companies Act of 1856 failed to make profit-and-loss statements mandatory, perhaps because of the difficulty in defining net income.[15] Cost accounting was even less typical. Evidence strongly suggest that manufacturers of the period tried to cut their production costs (for example, by replacing expensive materials with cheaper ones), but they appear to have done so without systematically accounting for those costs.[16] Moreover, the methodologies used were unique to each company and applied on an ad hoc basis. Rather than striving for uniformity across firms, businesses of the period appear to have treated their cost-accounting methods as a source of competitive advantage and did not share them with other firms.[17]

Very little, therefore, could be known for sure about a business's liquidity—how much cash or cash equivalents it had on hand with which to pay its debts. Edwin Freedley's *A Practical Treatise on Business* advised that a "reserve capital should always be easily convertible into money, as the exigencies of trade may require."[18] But for creditors, knowing precisely how much of these "easily convertible" assets a business had was next to impossible. In 1864 the Mercantile Agency's reference books began including estimates of capital strength, expressed via rating keys; it was the first reference book to do so on a regular and systematic basis. But although convenient, the rating keys did not distinguish among the types of assets owned, whether cash, real estate, inventory, securities, or other personal property.

Such information would have been useful to creditors because of developments in state law. Homesteads, for example, counted as part of a borrower's "capital strength," but state exemption laws increasingly were placing these assets beyond the reach of creditors (although they could, of course, still be used by the debtor as collateral to raise cash). The Married Women's Property laws, enacted in many states beginning in the 1830s, made it easier for merchants to shelter their assets from creditors by conveying them to their spouses. The R. G. Dun records provide ample evidence that this practice was widespread.

Determining the true value of a business's inventory was yet another problem. Credit reports frequently complained that merchandise was probably "overestimated." No standards for valuation existed. Instead, merchants used whichever method yielded the highest valuation, and many made no provisions for old, broken, or outmoded stock. The conscientious ones tried to convert these items into cash by auction or sale at the end of each season, but less scrupulous traders clung to defective merchandise and reported them at full market value. Samuel Terry's handbook for retailers warned that "old goods—soiled, faded, tarnished, rumpled or out of fashion" were often "held at the full original price, when there is . . . a depreciation of possibly one-fourth their value."[19]

Faced with these obstacles, how did mercantile creditors determine whom to trust? Compared to more modern methods, determining creditworthiness in the nineteenth century was more art than science, in keeping with the general practices of the period. Even so, the process was not purely guesswork. Examination of sample and actual credit reports, as well as business handbooks and articles spanning the period from the 1820s to the end of the 1860s, indicates that the process of assessing creditworthiness was not arbitrary. Although determining creditworthiness was not formally codified and lacked the sophisticated risk models that were developed during the second half of the twentieth century, a true method nevertheless existed. It became widely accepted by merchants, bankers, and others who transacted in an increasingly complex, credit-dependent economy.

Calculating Creditworthiness

Credit reporting agencies engaged local correspondents, primarily attorneys, to make twice-yearly reports on the businesses in their districts (see Chapter 2). Small-town attorneys were well placed to collect this information because they were at or near the center of community and business life. Relying on local knowledge made sense, even if the task of obtaining it was by no means easy. "We are aware that in all cases it is difficult—in some impossible—to give categoric answers," a Mercantile Agency circular acknowledged, "but as the past experience of correspondents has given them more or less acquaintance with the great body of traders in their County, a reasonable amount of diligent inquiry will suffice to make a highly satisfactory return."[20]

Public records like mortgages and taxes paid on real estate were available for correspondents to examine. Newspapers were another easily accessible source of information; even small towns had at least one weekly or daily. Reportage on specific firms was not extensive, but newspapers were heavily dependent for their revenues on commercial advertisements and notices, and they typically devoted nearly one-half of their pages to these items. In an early circular, Lewis Tappan specifically requested that correspondents send him their local newspapers so that he might study the advertisements.[21] Advertising sections, akin to the classified ads of modern-day newspapers, chronicled the creation of new firms, the dissolution of existing ones, and the sales of bankrupt stocks. These notices in no way formed a comprehensive record of a town's business life; in his study of frontier Midwestern merchants, Lewis Atherton estimated that less than one-half advertised regularly in their town newspapers, and in some localities only about one-third advertised at all.[22] Nevertheless, the notices provided a number of important clues to the condition of many businesses as well as a crude index of the local economy's health.

After exhausting these publicly available sources of information, correspondents could supplement what they had gathered by other methods. Useful impressions could be obtained by visiting an establishment and observing how well the store was kept, whether or not the stock on hand was fresh and appealing, and how many and what type of customers were in the store. An informal visit by an agency correspondent could determine how successfully traders were coordinating their merchandise with the demands of their market. (In the early years, such visits were made discreetly, even surreptitiously, because correspondents were not eager to reveal that they worked for credit-reporting firms.) Town directories, used as boostering devices by large and small towns alike, may have been another important source of information. With a map and the most recent town directory in hand, one could gain quick insight into an establishment's geographic and competitive position.[23] Business handbook writer Freedley expressed the conventional wisdom that a store "should be situated where the principal stores in the same line of business are" and that a "retail store should be established on some leading thoroughfare."[24] Directories and maps allowed distant creditors and their agents to determine quickly whether this was the case for a particular business.

Credit reports became increasingly detailed and their coverage more extensive. But creditors had to decide whether they would avail themselves of the full reports, as opposed to confining their investigations to published reference books such as those pioneered by Bradstreet and the Mercantile Agency. As discussed in Chapter 2, the reference books conveyed general information on individuals and firms via a series of rating keys. In its 1864 volume, the Mercantile Agency for the first time included broad estimates of "capital strength." It is not possible to determine what proportion of subscribers availed themselves of the full reports, but the leading credit-reporting agencies repeatedly urged their subscribers to do so.

If a creditor decided to order a full credit report on an existing or prospective customer, what financial information could he expect to gain? Fortunately, a number of sample reports, as well as numerous actual reports from the R. G. Dun and Company ledgers, survive. The following early sample report appeared in a June 1835 circular issued to correspondents by New York's Griffin, Cleaveland, and Campbell, one of the earliest known credit-reporting agencies and a predecessor of Lewis Tappan's Mercantile Agency. These samples were meant to provide correspondents with guidelines for the type of information the agencies believed was obtainable with a reasonable, although presumably not excessive, amount of effort. (Note the scarcity of financial information, here italicized for emphasis):

> John Doe & Richard Roe, Buffalo City, Hardware. Both educated to merchandise, and been in business about ten years; men of correct business habits; honest, intelligent, and prudent. Doe aged 36, married, *worth $15,000*. Roe aged 30, single, *worth $10,000—about half their property in real estate;* able friends, and engaged in no other business. They are very safe men.
>
> Orleans county, Town of Barre, Rush Village, Denn & Fenn. John Denn & Richard Fenn, Druggists. This firm have been in business about three years; Denn is unmarried, and was educated as a physician; *brought into the concern $4,000,* and is a *dashing* fellow. Fenn was formerly a clerk in a large drug establishment in ___, and *put into the concern $2,000*. Business much extended—engaged in speculations in real estate. Both rather visionary in their calculations. Denn married— Credit here tolerably fair *now*.[25]

Judging from these sample reports, Griffin, Cleaveland, and Campbell expected their correspondents to supply the following information: name(s), town or village, type of business, experience, age, marital status, estimate of assets, proportion of assets consisting of real estate, and character traits relating to "business habits" and "honesty," among others. Later, agencies also sometimes requested that correspondents determine whether the subjects of their reports carried fire insurance.[26]

The template used by Griffin, Cleaveland, and Campbell was widespread by the 1850s. A circular issued by the Mercantile Agency in 1853 instructed its correspondents to report the following information: "Age; length of time in business; success, prospects; moral character and habits; capacity; industry; amount of business; capital invested; entire means (noting Real Estate, and encumbrances, if any); home credit, and indebtedness there; with any peculiarity of position that may affect responsibility." The circular exhorted correspondents to give more information on capital: "An estimate of means should be made in every case, so far as it is possible to do so. The report 'good' signifies nothing, unless we know how much the trader is good for . . . or if he has no means, what makes him 'good.'"[27]

Michigan attorney Elijah W. Morgan, a correspondent for a number of credit-reporting and collection agencies during the 1850s, received this sample report from the American Collection Agency. (Again, note the paucity of financial information, here italicized for emphasis):

> Jones, Smith, & Brown
> Alfred Jones, John Smith, Wm. Brown, Gen'l Dealers
>
> "J." is about 50 years old, and a merchant at this place for 20 years, during which time he has been doing a good business and has made money, never failed, is of good character, and a shrewd business man. Is now estimated *worth about $25,000, of which $5,000 is in unincumbered real estate.* He does a legitimate business, and never ventures into rash speculations. "S" and "B" are each about 35 years old, and smart business men. "S" had been in business and failed, settled honorably, acted as clerk, for "J." for two or three years, and was admitted a partner some two years since, *paying in $5,000 in cash, principally a gift from his father, who is well off.* "B" has been a clerk in the house about four years, and a good and popular one, is just admitted a partner, but does not add any capital. They continue to do a good business, are in good credit, and worthy of it.[28]

According to the report the senior partner (Jones) was deemed to be worth some $25,000, of which $5,000 consisted of "unincumbered real estate." But of what, exactly, did the remaining $20,000 consist—cash, securities, merchandise, or personal property? The report does not say. And what of the real estate? Was it the owner's home, a property he rented out, a store? The report indicates that one of the junior partners, Smith, paid in $5,000 in cash when he was admitted into the partnership. But that was a full two years earlier, which means that the financial information, even if it was reported by the correspondent within the last six months, was at least two years out of date. The $5,000 was "principally a gift from his father, who is well off," but there is no precise measure of the father's wealth nor any indication that he would be willing to contribute more cash to the business.

These examples are idealized reports detailing the information that agencies believed ought to be available. Surviving reports, such as those of the R. G. Dun agency, followed the sample reports fairly closely. During the credit-reporting agencies' early years, correspondents were supplied information on real estate owned, the amount of merchandise on hand, estimates of total worth, and the amount of credit that could safely be extended.[29]

The Meaning and Function of "Character"

Trade creditors had access to a number of different sources allowing them to determine the creditworthiness of businesses located in distant towns. Local correspondents consulted official records, including land titles and tax rolls, for information on real assets. Newspapers provided notices of bankruptcies, partnership dissolutions, and the formation of new businesses. Directories and city maps, too, could furnish some indication of a business's location and its competition. Surviving credit reports indicate that local correspondents were able to provide some information on capital strength, including the approximate value of the stores' inventory and the owners' real property. After the Civil War, the reports began more regularly to include such items as annual sales, accounts receivable, cash on hand, and liabilities.

Yet, almost invariably, any pronouncement about creditworthiness involved an appraisal of the borrower's character. It is worth looking again at the sample report on Jones, Smith, and Brown, this time with the borrowers' character traits and experience italicized:

Jones, Smith & Brown
Alfred Jones, John Smith, Wm. Brown, Gen'l Dealers

"J." is about 50 years old, and *a merchant at this place for 20 years*, during which time he has been doing a good business and has made money, *never failed, is of good character*, and a *shrewd* business man. Is now estimated worth about $25,000, of which $5,000 is in unincumbered real estate. He does a legitimate business, and *never ventures into rash speculations*. "S" and "B" are each about 35 years old, and smart business men. *"S" had been in business and failed, settled honorably, acted as clerk, for "J." for two or three years, and was admitted a partner some two years since*, paying in $5,000 in cash, principally a gift from his father, who is well off. *"B" has been a clerk in the house about four years, and a good and popular one, is just admitted a partner*, but does not add any capital. They continue to do a good business, are in good credit, and worthy of it.[30]

Apparently, the agencies expected their correspondents to comment on borrowers' experience, failures (if any), business ability, propensity to speculate, and a constellation of other items that made up what was known as character.

The continuing reliance on character traits can be explained not only by the paucity of good payment and financial information but also by the fact that credit terms spanned from six to twelve months or longer. A borrower's current financial circumstances, therefore, were less significant than his or her past behavior. Moreover, legal developments increased the ability of debtors to protect their assets from creditors in the event of insolvency. The Married Women's Property laws, enacted in many states beginning in the 1830s, made it easier for borrowers to convey assets to their spouses. State exemption laws also allowed debtors to shield homesteads and personal property from the reach of creditors.[31] For these reasons, some business writers advised creditors to pay more, not less, attention to character traits. According to Samuel Terry, "Wherever the laws shield a debtor, as they do so generally throughout the United States, the best guaranty for payment that a creditor can have, is the moral and equitable obligation to pay, in the heart of the debtor."[32] Information on a debtor's ability to pay had to be supplemented by some indication of his or her willingness to do so.

Some disagreement existed over the relative importance of capital versus character. Griffen, Cleveland, and Company placed greater emphasis on character, telling its correspondents in 1835 that the "information wanted may be reduced to answers to the following questions. *First*—Is he a man of fair character, and good business habits?" Only after this had been determined should other considerations, such as experience and capital worth, be scrutinized.[33] An early competitor of the Mercantile Agency wrote to its correspondents, "Many a worthy man, has been refused credit, because he had not the requisite amount of capital when if his *character* and *business habits* had been thoroughly understood, he could have had credit as freely, and bought goods as cheap, as his more wealthy neighbor, who is better known."[34] But not all creditors were convinced of this reasoning. "Some of our merchants regard character and capacity as of the greatest importance," stated a Mercantile Agency circular dated 1853, "while others will not sell even to an honest, capable man unless he has *capital*, particularly if he is advanced in years."[35]

The idea that certain character traits were an integral part of a borrower's creditworthiness was already well established.[36] According to historian Ralph Hidy, Thomas Wren Ward, the American merchant hired by Barings to assess the creditworthiness of its U.S. business associates beginning in 1829, reported on the following items: "the location of the firm, its capital, its particular preoccupation . . . its character—whether trustworthy and honorable or unreliable, the amount of credit that it was safe to give to it, the conditions under which the credit should be given, and any special items that might have a bearing upon the business activities of the house." Ward's notes and reports reveal that although "a large capital was an attractive attribute . . . the personal integrity of the leading partner or director of the firm was of greater importance," writes Hidy. "Prudence and integrity were, indeed, the main indices of reliability and trustworthiness."[37]

Ward devised a credit-rating system, ranging from 1 to 11, which differentiated between a firm's character and its capital strength. Those he designated a "2" were ones that he considered "not only entirely safe for what they may do, but likely to continue so under any possible circumstances." He added, "They possess of course different degrees of wealth, but are placed together in this list on account of wealth, character and habits of business taken together." Those designated a "4" consisted "of a class many of whom I should consider safe and some even comparatively rich, but who from the smallness of their transactions, or from their having no abiding place . . . would not seem to belong to a class to be trusted much." However, he added that the list "contains few or none whose *morals* so far as we know is exceptionable." Customers who were rated a "5" were designated as "*No trust*. This column consists of those who either have not capital or are not of that character to render it desirable to trust them at all."[38]

Theoretically, the manifestations of an individual's character are numerous. Credit-reporting firms, however, concentrated on a very specific set of traits: honesty, punctuality, extravagance or economy, the borrower's "energy," and evidence of excessive drinking and gambling. Also important were the individual's previous experience, age, and marital status. In general, the credit correspondents did not focus on traits that, on the surface, were closely linked to an individual's character. Whether he or she attended church, much less which particular denomination, rarely appeared as an indication of creditworthiness. (As Chapter 4 explains, Jews were an important exception.) Reports of adultery appeared far less frequently than one might expect in this puritanical society and usually only if a merchant had set up a separate household that was financially dependent on him. Nor were memberships in political or social clubs typically noted, even though this information was readily available to correspondents living in the same communities as the subjects of their reports.[39]

In the absence of perfect financial information, each character trait came to have a specific meaning. When one looks beyond the moral language of the reports, a common and very precise set of standards for creditworthiness emerges—standards that allowed creditors and agencies to assess the ability of borrowers to remain financially solvent, as well as their willingness to meet payments or make good-faith arrangements when their liquidity was threatened.

Honesty

Agency correspondents may not have had access to specific payment records, but they could often make a reasonable assessment of an individual's willingness to pay. Informal channels of communication, including impressions gathered from local businesspeople, bankers, sheriffs, and attorneys, provided valuable information. A good deal of hearsay was reported as hearsay. Phrases such as "it is said that," "is rumored to," and "is believed to be" appear frequently in the credit reports. Gossip of this sort had to be reported cautiously, especially when courts began penalizing the agencies for spreading libelous information.

Creditors and agency correspondents were constantly on the lookout for businesses in trouble, but they tried to make careful distinctions as to the cause and the likely response of the owners. As far back as the seventeenth century, English writers had observed how unexpected developments could derail the best and most careful of merchants, a sentiment echoed nearly two centuries later by New York's J. N. Bellows: "[The merchant] does not control the currency, the government, the trade of the nation. Property falls; money is scarce, the crops are cut off; acting in good faith, supported by experience, still his hopes are disappointed, and his goods are sold under the hammer, and he has not a shilling in the world."[40]

Because the business cycle could turn so quickly, the mere record of having failed did not necessarily brand a business as a bad risk. The sample report on Jones, Smith, and Brown presented earlier illustrates that credit reporters were instructed to discriminate between those who failed "honestly" and those who did not. Failures that were the result of endorsing—when an individual with good credit acted as a guarantor for others who subsequently failed and brought the endorser down with them—usually received more lenient treatment.[41] Soon after the Mercantile Agency began publishing its failure statistics in 1857, it separated "swindling and absconding debtors" from ones that were "not classed dishonest, but will pay little or nothing" and those "likely to pay in full."[42]

Merchants who had a reputation for honesty and ability but who ran into temporary difficulties were frequently allowed by creditors to continue operating their businesses in the hope that they would pull through. Business writers pointed out the practical value to being honest with one's creditors: "These houses which have become insolvent or embarrassed, and have made a clean showing of their affairs, have found much sympathy and no difficulty in arranging a settlement."[43] Of course, large debtors had an advantage because of the sheer size of their debts. The experience of New York wholesaler Arthur Tappan, outlined in the previous chapter, was one prominent example. Forced to ask for a general extension of the $1.1 million it owed, the firm was allowed by its creditors to give notes for eighteen months. Tappan and Company paid an estimated $100,000 in interest costs during this period, but creditors did not institute proceedings. Instead, the firm continued to operate, and the general extension on previous debts did not prevent it from obtaining some 1.5 million dollars' worth of new merchandise.[44]

Honesty was valued because debtors could so easily hide the true condition of their businesses. Even those who met their payments on time could, unbeknownst to their creditors, be sinking deeper and more hopelessly into debt. For example, some debtors paid their main suppliers punctually while letting payments to others run late; thus, a supplier thinking that an account was good could suddenly learn that the business was on the verge of insolvency. At times the borrower was aided by certain of his creditors, who hoped to recover some of their money by recommending the troubled debtor to other suppliers.[45] In this way, an insolvent business "may, by private assistance, still keep up an appearance of solvency."[46] Writers stressed that debtors who found themselves in deep trouble owed it to their creditors to declare insolvency immediately. Defoe had urged long before that "honesty obliges every man, when he sees that his stock is gone, that he is below the level, and eating into the estates of other men, to put a stop to it; and to do it in time, while something is left." He exhorted the debtor to "call his creditors together, lay his circumstances honestly before them, and pay as far as it will go . . . By breaking in time you will first obtain the character of an honest, tho' unfortunate man."[47] Declaring insolvency immediately would ensure that creditors received a proportionally bigger dividend than they would later, when the business had become utterly worthless.

Other instances of dishonesty included designating "preferred" creditors, usually associates or relatives, who were paid before other creditors. Although the practice was legal, it could easily be abused and so was carefully noted by creditors and credit reporters.[48] In England, preferences had been declared unlawful, but in the United States the practice continued to have the support of state legislatures and courts. The problem was that preferences could be used fraudulently, as when a debtor conspired with a preferred creditor to reassign to him (the debtor) part or all of the estate, leaving nothing for other creditors.[49] This was easy enough to do, as debtors had wide latitude in apportioning assets among creditors. Under a voluntary assignment, a debtor could transfer his assets to an "assignee," who acted as trustee over the estate. The trustee was responsible for converting the estate into money to pay creditors. Failing debtors could name a preferred creditor to act as the assignee, and assignments often required creditors to release the debtor from all legal liability. Unless creditors already held security, such as a mortgage or a lien, they had no choice but to acquiesce. Reforms were put in place by the Bankruptcy Act of 1841, but they met with only limited success.[50]

At times, a shrewd debtor gained almost complete control of the process and dictated terms to his hapless creditors. The insolvent, complained Pennsylvania Congressman Joseph Hopkinson,

> sits down to make, at his pleasure, what he calls an assignment; he deals out his estate to such persons, and in such portions, as he may deem most expedient for himself, or find most agreeable; he dictates the terms, having a special regard to his own interest, on which ten per cent. or five per cent. shall be paid to the claimants; he selects the persons, of course his kindest friends, who shall execute these trusts; and when everything is thus decided and prepared he summons his creditors to a meeting, not for consultation, not to learn their wishes and opinions about their own rights and interests, not to ask them what he shall do, but to inform them of what he has done.[51]

Hopkinson warned that the greater part of the property typically was given to preferred creditors, including those who had endorsed for the debtor. The practice of designating preferred creditors cut across all ethnic lines, but the R. G. Dun records indicate that Jewish merchants were singled out for paying their Jewish creditors first.

The preferred-creditor arrangement was hotly debated, but it proved difficult to end. A uniform national bankruptcy law would have solved the problem; not surprisingly, supplier-creditors in the country's large urban commercial centers, who were often disadvantaged relative to local creditors, were the law's most vocal supporters. Article I, Section 8 of the federal Constitution imposed on Congress the obligation to make a national bankruptcy law, but widespread resistance made the goal difficult to achieve. Many Americans believed that laws administered by federal authorities to further the interests of distant creditors should not replace what legal historian Tony Freyer calls the "associational" economy that was characteristic of local communities.[52]

Defenders of the preferred-creditor arrangement argued that some creditors simply deserved to be treated with more consideration than others and that insolvent debtors themselves should have the right to determine how their assets were divided. A letter to the editor of a Gainesville, Alabama, newspaper stated,

> Upon the whole, it seems to us there is nothing immoral in a debtor's preferring one creditor over another under peculiar circumstances, but on the contrary to neglect to do so would be the more unconscientious course . . . The unfortunate debtor who is unable to pay all he owes, cannot possibly give satisfaction to all his creditors, whatever course he may pursue. If all are placed upon an equality with respect to the division of his estate those whose claims stand upon higher grounds than others, will clamor against his ingratitude.[53]

Preferences appeared logical in light of practices such as endorsing, which placed a moral and psychological claim on the debtor to reciprocate favors that had been extended to him. The problem of preferences continued throughout the nineteenth century until the passage of a permanent national bankruptcy law in 1898 helped to resolve the issue.

Formal collection laws existed, but they were not uniform across states. Charles Francis Adams and Robert Hare argued that better laws were the key to preventing losses.[54] Some creditors, however, deemed the current laws to be so ineffectual that they actually argued against having any laws at all. Instead, they insisted that informal norms, such as an individual's sense of honor, remained the most effective guarantee of full repayment.[55] "If there were no laws for collecting debts," wrote one, "credit would be more generally founded upon character and debtors would, when unable to pay, lose caste . . . The force of public opinion influence[s] debtors more than law." Formal collection laws, moreover, involved high costs. The writer speculated that "more money, including the value of time spent in law suits, has been expended during the past thirty years than has been recovered by the aid of the collecting laws."[56]

"Honesty" and "honor" also encapsulated a set of shared assumptions about moral hazard versus the desire to encourage risk taking and entre-preneurialism, assumptions reflected in the changing bankruptcy laws in both Britain and the United States. Conceptions about debt and moral culpability shifted in the increasingly unstable, unpredictable economic environment. In the late seventeenth century, Cotton Mather had insisted that debtors were morally bound to pay their debts.[57] By the mid-eighteenth century, however, many writers exhibited at least partial acceptance of the idea that debts could be discharged under certain circumstances.[58]

Although ideas about moral culpability and the obligation to repay all of one's debts persisted, antebellum writers placed much greater stress than did their predecessors on the shared nature of the risk. Mercantile credit, they argued, was extended not as a favor but with the intention of making a profit. Creditors should therefore refrain from being overly harsh with debtors who were struggling to meet payments. In a lecture in the mid-1850s to the Young Men's Christian Union in Boston, one J. H. Allen stated that with "the utmost degree of circumspection, losses will occur." The creditor "spurns the idea of an advantage over his neighbor . . . Neither will he, if the bankrupt appear to be honest, oppress the spirit bowed down with sadness."[59] "It must be kept in mind," wrote J. N. Bellows of New York, "that the seller walks with his eyes open. He can select his own agents; give or refuse credit; easily learn the state of him to whom he intrusts his property. Moreover, the obligation is not on one side; it is a mutual risk."[60]

The very nature of mercantile credit forced creditor and debtor into partnership, for unlike bank credit, it was extended without collateral or liens. And although the goods could be seized if the debtor failed to pay, creditors knew that the process was cumbersome and expensive and that the seized goods would likely be sold at a steep discount. Overall, it was in the creditor's interest to give as much leeway to the unfortunate debtor as possible—provided, of course, that the debtor was operating honestly and in good faith. Defoe had made the argument for leniency on practical grounds, pointing out that it was in "the creditor's true interest." If the creditor "finds the debtor inclin'd to be honest, and he sees reason to believe he makes the best offer he can; he should accept the first offer, as being generally the best the debtor can make."[61] Business writers of the antebellum decades appear to have come to similar conclusions.

There was also concern that overly exacting standards of honesty—insisting on full payment of debts in an unstable economy—could be detrimental to the individual, his or her family, and society at large. Business writers urged creditors to balance toughness (to guard against fraud) with flexibility (to encourage legitimate business activity and entrepreneurship). Responding to stories about those who strove heroically to pay off all their creditors, one writer questioned the wisdom of the anecdotes, arguing that "they substitute a wild heroism of action which in grasping at one noble act tramples in the dust some humble virtues":

> Let us suppose, to illustrate our meaning, that the day-laborer . . . in putting before his mind this exciting object [of paying back all of his creditors] . . . neglected his health, his home, his children; gave nothing to schools, to religion, to public improvements. Absorbed in this one object, every thing else was forgotten, and his duties as a husband, a father, a citizen, a being dependent upon God, were made to yield to this chivalrous act of honesty. We say in such a case the infatuation of the man is an object of pity, and we must think better of his heart than of his head.[62]

Punctuality

The webs of credit relationships that characterized the American economy made stability dependent on the solvency of every merchant. Liquidity was as much a psychological as a purely practical problem: for the credit system to work smoothly, all merchants had to remain reasonably confident that bills would be paid and that the volume and velocity of trade would remain at a constant level. One large merchant's failure to pay a bill could have serious reverberations. At its worst, the result was a downward spiral, in which the collapse of confidence led to a rapid contraction of trade and then to an even greater loss of confidence. Business writers therefore insisted that failure to pay one's debts not only was immoral in the abstract but also had a palpable effect on the rest of society: "So dependent are business men upon one another," one writer declared in 1842, "that no man has the right, as a member of the mercantile community, however much his interests require the step, to voluntarily destroy one wheel of it . . . How many operations may be based upon his solvency!"[63] Another stated, "Many and many a time has the failure of one man to meet his obligations brought on the ruin of a score of others."[64]

Yet the traditional flexibility of trade creditors, arguably a positive trait in a volatile economy, compromised the strict punctuality with which debtors were expected to meet their payments. After the Civil War, it became more common for large jobbers to deposit notes at a bank payable at a certain date to their creditors—an instrument similar to a postdated check. According to one handbook, however, the numerous small retailers scattered around the country "shrink from giving a note payable at bank; and some altogether refuse to do so. They wish to buy on open account; or to give a note to be paid at maturity, if convenient; otherwise not. The number of really prompt and punctual men, as compared with those who are otherwise, is very small."[65]

Even in Defoe's time, it was understood that payment was contingent on the debtor's ability to achieve the requisite level of sales. Defoe singled out book credit transactions as "the loosest article in a tradesman's payments" and estimated that "not one man in twenty keeps to his time; and so easy are tradesmen to one another, that in general it is not much expected."[66] That lax attitude was much in evidence in the United States, where buyers, especially those who had a generally good credit record, regarded suppliers' refusal to extend payment schedules during tough times as a personal slight. Samuel Terry reported that a trader who found himself unexpectedly short of cash often preferred "as the least of two evils, to ask his creditor to extend [the payment terms], rather than to borrow from his friends or ask them to endorse a note, to raise the necessary funds."[67] Debtors with good reputations were often allowed to miss payments, and suppliers simply tacked on an interest rate to the balance. When they were unable to collect, creditors in the northeast increasingly could rely on banks to supply them with accommodation facilities, similar to a modern overdraft.[68]

Storekeepers were the first, crucial link in the chain of credit. Those in the West and South were criticized for their inefficiency in collecting from customers, who were mostly farmers.[69] The Mercantile Agency warned its correspondents about the lack of punctuality of "country" merchants:

> In our Cities the maker of a Note understands that he assumes a solemn obligation, to be paid at maturity, and he holds his paper as sacredly as our banks their issues. Their Bill Book is kept accordingly, and a protest is regarded as evidencing, at the least, a want of business promptness and accuracy. In the Country, generally, there is a different view taken. The trader gives his note at six or eight months, and about the time it falls due may recollect it or he may not. He may wonder to himself when it is due, and he may anticipate or fall behind. He believes that the fact of a protest in his case does not affect his standing or general credit . . . The system of "open accounts," which may imply six months and involve twelve is a wrong one.[70]

Another circular expressed the agency's opinion that the "Jobbing Merchant's embarrassments arise mostly from the want of promptness on the part of his country debtor; no definite time being fixed when the debt *must* be paid." The agency argued that country storekeepers should sell only for cash or short credit, for "the prosperity of the manufacturer, importer, banker, and jobber is largely dependent on the manner in which the country merchant does his business," and "his course tends to make or break all those above him."[71]

Country storekeepers themselves sometimes tried to implement a strict cash policy for their customers, but they were never able to sustain it because farmers simply did not have adequate cash to pay for store-bought goods. Writers often observed that credit relationships obliged local storekeepers to monitor their customers' behavior, "to see that they are not becoming irresponsible," according to Samuel Terry. He estimated that more than one-half of a retailer's time and energy was occupied by credit and collections, significantly more than was devoted to "the actual business of buying and selling."[72]

Edwin Freedley acknowledged the inherently contingent nature of the trade credit contract: "Creditors generally compel their debtors to fix a time of payment, and these promises are made, and understood to be made, conditionally on the fact of having the money at the time, which is not always the case." Because of this contingency, honest communication between debtor and creditor was critical to maintaining trust and confidence. "Punctuality," in other words, could be defined as informing one's creditors whenever, and for what reason, a payment would be late. A "punctual man will not keep his creditor in suspense as to the cause [of late payments], or put him to the trouble of calling to ascertain it; but *will give him timely intimation of the fact by sending him a note or an agent, or calling himself, and renew the promise.*" Freedley assured readers that such a man, "though he fails a dozen times in the same transaction, is more worthy of credit than the clown who, besides keeping you out of your money, consumes your time, and causes uneasy and unhappy feelings."[73] Relationships that were personal and not merely contractual could weather the inevitable delays imposed by an unpredictable economic environment.

Extravagance/Thrift

The term "extravagant" was frequently used to describe merchants who operated on too high a ratio of expenses to income or whose level of inventory was inappropriate for the amount and type of trade they were doing. There was little agreement about what constituted safe ratios. (Samuel Terry in 1869 made one of the earliest attempts to recommend one: "[A] retailer's total expenses, including those of his private living, ought not to exceed one-half the gross profit of his business." Losses "will take from fifteen to twenty-five per cent more of the gross profits to cover them." A retailer's typical net profits, then, were between twenty-five to thirty-five per cent of gross profits.)[74] Writers urged tradesmen to be realistic about the demand of their markets and to try to fulfill it accurately. Overbuying, or tying up capital in goods that were not likely to sell quickly, was a sign of trouble. So was high overhead, the "marble palaces, granite buildings, pediments, columns, tiled floors, painting, gilding, &c.," which "have a tendency to foster a sprit of extravagance in trade that leads to ruin."[75] Instead, moderation "often proves to be a safeguard," Thomas Cary lectured in 1846, "for in numerous cases, those who make the largest purchases find that, through unforeseen changes, they have the most to regret before their engagements become due."[76]

Because financial statements gave only a poor indication of a business's liquidity, evidence of thrift was an important signal that borrowers were managing their cash responsibly. Credit-reporting agencies extended their scrutiny to borrowers' household and personal spending habits, a practice that opened them to charges of spying. Yet the structure of proprietorships and partnerships mandated such close, even intrusive, examination because the expenses of both household and business were paid from the same funds. The *Providence Journal* made the connection when it remarked, "It cannot . . . be a matter of surprise that the present general prevalence of an unrestricted indulgence in showy habits of dress and of living, should cause the failure of nine-tenths of the men who embark in business."[77]

The close association of thrift and household consumption highlighted the role of women in maintaining a household's solvency. Writers of fiction exploited the subject as a fertile source for concocting morality tales.[78] Newspapers also weighed in. "We care not how much money a man may make," the *Illinois Daily Journal* stated, "if his wife does not second his endeavors, he is just as sure of dying poor as if he had kept a grocery and trusted every body."[79] Business writers counseled men to inform their wives and children of the close connection between their spending habits and the reputation of the family firm. A merchant whose business cannot support his living expenses, according to the *Philadelphia Merchant,* should "explain his condition to his wife and family, who have an equal interest with him in sustaining his reputation and standing, as an honorable business man . . . He is not a good business man who keeps his wife and family in ignorance of his ability to indulge their fancied requirements."[80]

Ideas about thrift were influenced by a more-sophisticated understanding of opportunity costs, or the value of all goods and services forgone in the pursuit of particular goals. Interest earned on savings, for example, were an opportunity cost when individuals chose to spend rather than save their money. Antebellum Americans were fascinated by the power of compound interest, which turned small, regular savings into impressive fortunes. The *Providence Journal* calculated in 1850 that a "six cent piece saved daily" over a number of years "would provide a fund of nearly $7,000, sufficient to purchase a fine farm." A tradesman "who can lay by about a dollar per day, will find himself similarly possessed of one hundred and sixteen thousand dollars, and numbered among the one hundred and seventy-five rich men who owned one-half of the property of the city of Providence." Given those bullish returns, spending money on frivolous pleasures seemed to make even less business sense.[81]

Ironically, thrifty behavior became more difficult to maintain in an increasingly consumer-driven society. The literature of the period displayed the tension between the desirability of producing and selling ever-larger amounts of consumer goods and the censure against extravagant consumption. The *Illinois Daily State Journal,* for example, preached against "nobby" (dandified) behavior in young men: "Employers cannot be too careful of 'nobby' young men. Temptation cannot be always resisted either by weak or immoral natures." But the *Journal* acknowledged that its own survival depended on selling advertising space to stores that catered to these dandies: "So important . . . has the 'nobby' branch of business become, that some newspapers live by recording the constant changes in the fashions of 'butterflies, suspenders, shirt collars, and gaiters.'"[82]

Vices

The range of behaviors that could be termed "vices" was potentially wide. Credit-reporting agencies, however, restricted their reporting to only two: excessive drinking and gambling, the habits most likely to affect an individual's business performance in a negative way. Reports were reticent or silent about other foibles, such as licentiousness. Occasionally reports commented on sexual misbehavior.[83] But such censure was rare, even though correspondents were privy to local gossip about the sexual behaviors of its businesspeople.

Reports of drunkenness were far more typical.[84] Temperance was an explosive issue throughout much of the nineteenth century, when the "vice" of drinking became linked to middle-class assumptions about respectability and business success. Like Europeans of the period, eighteenth- and early-nineteenth-century Americans drank large quantities of alcohol, in part because reliable sources of clean, fresh water were difficult to secure. Improvements in distillation beginning in the early nineteenth century and the growing national and international markets for grain provided surplus corn that could be turned into whiskey, which became plentiful and cheap—cheaper even than coffee, tea, or milk. Whiskey was drunk by both sexes and among all classes; even older children consumed it. Cider, produced in great quantities in apple-growing regions, was another popular drink. After 1800 the total quantity of alcohol consumed shot upward until it reached nearly four gallons per capita in 1830, the highest rate of consumption in American history.[85]

A temperance movement began among the Protestant clergy, and temperance associations were established in New York in 1808 and Massachusetts in 1813. The movement spread quickly, fanned by the Second Great Awakening; by 1834 the American Temperance Society claimed more than seven thousand local associations with more than 1.2 million members. The movement appears to have had an impact, for alcohol consumption fell sharply: from 1840 until the late twentieth century, the highest levels of consumption never exceeded two gallons per capita, or less than half the rate of the 1820s. The changing structure of the grain market helped bring about the success of temperance advocates. As distilling and marketing became a more interregional business and less of an activity engaged in by one's neighbors, it became easier to mount an organized opposition. Whiskey and other spirits became associated with moral and spiritual degradation. Many Americans, especially those living in small towns, rural areas, and middle-class neighborhoods, advocated complete abstinence. Prior to the Civil War, men led the temperance movement, but afterwards women became the driving force.

A reform movement that had its roots in religion became inextricably tied to the needs of capitalist development.[86] Credit reports explicitly and directly tied sobriety to individual success, while the business press linked the abuse of alcohol to inefficiency and reduced profits. "To dissipate is not alone to trifle with health and reputation, but to rob the employer of a portion of the time for which he pays," wrote *Hunt's*. A young man "must be as regular in his habits away from business as when in business."[87] The *Philadelphia Merchant* stated, "In the ratio that the bar-room prospers, the merchant suffers loss . . . The liquor seller is directly pitted against the dealer in all wholesome and useful articles of consumption, and we submit that all merchants . . . should array themselves promptly and decidedly on the side of temperance and against all forms of alcohol as a beverage."[88]

Energy/Focus

"Energy," the quality of being "wide awake," was lauded in the credit reports and the business press. Yet there was concern lest mere energy supplanted good judgment and caution. The tension points to a definitional problem that many theorists of entrepreneurial capitalism still must resolve. As Julian Hoppit points out, historians tend not to differentiate between the terms "businessman" and "entrepreneur"; consequently, "definitions of 'entrepreneur' have multiplied with ever-diminishing returns. Confusion has arisen because the dividing lines between inventive, innovative, and imitative businessmen are hazy and unclear."[89] Similarly, Thomas Doerflinger writes in his history of late-eighteenth-century Philadelphia merchants that one must distinguish between the "atavistic" and speculative capitalism practiced by some, particularly during boom times, and "the icy worldly asceticism of Weber" that was practiced by others.[90] Some business owners resisted the call to be aggressive, pushing, and intensely competitive. Instead, they emphasized the independence conferred by having one's own business and took pride in their reputations for integrity and steadiness. The outlook was particularly marked among self-employed artisans such as blacksmiths and carpenters.[91]

Along with many business writers of the period, credit reporters tended to reject the older artisanal outlook, which was content with establishing an independent living and which regarded the overbold ambitions of the mercantile class with distaste.[92] R. G. Dun differentiated between the caution necessary among bankers and the greater risk taking demanded by trade. "The Banker," according to the 1859 edition of Dun's reference book, "loans his money on interest. Having no other consideration, it should be a fundamental principle with him, in all cases to be secure. His judgment should be rigid." The importer, manufacturer, and jobber, by contrast, were driven by "the stimulus of good profits." Thus, "a larger liberality is expected. Holding these views, we have adapted our markings accordingly."[93]

Tolerance for risk taking and speculation increased during the nineteenth century, to the point where some business writers began to equate excessive caution with stagnation and idleness.[94] In 1853 *Hunt's* wrote, "There is nothing gained by idleness and sloth . . . Men must be active, persevering and energetic."[95] Another writer remarked, "In this active, stirring country of ours there is no room for the lazy, prodigal spendthrift of time . . . the world cannot afford to wait for him, and if he wishes to be in the first rank, he must be up and dressed, ready at the instant, and setting this good example to others he will reap the fruits which they may find sometimes snatched from their grasp."[96]

The relentless boosterism in the Old Northwest and West encouraged men to be aggressive and expansive. Boosters publicized their towns widely to outsiders and mailed promotional materials and newspaper clippings to interested parties as far away as Europe.[97] Town histories began appearing when many of these localities were only a few decades old, and they became effective promotional vehicles as well as sources for information on local businesses. Newspapers pushed the benefits of advertising by appealing to this aspect of the business culture. The nineteenth century, wrote the *Illinois Daily Journal,*

has opened a new era in mercantile enterprise . . . Our merchants have received, as it were, a new revelation.—Eschewing the stereotyped ideas of former generations, they have liberalized their policy;

abandoning the contracted sphere to which their predecessors confined themselves, they have extended their operations far and wide, annihilating distance, surmounting difficulties, and defying competition . . . Those who have acted on this principle have given new impetus to business, and gained vastly on the more cautious dealers who have resisted the tide of progress and stand where they stood a quarter of a century since.[98]

Even writers such as Freeman Hunt, who lectured young men to choose a salaried occupation over starting a business, expressed deep admiration for risk-taking entrepreneurs.[99] The attitude intensified after the Civil War, when extreme cautiousness became more closely equated with the "plodder," the man so "chicken-hearted" as to be a failure even when he was not literally insolvent.[100]

Sometimes, however, an entrepreneur could be too energetic—that is, unfocused, with "too many irons in the fire." The temptation was especially strong among merchants, lawyers, financiers, and builders, the men who were most likely to be involved in speculative ventures and who comprised the largest portion of the bankruptcy rolls.[101] The inability to remain in one pursuit was as much a sign of danger as was the lack of enterprise. Business writers warned against the perils of tying up capital, time, and energy in outside ventures. (Ironically, both Lewis Tappan and Robert G. Dun were themselves guilty of having too many pursuits.)[102]

Of the character traits, "energy" was the most explicitly gendered: credit correspondents tended to praise the quality in men and ignore or downplay it in women. Business writers were more likely to admire women for their industriousness rather than their attempts to enlarge their businesses or take entrepreneurial risks.

Experience

Technically, experience belonged within the category of "capacity" (business ability). Certain elements, however, clearly shaded into the area of character. The best new firms were generally deemed to be those owned by former clerks in the same line of business who had financed their new store with money saved from their salaries.[103] Capital of that kind was proof of thrift (good cash management) as well as experience.[104] Lewis Atherton found that 46 percent of the country merchants he investigated began as store clerks, saving money until they could start a business of their own.[105]

Storekeepers often hired clerks with the understanding that they would someday become junior partners—future financial reward for the hard labor the young men provided during their apprenticeship years.[106] Clerking could be a strenuous occupation; some establishments required its staff to work "from early dawn almost, till ten o'clock in the evening and sometimes up to midnight," according to one concerned letter-writer to the *Daily Illinois State Journal*.[107] Relatively few young men were up to that challenge. One writer claimed to have met during a twelve-year period more than four hundred dry goods clerks in New York City, of whom he could not "find ten of the number now in successful business. One in fifty is a fair estimate of the number of clerks that succeed in business for themselves." Too many "country boys" crowded into New York City looking for a well-paying white-collar job, but few lasted the course: "Those who are not ruined by dissipation, waste five or six years of their lives in learning a business, and then return to some profitable employment in the country, or go to California."[108] The amount of capital required to enter the retail sector remained relatively low compared to opening a wholesaling or manufacturing concern, and the low barriers attracted individuals who lacked the requisite experience, talent, and stamina. One of the beneficial effects of the Mercantile Agency, according to its supporters, was that it would force out those who were unsuited. As one writer remarked, "Trade is a science, to which many, who would make excellent mechanics or agriculturists, are wholly incompetent."[109]

Credit reports noted whether individuals were "educated" to the trade, referring to apprenticeships rather than formal course work. At any rate, few courses on mercantile subjects were available in colleges and universities; the "mercantile" departments in the law schools of Harvard and Yale, which offered lectures on commercial law, were among the few exceptions.[110] Curriculums specifically designed to teach proper business methods were increasingly proposed throughout the North and South in the decades before the Civil War.[111] Until the end of the nineteenth century, however, business education consisted of an eclectic mix of formal apprenticeships, informal on-the-job training, and courses offered by small schools run by enterprising individuals. These schools first began appearing in the 1820s, and although not numerous, they dominated the field of business education until about 1890. Run as money-making operations, the owner sometimes comprised the entire faculty and may also have written the textbook that students were required to purchase. Students typically were employees in business establishments and took courses in the evenings. Courses were restricted to only three subjects: arithmetic, book-keeping, and penmanship (considered a technical skill until the advent of the typewriter). There were no courses on the theory behind mercantile practices and nothing on credit.

By 1850 about twenty such business schools operated in various cities throughout the East and Middle West. Among these were Dolber's Commercial College (founded in New York City in 1835), Duff's Mercantile College (Pittsburgh, 1840), Comer's Initiatory Counting Rooms (Boston, 1840), Jones Commercial College (Saint Louis, 1841), Scholfield's Commercial Academy (Providence, Rhode Island, 1846), Spencerian Business College (Cleveland, Ohio, 1848), French's Business College (Boston, 1848), and Paine's Business College (New York, 1849).[112] Business writers generally had a poor opinion of these schools. Freedley, for one, strongly recommended against a liberal arts or business school education in favor of two years in a counting house, followed by a course of study in mercantile law.[113]

After the Civil War, Andrew Carnegie famously remarked that college graduates did not make for successful businessmen.[114] Working as a clerk in a mercantile establishment still was considered far more important than a formal education. Credit reports continued to view clerkships approvingly. Increasingly, they also tracked borrowers' experience across multiple locations, information that was critical in a large country with a highly mobile population.

Age and Marital Status

Credit-reporting agencies were not always successful in discovering the ages of business owners, particularly women. Even so, age was considered a critical piece of information. Younger proprietors who already had some experience in trade were deemed the best prospects; older ones, by contrast, had less time to settle a bad debt. A Mercantile Agency circular observed that some merchants "will not sell even to an honest, capable man unless he has *capital*, particularly if he is advanced in years."[115]

Marital status was considered important for a mix of reasons. Married men generally were regarded as more stable, and having a spouse and children to help run the business was a positive attribute. Although divorce was relatively rare, it could affect the financial standing of a business. (The notorious *Beardsley* case, for example, turned on rumors about John Beardsley's impending divorce from his wife, Mary.)[116] Marital status also became an important practical consideration when the Married Women's Property acts, first enacted in the South during the late 1830s primarily to protect the assets of wives from their husbands' creditors, removed many of the obstacles to owning and operating a business. *Hunt's Merchants' Magazine* recognized the significance of the statutes, observing in 1850 that any laws "making or tending to make the wife an independent person as respects property, are of great mercantile interest, not only because they alter the relations of business men, but tend to create a new mercantile class—business women."[117]

The new laws had an unintended effect: they allowed men to protect business assets by legally transferring them to their wives through instruments such as chattel mortgages, a practice that credit reporters frequently recorded.[118] An anonymous credit-reporting journal kept by an individual living in Jackson, Michigan, was typical. It stated that the wife of one P. J. Avery, owner of the town weekly, "has some property. *All* the property I think is in her name and would be difficult to reach if a collection were forced."[119] After transferring a business's assets to his wife, a man could resume as her "agent," in the knowledge that her property could not be seized to pay off his old debts. The more obviously fraudulent transfers were declared illegal by the courts, but the ploy often succeeded.[120] Another way to protect family and business assets was for the husband to set up a trust, managed by a third party (trustee), which reserved property for his wife and children.[121] How the Married Women's Property laws affected the actions and decisions of women engaged in business is unclear. Despite the growing literature on this subject, scholars have paid more attention to how the laws benefited men and families rather than to how women themselves may have exploited the laws.[122]

Marriage had a mixed effect on women's creditworthiness because the occupations and financial worth of husbands varied widely. In some instances, marriage did not necessarily lend stability to women's businesses because their husbands held jobs that were insecure or low paying. Conversely, women who married men with stable occupations and a significant financial worth saw their creditworthiness improve.[123]

Women- and Black-Owned Businesses

Participants in business were a diverse population. Credit reports reflected that reality and included significant numbers of women and blacks. Women appeared in greater numbers in the credit reports than did blacks, but both groups tended to operate smaller businesses in the service sector and on the retail rather than wholesale level. Proportionately fewer retailers than wholesalers were covered by the agencies prior to the Civil War; as a result, R. G. Dun rarely reported on women- and black-owned businesses during the 1840s and 1850s but covered a larger portion of them during subsequent decades. Too small to command much credit from large wholesale houses in the country's commercial centers, most were dependent on local suppliers for much of their mercantile credit.[124]

Sex and race were central considerations in a credit report; no individual was perceived purely as a businessperson, without the qualifiers male, female, white, or black either explicitly reported or implicitly recognized. Yet it is also true that credit reports tried to include details about the capital strength, business ability, and character traits of all individuals, regardless of sex, color, or ethnicity; moreover, judgments were fluid and subject to revision. Widely held prejudices were modified or reinforced according to behaviors observed by other members in the individual's community or, less frequently, by outside suppliers who had previous dealings with the individual. The categories of race, ethnicity, and gender were therefore not static but always somewhat unstable. Credit reporters and their informers constantly reconstructed these categories in the process of reevaluating their subjects' behavior over time.

A small but significant minority of women—about 145,000 in 1870— was engaged in business pursuits, and women made up about 10 percent of urban businesspeople. As with Jews in the clothing industry, the large number of reports on women reflected their numerical importance in specific trades, especially those—such as millinery and dressmaking—that served primarily female customers. In 1870 these two trades made up the fourth most important occupational category for women, who accounted for some 98 percent of the trades' workers.[125] The vast majority of women-owned businesses was small; some were minuscule. Even after the Civil War, a reported total worth of only a few hundred dollars was not unusual. Yet business ownership was an important source of income for women. In the midwestern states of Illinois, Indiana, Iowa, Michigan, Minnesota, Ohio, and Wisconsin, for example, the number of women in business was roughly equivalent to that of female teachers and higher than the number of female factory workers.[126]

The mortality rate for women-owned establishments appears to have conformed to the average for all businesses. An investigation of male- and female-owned businesses in Poughkeepsie, New York, between 1843 and 1873 found that 60 percent closed before they were four years old. That figure mirrors Lucy Murphy's findings, based on 213 female business owners in Illinois, that the average concern lasted 3.74 years.[127] Yet contemporaries perceived female-run businesses as peculiarly short-lived. "The want of perseverance is sometimes said to adhere very generally to the female sex, when they are employed in business pursuits," observed Samuel Terry. He speculated that the reasons had less to do with lack of ability than the widely held sentiment among female proprietors "that the business is not of essential importance in itself, and is only a make-shift or stepping stone, as in their case it must be regarded, to the higher aims of existence"—presumably, those of marriage and raising children.[128] The perception, widespread in American society among both sexes, was already well entrenched during the colonial period, when women in business were assumed to have entered the field only on a temporary basis, usually upon the death of a husband or male relative. Historians have confirmed that women's motivations in the business realm generally differed from men's. For women, business tended to be "a rather humdrum practical affair, where money is made rather than accumulated, where growth and expansion is the exception rather than the rule," writes Mary Yeager. Business "was more often than not simply 'work'—a way to make a living and survive."[129]

Moreover, the vast majority of women-owned businesses was thinly capitalized, and this, rather than the owners' sex alone, made credit correspondents wary of recommending women for credit.[130] Of the Boston milliners and dressmakers who appeared in the Dun ledgers, 62 percent were reported to have "no means" or "small means" of $1,000 or less.[131] In 1857 a correspondent in Springfield, Illinois, observed that milliners there seldom or never owned real estate and generally had only a small amount of merchandise on hand. During the 1860s $1,000 to $2,000 was sufficient to run a millinery business in a small town such as Springfield, Illinois. By contrast, the average business means of Springfield's dry goods establishments in the period 1848–1858 totaled $8,700; for clothing businesses, the figure was $4,500. In the 1870s, most of Springfield's milliners continued to operate with a relatively small amount of capital invested in their businesses, mostly in the form of inventory. Throughout the nineteenth century, the typical millinery business in the United States continued to be thinly capitalized. In 1900 the *Illustrated Milliner* estimated that 78 percent of these businesses were worth $1,000 or less.[132]

A small asset base, irregular cash flow, and a perceived lower commitment to the business were among the risks associated with female-owned businesses. Indeed, the male-dominated wholesaling establishments that specialized in supplying milliners were known to be less profitable and successful than their counterparts in other lines.[133] The risks were especially high for out-of-state creditors. Local ones, favored by state laws and courts as well as by geographical proximity, could collect payments more easily than could outsiders—who, presumably, were the Dun reports' main target audience. Surviving credit reports indicate that milliners could often obtain credit from local suppliers, but distant ones were warned to be careful.[134]

Like the Jewish clothing establishments discussed in Chapter 4, many women-owned businesses were difficult to assess. Reporters often had trouble distinguishing women-run businesses from those nominally owned by women but in fact run by husbands or male relatives. Those that operated from homes rather than shops presented the further problem of being inscrutable; agency reporters could not inspect them as they could a store for evidence of good stock turnover, decent fixtures, or overtrading, nor could they gauge the success of the business by the number of customers patronizing the shop.

Yet correspondents expressed little of the distrust of women-owned businesses that pervaded the reports on Jewish businesses. Instead, the credit-reporting firms accepted that the opacity of women-owned establishments was the result not of "trickery" but of their small scale and the fact that many were operated out of private homes. Milliners, in particular, were regarded not as outsiders but as respectable members of the community. Christie Daily's work on Iowa milliners notes that the social columns of local newspapers often featured these women alongside the town's leading citizens.[135] Although the middle-class concept of separate spheres endorsed a "cult of domesticity," positive views of women in business were by no means lacking in the popular media.[136]

Relegating women to a separate sphere confined them to certain occupations, most notably food preparation and distribution, lodging, and the production of women's clothing. Yet the sexual division of labor may also have protected women from having to compete with men in these trades.[137] Writers sometimes waxed indignant when men occupied jobs that the writers believed should have been reserved for women.[138] Within the "women's" trades, female ambition was not only acknowledged, but institutionalized. As Wendy Gamber points out, "the desire to get ahead was built into the very structure of the [dressmaking and millinery] trades." A milliner began first as a "maker," who produced the body of a hat, and then proceeded to "trimmer," decorating the hat with feathers, ribbons, lace, and other trimmings. After about a year, the ambitious apprentice might be expected to open a shop of her own, a move that entailed considerable financial risk, or to begin doing customized work from her home.[139]

Yet approbation of female enterprise had its limits, and "energy" was overwhelmingly deemed a masculine trait. Although women were frequently described as "honest," "industrious," and "respectable," words such as "enterprising" were reserved for men. Women appeared in the credit reports not as "risk-taking capitalists," according to Susan Ingalls Lewis, but as "'self-employed' artisans, shopkeepers, and petty manufacturers."[140] To be sure, these characteristics could sometimes make women better credit risks than men. Peter Earling summed up several decades' worth of experience when he wrote that women in business were usually cautious, economical, not overly ambitious, and therefore risk averse. They tended not to indulge in the vices that plagued so many men: little if any of their money was spent on smoking and drinking, for example. As a result, "the financial status in which women receive credit would not warrant us in giving credit to men, whatever their business might be."[141] A study of Denver covering the period from 1859 to 1877 concluded that Earling's comments were generally accurate. Women deemed to have good character and habits were assessed favorably, even at times outdoing their male counterparts. In Denver, saloon keepers rather than women or ethnic minorities received the harshest appraisals, perhaps because these establishments were considered a threat to the community's stability and business reputation.[142] Credit reporters declined to apply to women the harsh descriptions ("no good," "worthless") that they unhesitatingly used on men.

For blacks, business opportunities were even more circumscribed. In the first half of the nineteenth century, most enterprising blacks were relegated to occupational lines such as catering, barbering, and the tailoring trades, whose customer bases were overwhelmingly white.[143] Yet entrepreneurial activity occurred even among individuals who were enslaved. Slaves could not legally engage in independent economic activity, yet they did so and at times openly. Court cases from the eighteenth century to the Civil War demonstrate that at least a small number of slaves operated with a great deal of independence; they performed supervisory and managerial work, sometimes over white workers, and a few appear actually to have owned their businesses. These were rare exceptions, to be sure, but such activity was not unknown. More common was the phenomenon of slaves hiring themselves out, usually (but not always) with their masters' consent.[144]

In her groundbreaking history of black enterprise, Juliet E. K. Walker estimates that five thousand businesses were established by free blacks in

1860, a participation rate of one business per one hundred free blacks. Even during and after Reconstruction, when increased industrialization along with rigid black codes and Jim Crow laws placed serious barriers to the establishment and successful running of a business, blacks continued to be active in doing so. They were, however, unable to participate in the ownership of large industrial concerns, and opportunities in at least one traditionally black-dominated field (catering) diminished.[145]

Credit reports almost always indicated when a business was black owned. These individuals were designated as "free men of color," "darky," "negro," "colored," "quadroon," "mulatto," and—infrequently—"nigger." As with Jewish business owners, the agency reports sometimes noted that an individual was a good risk despite belonging to a suspect group. Apart from the specific allusions to race, black businesses generally were described in terms similar to those used for white businesses: some large, well-established concerns were granted a rating of "A-1." (New Orleans, in particular, had several large black-owned businesses, including commodity brokers and commission merchants, land speculators, real estate brokers, and developers.) Good character and habits, or the lack of them, were appraised separately from capital strength. Slow payments, the issuance of notes, and discounting at banks also were reported.[146]

By the mid-nineteenth century, a recognizable method for assessing creditworthiness had emerged among American merchants, which the new credit-reporting agencies helped to transmit. The method was shaped by the obstacles faced by creditors, particularly their limited ability to procure the payment records of individuals. Instead, creditors and credit-reporting firms focused their attention on business owners, scrutinizing their financial standing and patterns of behavior for clues about their ability and willingness to pay debts.

Aside from insurance and railroad firms, however, businesses did not make their financial records public, and there was no expectation that they should do so. Statements, when made at all, were used primarily for internal administration. Long after the first credit-reporting firms were established, the notion persisted that being asked to give a statement impugned an individual's honor. Fearful of alienating buyers, many suppliers declined to ask for statements, and credit reporters found much resistance when trying to obtain them.

The method for calculating creditworthiness was also shaped by the long credit terms of the day. When most lending is short term (thirty to ninety days), cash flow and liquidity are the most important considerations. Longer terms, however, make information on past behavior more important because information on a trader's current cash position is of little value if payment is not due for several months. In these cases, the proven willingness to meet one's obligations becomes a more telling indicator of creditworthiness.[147]

Because individuals' payment records were largely unavailable, "character" traits served as a proxy for the willingness to pay debts. As discussed in this chapter, credit reports emphasized a specific set of traits: honesty, punctuality, extravagance (or thrift), the vices of drinking and gambling, energy, focus and perseverance, experience, age, and marital status.[148] The reports tended not to contain information such as membership in political parties, a significant omission in a period when these institutions played an important role in the construction of (white) men's social identities. Nor did reports tend to note membership in social clubs or churches—again, a noteworthy omission given the crucial position these institutions held, especially in small-town life.

The omission of membership in Protestant denominations is particularly puzzling. In "The Protestant Sects and the Spirit of Capitalism," Max Weber noted that in the United States, membership in Quaker, Baptist, Methodist, and other denominations created networks that facilitated economic activities, including the granting of credit.[149] Why, then, did the credit-reporting agencies not include information that would presumably have been of interest to wholesalers who may have been members of these national Protestant denominations? Procuring the information would not have involved much additional cost. The fact that the agencies never chose to include it suggests that, contrary to Weber's observation, American creditors did not rely too heavily on membership in specific religious groups as a sign of trustworthiness. Indeed, they did not pay much attention at all to individuals' religious activities, including regular church attendance.

With regard to women and black business owners, at least two historical problems arise. First, how were they appraised? Second, how did these appraisals affect the structure and nature of the American economy? Researchers have only begun to investigate the first of these questions. But the second—in particular, whether credit reporting helped to segment the economy more rigidly by sex, race, and ethnic origin—has yet to be systematically investigated. Reflecting the attitudes of the larger society, credit reporters accepted recent immigrants, blacks, and women as participants in the mercantile and agricultural sectors. But as owners and managers, these individuals were concentrated overwhelmingly in small establishments. They were far less numerous in the wholesaling sector, and virtually nonexistent in the large, capital-intensive industrial enterprises that became more numerous after the Civil War. What role did credit reporting play in that historical development? The institution embedded ways of doing and thinking about business more deeply into American culture and helped naturalize ways of thinking about types of businesspeople. In the same way that opaque business practices were not granted legitimacy by credit reporters, neither (for example) were "female" ways of doing business. These included the greater propensity of women to shuttle between the responsibilities of home and work, behavior that was interpreted as women's "want of perseverance." The institution of credit reporting may well have helped to preclude the development of a viable, female-centered tradition of doing business that would have better accommodated women's domestic and family responsibilities.

Yet the very fact that women and blacks appeared at all in the Dun ledgers, and in great numbers, deserves some comment. Had these individuals been dismissed as undeserving of credit by the fact of their sex and race alone, the credit-reporting agencies would not have wasted the resources to report on them. Or, even more proactively, the agencies might have issued blacklists warning that particular businesses were female or black owned and that creditors should steer clear of them. But neither of these scenarios occurred. To the contrary, the agencies reported on tens of thousands of female-owned enterprises and on a lesser (but still substantial) number of black-owned ones, some in great detail and over a number of years. Competition among credit-reporting agencies beginning in the 1860s may well account for the inclusiveness; comprehensive coverage of a locality's business establishments became equated with superior service and better value for subscribers' money. The agencies were also simply bowing to actual practice: because many suppliers wanted to extend credit to these individuals, the agencies were obliged to include them.

In light of recent scholarship, it is also important to note that the agencies reported both positive and negative information. Trade protection societies, by contrast, focused almost exclusively on negative information because members feared losing their good customers to other members.[150] Recent studies have found that reports containing both positive and negative information allow creditors to assess more accurately the likelihood that a borrower will default. Moreover, reporting negative information alone has socially undesirable effects: it hurts younger and lower-income borrowers and those who have been at their job or residence for only a short time.[151] Good borrowers, too, are penalized under this system, because they are prevented from broadcasting their good records to other lenders.

Unlike arrangements designed merely to alert creditors about bad debtors, the credit-reporting system consisted of narratives that attempted to capture the paradoxes and complexities of individuals' business experiences. Thus, an individual could be described as both wildly extravagant and honest, or as occasionally intemperate but well thought of by the trade. Detail and history mattered a great deal, and the agencies instructed their reporters to provide as much of this as possible. "We are unwilling to assume the responsibility of reporting any person good or safe without accompanying it with qualifying remarks," the Saint Louis office of the Mercantile Agency wrote to its correspondents in 1851, "and where they are reported bad or unsafe, we wish to have the report enable us to state why they are so; whether through dishonesty, want of means, or deficient business knowledge."[152]

As late as 1860, the Mercantile Agency's New York office refused to issue written reports to subscribers, insisting that they personally visit the firm's office. Some records stretched back several years and contained indications of both success and failure. No written summary, the agency argued, could do justice to such a complex narrative:

> When reports are *written,* they necessarily are given in a *condensed* form; and, where the *history* of a trader *covers nineteen years,* there are so many points to be considered, that *different* minds would form *different impressions.* Clerks might form an opinion that the subscriber would not, and, to protect himself in each case for *each* case is important, he should have the Records read to him, bringing his *own mind* to bear on the subject, and eliciting the truth, referring in doubtful cases to one of our firm.

Subscribers living far from the firm's offices received written information, "but invariably under a very especial supervision." Moreover, the New York office required them to obtain their semiannual reports in person.[153] In 1865 the manager of the Chicago branch wrote to his subscribers cautioning against relying exclusively on the published reference books: "It is not intended as a substitute for the detailed reports upon our Records; no work of this kind can possibly supply their place."[154]

These urgings were no doubt prompted in part by the fear of lawsuits, which encouraged the agencies to emphasize that decisions about whom to trust ultimately were the responsibility of creditors alone.[155] But these comments also reflected the tendency of nineteenth-century business writers to regard human nature as malleable. Individuals changed; they became better merchants or, conversely, fell into dissipation and ruin. From a wholesaler's point of view, these individuals—changeable and difficult to put into static categories—were the higher-risk customers who might nevertheless prove profitable. New customers were important because a supplier's customer base was dynamic and constantly shifting; individuals continually pulled up stakes and moved or left retailing altogether. Success, as well as failure, prompted these decisions. Lewis Atherton, for example, found a tendency among successful storekeepers in the Midwest to shift to occupations, such as banking or politics, which were considered more prestigious.[156]

Although rational, the method for determining creditworthiness was not optimally efficient because creditors and correspondents were characterized by as many levels of ability as were the subjects of credit reports. Some correspondents, especially during the agencies' early years, submitted information that was confused or simply wrong. And the subjects of the reports at times confounded the odds: drunkards and gamblers prospered (to the evident disgust of the reporters), while able and honest merchants failed and did not recover. Yet the business literature of the period assumed that successful lending and borrowing were not purely a matter of luck. No method could ensure success every time, but in the absence of completely reliable information, specific steps could still be taken to decrease the chances of making a bad decision. The conventions that came to define credit reporting may be compared to those in accounting, which also evolved over time and contain a degree of arbitrariness and imprecision.[157] Like accounting, credit reporting simplified reality and rendered items more comparable, making it easier for creditors to make more "rational" decisions.[158] The terse quality of the reports did not completely mask the complex experiences of individuals whose fortunes were documented over a number of years.

A homely, folksy quality pervaded the method employed by nineteenth-century creditors, which might tempt modern analysts and scholars to dismiss it. Yet these very qualities are what account for the method's historical importance. Thomas Haskell uses the word "recipe" to describe the attempts to solve business and social problems, which burgeoned beginning in the eighteenth century: "It was not only the exotic achievements of Newtonian science or dramatic labor-saving devices like the steam engine that underwrote the Enlightenment optimism but also the buoyancy supplied by a surge of homely recipes for getting things done."[159] "Recipe" appropriately describes the method of determining creditworthiness that evolved during the first half of the nineteenth century. Precisely because it was simple, the method was perceived as widely accessible rather than confined to those with special privileges, training, or knowledge. Douglass North has argued that by standardizing expectations and lowering the costs of monitoring, such informal rules encourage spontaneous cooperation and a greater willingness to trade.[160] The assumption that creditworthiness could be determined through simple and careful calculation by any reasonably intelligent creditor may well have increased the number who were willing to try.

4

Jewish Merchants and the Struggle over Transparency

Mid-nineteenth century Americans found much to respect about Jewish ways of doing business. Jewish merchants were perceived to be thrifty, orderly, "wide-awake" go-getters in a country that had come to embrace the values of the market and the ideal of the self-made man. American elites could afford to be indulgent. The number of Jews in the United States was small, and they were deemed less threatening than were the "disorderly" and "intemperate" Irish (and to a lesser extent Germans) who emigrated to the United States in large numbers beginning in the 1840s. The absence in Judaism of a central political-religious authority further distinguished Jews from Catholic immigrants ("papists"), whose mass arrival inflamed nativist sentiments and fundamentally altered the American political party system.

Nevertheless, specific Jewish practices clashed with the assumptions that underlay the practice of credit granting, which the new credit-reporting agencies were embedding into American business culture. The struggle was peculiarly visible because Jews were the only immigrant group that succeeded in establishing their own mercantile distribution networks. These stretched from small towns all over the United States to the large commercial centers and as far as Europe in a few cases. American Jewish merchants bought and sold goods on a massive scale, and their representation in the ledgers of credit-reporting firms was correspondingly high.

Credit reporters' criticisms of Jewish businesses fell into two interrelated patterns, both of which give insight into the push for more transparency. First, although Jews were highly visible in their communities, their business ownership and financing structures were opaque and depended on a distribution network that was unusually close-knit and secretive. In effect, American Jews represented an alternative, "other" way of doing business, against which the evolving ideology of transparency could be opposed and, thus, defined.[1] Second, the credit reporters perceived Jewish merchants to have a lower level of commitment to the communities in which they operated, circumstances that can be explained by the patterns of migration and economic mobility that evolved among American Jews prior to the Civil War. Their preference for settling in urban areas involved Jews in the intense competition for migrants and capital among new towns. Jewish migratory patterns ran afoul of ambitious local elites who had a stake in their communities' future prosperity. Jews were accused of being, in the words of some credit reporters, mere "birds of passage," who settled in communities only to make money before moving on.

Certain assumptions about Jewish business owners became so widely shared that "Jew" evolved into a shorthand for specific business risks: secretiveness, trickery, and deceitfulness. The term "Jew" even entered American slang as a verb, meaning to haggle aggressively with or to cheat another. (The more respectful term, and the one that Jews themselves preferred, was "Israelite.")[2] These prejudices were also present in Britain. During the eighteenth century the English showed a great deal of hostility to Jews, whom they regarded as dishonest. The Bank of England's directors, for example, were widely known to be anti-Semitic. Even so, by the end of the eighteenth century, a number of successful Jewish merchants and bankers had established themselves in London, with the Rothschilds perhaps the best known.[3]

Unflattering Jewish stereotypes were widely accepted in Europe and the United States. Yet American credit reporters displayed no systematic discrimination against Jewish merchants. Intense competition for new business—the very pressures that led suppliers to prefer transparency and to rely on community monitoring of borrowers—combined with a genuine ideology of openness and opportunity to work against exclusion.[4]

Settlement and Occupational Patterns

The Jewish population in the United States from 1840 to 1880 can properly be described as minuscule. Nevertheless, their settlement and occupational patterns gave Jews a visibility and importance that were out of proportion to their small numbers. From fifteen thousand at the beginning of the period, the Jewish population reached fifty thousand by 1850. Even with the huge increase in immigration during the next decade, by 1860 American Jews totaled only 150,000 out of an overall population of

31.4 million. (These numbers are necessarily estimates because, unlike Europeans, U.S. census officials did not place Jews in a separate ethnic or religious category.) Most Jews lived in the North and West. At the start of the Civil War, only about one-quarter lived in the South, and the proportion declined to 14 percent by 1878.[5] The majority arrived from the German states, a region in the throes of political and economic changes following the Congress of Vienna in 1814–1815.[6]

Jewish settlement and occupational patterns in the United States continued those that had evolved in Europe, where Jews had long been accustomed to living as a separate group. Their separate status, imposed by law in much of the Old World, nevertheless allowed them to preserve religious traditions; at the same time, they interacted with non-Jews, mostly in a commercial capacity.[7] Accounting for only a tiny proportion of the overall German migration to the United States (2 to 3 percent of the more than 1.2 million Germans who arrived between 1820 and 1855, according to one estimate) Jews exhibited distinctive characteristics, including a much stronger preference for settling in urban areas and a greater tendency to engage in commercial rather than agricultural activities. In these early decades, single male migrants predominated among Jews, whereas German Gentiles were more likely to travel in family groups.[8]

In another pattern that mirrored the Jews' experiences in Europe, substantial Jewish communities emerged in only a small number of cities and towns. New York was the Jewish immigrants' most likely destination, and that city's Jewish population grew exponentially, from approximately 500 in 1825 to 40,000 (out of an overall population of 805,000) in 1860. That year, two-thirds of all Jewish Americans lived in only fifteen cities. In the following decade, only 160 urban areas had Jewish populations of one hundred or more, and together these places contained 84 percent of all American Jews. By 1880 New York was home to 35 percent of the country's 280,000 Jews, and Philadelphia, Baltimore, Boston, and New Jersey combined accounted for an additional 19 percent.[9]

Along with this concentration occurred a wide dispersion. Compared to German Gentiles, Jews were more likely to head west, and by 1880 they made up 1.5 percent of the populations of California, Oregon, and Washington, versus only 0.5 percent of the American population as a whole. In 1870 nearly nine hundred small towns throughout the United States had at least some Jewish residents. These places had fewer (oftentimes considerably fewer) than a hundred Jews, who almost always worked in a retailing capacity.[10] Commercial districts in small towns consisted of only a few downtown blocks, and Jews typically sited their stores near one another, with many owners living in or near their stores. Their heavy concentration in the retail sector obliged them to interact extensively with non-Jews, who made up the bulk of their customers. So although the overall number of Jewish immigrants during this period was small, they were a highly visible minority. Substantial Jewish communities existed in the country's largest cities, and the Jewish clothing or dry goods dealer became a familiar figure in many small towns and villages. Even isolated farm households were likely to have encountered Jews, who made up a large proportion of the country's peddlers beginning in the 1840s.

The clothing sector became the largest employer of Jewish immigrants. By the 1830s, Jews had established their dominance in the secondhand clothing trade, a significant business before mass production and the resulting wide availability of cheap new clothing had fully taken hold. As a number of recent community studies indicate, the clothing business continued in the following decades to be the most important source of employment for American Jews.

The arrival of Jewish immigrants coincided with the rise of the ready-made clothing industry in the United States. By 1859 New York City had at least 141 Jewish-owned garment wholesaling firms, and the trade grew rapidly in the new inland commercial centers, especially in Cincinnati and, later, Chicago. The invention and refinement of the sewing machine in the 1840s and 1850s and the large demand for uniforms during the Civil War laid the groundwork for further expansion. After the war, Jews were in an advantageous position to move into clothes manufacture, and they did so in large numbers. Jewish wholesalers and manufacturers frequently used their businesses as platforms to launch other enterprises. A notable portion of the business elite who emerged between 1860 and 1880, particularly those in New York City, originally made their fortunes in the clothing business.[11] Their dominant position in this important industry was reflected in the records of the credit-reporting firms.

Of all the immigrant groups of this period, only the Jews succeeded in forming business networks, that stretched from the country's small inland towns to its large commercial centers. Even small-scale establishments were potential suppliers to the thousands of Jewish peddlers who plied their trade throughout the country. The diary kept by twenty-three-year-old Abraham Kohn, who arrived with his brothers in New York in 1842, illustrates how quickly young Jewish men could find work peddling goods for Jewish suppliers.[12]

Proportion of American Jews in Clothing and Allied Businesses

Place	Year(s)	Index of Participation
New Orleans	1841–1861	More than half of 245 Jewish-owned businesses were in clothing or dry goods.
Springfield, Ill.	1841–1889	Jews owned more than one half of clothing establishments.
Cincinnati	1860	Jews owned 65 out of 70 clothing businesses.
Indianapolis	1860s	Jews owned 70 percent of all clothing stores.
Milwaukee	1862	Jews owned 5 out of 14 of the largest clothing businesses.
Columbus, Ohio	1872	Every Jewish family except one worked in clothing, and Jews owned every retail clothing store.
New York City	1880	Jews owned 80 percent of all retail and 90 percent of all wholesale clothing businesses.
Nationwide	1880	Fifty percent of employed Jews worked in clothing and allied occupations.

Sources: Howard M. Sachar, *A History of the Jews in America* (New York: Alfred A. Knopf, 1992), pp. 42, 86–87; Elliot Ashkenazi, *The Business of Jews in Louisiana, 1840–1875* (Tuscaloosa: University of Alabama Press, 1988), p. 13; Olegario, "'That Mysterious People,'" p. 166; Stephen G. Mostov, "A 'Jerusalem' on the Ohio: The Social and Economic History of Cincinnati's Jewish Community, 1840–1875" (Ph.D. dissertation, Brandeis University, 1981), pp. 109–114; Judith Endelman, *The Jewish Community of Indianapolis: 1849 to the Present* (Bloomington: Indiana University Press, 1984), p. 25; Louis J. Swichkow, "The Jewish Community of Milwaukee, Wisconsin, 1860–1870," in *The Jewish Experience in America: Selected Studies from the Publications of the American Jewish Historical Society,* vol. 33: *The Emerging Community,* ed. Abraham J. Karp (New York: Ktav Publishing, 1969), p. 36; Marc L. Raphael, *Jews and Judaism in a Midwestern Community: Columbus, Ohio, 1840–1975* (Columbus: Ohio Historical Society, 1979), pp. 40–41; Naomi W. Cohen, *Encounter With Emancipation: The German Jews in the United States, 1830–1914* (Philadelphia: Jewish Publication Society of America, 1984), p. 29.

The early existence of these networks and the employment they provided may help to explain why Jews had a greater tendency to remain in their adopted country than did their German Gentile counterparts. Remaining in the United States had, in turn, a beneficial impact on the amount of business capital that Jewish merchants accumulated. As permanent residents, they did not dilute their capital by sending it to family members back in Europe. Instead, Jewish immigrants increasingly formed families or brought family members over and, with their help, immediately attempted to set up independent businesses. Again continuing their experiences in Europe, Jewish immigrants aimed to become proprietors rather than wage or salary workers. Owning a business helped to safeguard the independence to carry out religious traditions, along with providing some protection from discrimination.[13]

Their closed networks naturally made Jewish merchants taciturn about their sources of inventory and capital. Credit reporters frequently commented on the difficulty of ascertaining the true ownership of these businesses. In 1855 a reporter in Louisiana made a typical observation about a Jewish business run by two partners: "Both are Jews, keen & wide awake to their own interest (as much so, as any other two of that mysterious people that the sunlight ever has shown upon)."[14] The comment reflected the ambivalence of the larger business community, which mixed respect for Jewish commercial abilities ("keen & wide awake") with genuine perplexity about the true state of their business affairs. In some cases, the reporters could not be sure who actually owned the business. Was it really a branch of a larger parent company? Who was ultimately responsible for the business's debts?[15]

The typically opaque nature of Jewish businesses heightened fears that their Jewish creditors would be paid first, leaving nothing for the rest. Lacking information on how the businesses were structured and financed, the reporters often declined to recommend credit, especially since state laws increasingly favored local creditors rather than the outsiders who constituted the bulk of Bradstreet's and R. G. Dun's subscribers. Collection proceedings were a persistent problem in the United States throughout the nineteenth century, when insolvencies occurred without the legal mechanisms provided by a permanent national bankruptcy law. In the evolving legal climate, debtors frequently used both state and the temporary federal laws to evade their obligations and shelter property that would otherwise have gone to pay their debts in full.

Defenders of the highly controversial and short-lived law of 1841, which for the first time allowed debtors themselves to initiate bankruptcy proceedings, argued that voluntary bankruptcy could sometimes be a sensible business move because it gave debtors breathing room and increased the likelihood that creditors would eventually recoup their investments.[16] Many Americans, however, balked at the moral hazard that such a law presented. As one critic wrote in 1851, under the law a bankrupt was able secretly to buy up his own debts "at 30 or 40 per cent discount, and make a capital but dishonest speculation out of his own failure"—precisely the kind of conduct that alert credit correspondents tried to flag for their subscribers.[17]

Other problems included the widespread American practice, long illegal in England, of designating preferred creditors, who were paid first in the event of default. These creditors were usually the debtor's friends or the endorsers of his commercial paper. Besides being unfair to other creditors, the arrangements were sometimes fraudulent. Although the national laws aimed to end the practice, states allowed it because the arrangement worked to the benefit of creditors who lived in the same state as the debtor. Throughout the century, tensions between locals and outsiders were played out in the arena of bankruptcy law.[18] States steadily passed measures that shielded increasing amounts of debtors' property from the reach of creditors. To compound matters, the Married Women's Property laws, enacted in many states beginning in the 1830s, also made it easier for businessmen to shelter their assets by conveying them to their spouses.[19]

Most requests for information on Jewish businesses came from non-Jews residing outside of the locality, who would have been disadvantaged relative to the borrower's Jewish and local creditors. Given that reality, the reporters quickly flagged many of these businesses as risky. The fear surrounding illegal bankruptcies and under-the-table arrangements was not confined to Jews; credit-reporting firms made careful note of any business, Jewish or otherwise, that engaged in such transactions. Nevertheless, American Jews' propensity to form business networks, combined with their reluctance to provide ownership and financial information on their businesses, made them more vulnerable to accusations of engaging in illegal activities and of favoring their friends and coreligionists over their other creditors. In censuring these practices, the credit reporters frequently resorted to language that was based on negative stereotypes. Thus one Cincinnati reporter advised the creditors of a troubled Jewish business to "send their claims at once as delay is always dangerous with Jews."[20]

The reporters' fears were sometimes justified. Like their non-Jewish counterparts, some Jewish merchants made questionable arrangements with one another or placed businesses in their wives' names to preserve family assets. Elliot Ashkenazi gives several examples of how Jewish suppliers in New Orleans helped to prop up their ailing customers. In one instance, the wholesaler Goldsmith, Haber, and Company allowed one of its troubled debtors to lease back property—including his store, a parcel of land, and two slaves—that he had transferred to them as payment. Goldsmith, Haber then took the debtor on as an "employee." According to legal proceedings initiated by New York suppliers, Goldsmith, Haber, and Company earlier had allowed the debtor to use its name to buy merchandise in New York. Jewish creditors also sometimes permitted debtors to operate under their wives' names and to supervise the collection of their own accounts. More rarely, the reverse situation occurred, and strong customers helped a wholesaler who was experiencing temporary liquidity problems. No doubt these moves helped unfortunate debtors to stay in business, but it gave a false impression of their true ability to pay and intimated a too-cozy relationship between suppliers and customers that could prove unfair to other creditors.[21]

In theory, such arrangements were beneficial because they allowed businesses to survive what was usually only a temporary problem. By building flexibility into the contract between creditor and debtor, the arrangements may also have given Jewish entrepreneurs the confidence to expand their businesses in the risky American environment. This is not to argue that Jewish creditors regularly forgave debts; they, too, were looking for good returns. Nor does it deny the existence of intragroup prejudices, such as those apparently held by Jews from the southwestern German states against "Polish" Jews.[22] Nevertheless, contractual arrangements in closed networks tend to be flexible because lenders believe that helping debtors through difficult times will result in long-term benefits to themselves. Formal mechanisms such as written documents and lawyers are less necessary in closed networks. According to one scholar of ethnic entrepreneurship, these enterprises demonstrate "a flexibility not found among firms in the open market and, hence, a significant competitive advantage."[23] In fact, the introduction of more formal institutional mechanisms can sometimes negate the benefits of informal arrangements. Such was apparently the case in the Bombay Deccan during the nineteenth century, when the introduction of civil courts by the British discouraged lenders from assisting debtors through rough times.[24]

The catch is that, unlike formal institutions, informal arrangements usually are kept secret to allow lenders the widest possible discretion. Difficulties arose for American Jewish merchants when they were forced to operate their businesses under the prying eyes of credit reporters, who expressed no sympathy for these practices. Perhaps ironically, the networks that developed among American Jews, which might have helped to mitigate the market's volatility, became regarded with suspicion by credit reporters and the suppliers they served. During a time of relatively slow communication, distant suppliers were wary of arrangements wherein some creditors were obviously preferred over others. Instead, suppliers wanted to deal with businesses whose ownership and financial structures could be scrutinized and whose statements could be independently confirmed by local sources.

Opaque business practices became increasingly unacceptable to suppliers and credit reporters. The geographically large and dynamic American economy made the development of permanent networks difficult and encouraged suppliers continually to seek out new customers. Transparency became an index of creditworthiness, to the detriment of Jewish business owners.

Credit and Community

The distinctive migratory and occupational patterns that evolved among Jewish merchants ran headlong into other American anxieties. Old stereotypes of the "wandering Jew," long prevalent in the Christian world, were exacerbated by the peculiar pressures inherent in founding and funding new American towns. During the nineteenth century, towns in the United States were not established by monopolistic state and corporate bodies. Instead they were essentially private business start-ups forced to contend with others for people and capital.[25] Numerous boosterist town histories attest that the reputations of communities in the larger market played an important role in attracting resources. A town's economic base and its general reputation for stability, enterprise, and good business practices affected the amount of capital likely to flow in its direction. Enterprise combined with order, rectitude, and stability were highly prized as indicators of a town's overall economic potential. If "a mercantile community could be found whose every individual was known and acknowledged to possess strict and uncompromising integrity," declared *Cumming's Evening Bulletin*, "it would have a monopoly of the trade."[26] Yet the exaggerated optimism of boosterist writings masked a starkly different reality, consisting not of orderly growth but of feverish speculation, frequent bankruptcies, and the disturbing evidence of failure at every turn. In this environment, communities came to serve several economic functions, all of which had important consequences for American Jewish merchants.

For one, outside creditors considered local knowledge to be the best, most accurate information for making their decisions. In its 1851 article on the Mercantile Agency, *Hunt's Merchants' Magazine* stated, "Information of this character can, in general, be satisfactorily obtained only at the *home* of the trader."[27] Mercantile Agency founder Lewis Tappan regarded its system of local correspondents as a distinct advantage. The local agent, he wrote, "having his eye upon every trader of importance in his county, and noting it down, as it occurs, every circumstance affecting his credit, favorably or unfavorably, becomes better acquainted with his actual condition than any stranger can be."[28] Nearly all information in the credit reports originated from local sources, especially attorneys, merchants, government officials, and banks. The phrasing of the credit reports leaves no doubt that an individual merchant's local standing was considered a key index of trustworthiness. The importance of local knowledge tended to work against traders who had only recently moved into the community or who showed few signs of intending to stay.[29]

Jews were sometimes praised for their positive contributions to their communities, perhaps in implied contrast to the Irish and German laborers who were perceived by town elites to be less orderly and therefore less manageable. Writing about the opening of a new synagogue, a Syracuse, New York, newspaper declared that "The Jewish population comprises some of the most industrious and frugal of our citizens." The editors expressed the hope that "others of the same creed" would settle in the city. An editorial in the *Philadelphia Evening Telegraph* stated in 1872 that Jews brought "into every community wealth and qualities which materially assist to strengthen and consolidate its polity . . . No other element in the community is so orderly." Some western communities gave their Jewish residents gifts of land to build their institutions, and Jews held political office in a number of small towns.[30]

Yet the pattern of Jewish economic mobility fed the anxieties of residents who had a stake in their towns' success. Town boosters, allied with local newspapers, tried not only to encourage migrants to settle in their communities but also attempted to promote an image of stability, especially of their towns' local businesses. Town histories frequently showcased the communities' merchants, emphasizing the number of years they had operated in the area.[31] For many Jewish business owners, however, economic mobility was linked to geographic mobility: they progressed up the economic ladder in stages, beginning with a kind of apprenticeship period in smaller towns and, ideally, ending up in a large manufacturing and wholesaling center. The "particular small town in which they established a country store was chosen for purely economic reasons," writes Steven Mostov. "Often these were towns with no more than a handful of other Jews, and were not thought of as a place of permanent residence." The Jewish trader "spent much of his time out of town, either peddling in surrounding areas or purchasing goods in the larger cities. As a result he rarely became socially integrated into the local community, and often was barely known to the town's residents." In the Midwest, many Jewish entrepreneurs aspired eventually to settle in Cincinnati. Its Jewish population trebled from 3,300 in 1850 to 10,000 a decade later. Mostov found that one-half of a sample of Cincinnati Jews had operated businesses in some sixty small towns in the surrounding region before making the move to the "Queen City."[32]

Jewish settlement patterns of the 1870s suggest that the practice of initiating a business career in a small town was by then still widespread. During that decade, 329 places in the United States had no more than ten Jewish residents, and 190 had between eleven and twenty. Presumably, a number of these communities served as the first step in the career ladder for ambitious Jewish traders. Studies of larger cities, including Poughkeepsie, San Francisco, Atlanta, and Columbus, indicate that Jews were not necessarily more mobile than were non-Jews.[33] But "community" was a potent notion in nineteenth-century towns competing for migrants and capital, and individuals who showed little or no commitment to their town's well-being were chastised. As early as 1820, the editor of *Niles' Weekly Register* voiced his misgivings that the Jews' "interests do not appear identified with those of the communities in which they live, though there are some honorable exceptions to this remark." Instead, Jews preferred "to live by their wit in dealing, and acting as if they had a home no where." In Santa Cruz, California, state Speaker of the House William W. Stow, angered by a Jewish proprietor's refusal to support a Sunday closing law, proposed in 1855 that a "Jew tax" be imposed on all Jewish businesses. He argued that Jews came to California only to make money. Once this goal was achieved, they left without having invested in the state's future. California's Jewish leaders strenuously fought the proposal in the local newspapers.[34]

The disinclination of Jewish merchants to own real estate in the community caused further suspicion and resentment. Credit reporters of the 1840s and 1850s frequently noted the tendency of Jewish merchants not to own land. The Southern Mutual Insurance Company reflected these prejudices when in 1857 it instructed its agents to refuse policies to individuals of "bad or doubtful reputation," especially "Jews without real estate property."[35]

From a creditor's point of view, land was an excellent gauge of an individual's worth because its dollar value could be verified in the public records and it could also be mortgaged to pay for goods. (State exemption laws, however, made it difficult or impossible to attach real estate in the event of default.) In contrast, inventory was difficult to value with any certainty and, depending on shelf life, could depreciate rapidly. But Jewish merchants planning to move on to a larger town preferred to keep their money in inventory, not land, and that preference injured their creditworthiness.[36] The Jewish disinclination to own real property may have appeared especially striking when compared to German Gentile business owners, who were far more likely to own land and to buy a local farm after retiring. (However, German Gentiles suffered from their own negative stereotypes, including a reputation among credit reporters for being "phlegmatic"—that is, unambitious, in contrast to the "keen and wide awake" Jewish merchants.)[37] Not all Jewish business owners declined to invest in real estate; in later decades many owned considerable amounts. Yet the early connection that creditors and business writers made between real estate ownership and stability was not fanciful. Steven Hertzberg's study of Jews in Atlanta confirms that of those who owned real estate, only 8 percent in 1870 and 17 percent in 1880 lived in the city for fewer than ten years. In contrast, 55 percent of those who owned no real estate in 1870 and 58 percent in 1880 lived in Atlanta for less than a decade.[38]

The demographic makeup of early Jewish immigrants reinforced their migratory patterns. Prior to the Civil War a large proportion were young single men whose right to marry, work, and establish households had been legally restricted by the authorities in their native German states. These individuals, many from Bavaria, left for the United States to improve their economic and marital prospects. Later migrants were more likely to be part of a family group consisting of a married couple and their children, but during the antebellum period, large numbers were single young men or unmarried siblings traveling together. The predominance of single male migrants was evident in some American communities as late as 1870. In Atlanta that year, Jewish males outnumbered females in the group aged ten to thirty-nine years by more than two to one, and 83 percent of single adult males were foreign born compared to none of the adult females. The average age difference between husband and wife was nearly seven years, an indication of how long it took immigrant males to become economically secure before they could finally marry.[39]

Peddling was a popular occupation for early Jewish immigrants, and it further contributed to the negative stereotype. Beginning in the 1840s Jews took over the role that New Englanders had performed in the eighteenth and early nineteenth centuries. Many Jews engaged in peddling for only a short time, or during certain times of the year. Nearly eleven thousand peddlers (Jewish and otherwise) plied their trade in 1850, and the number increased to almost seventeen thousand a decade later. Available statistics confirm that peddling was an important occupation for Jewish men. In the 1860s 23 percent of Nashville Jews worked as peddlers, as did one-quarter of Boston Jews in the years 1845–1861, four-fifths of the Jewish residents in Iowa in the 1850s, and two-thirds of all Jews in Syracuse. Jewish peddlers continued to work in large cities and in underdeveloped rural areas until well into the twentieth century.[40]

Peddling attracted recent Jewish immigrants because it required only a small amount of capital to start and could be accomplished extensively on credit provided by fellow Jews. The trade was particularly well suited to the young, unmarried men who made up a large proportion of immigrants. Merchants such as Cincinnati's Kuhn family regularly hired Jewish males between the ages of fifteen and twenty to peddle shirts; Levi Strauss, who began as a peddler in San Francisco, was supplied initially by members of his family. Ambitious peddlers moved up the career ladder as they accumulated capital: pack peddlers graduated to wagon peddlers and then to store owners, who sometimes also continued to peddle during certain times of the year. Being highly mobile, peddlers were perceived as less committed than were stationary merchants to the communities that served as their home base.[41]

Whether Jewish or otherwise, peddlers were regarded with ambivalence. They were welcomed in isolated hamlets as distributors of the manufactured goods that people craved. But in more settled areas peddlers were regarded with resentment by local dealers. In 1852 one newspaper explicitly linked these itinerant sellers to a popular Jewish stereotype: "One of these wandering Jews stept into a counting room a few days since," began the story, which related how the peddler took advantage of a gullible buyer. After the experience, the buyer "resolved never to patronize a peddler, but to extend his patronage to those good tax paying citizens who have a local habitation and a name."[42] Public pressure led Massachusetts and other New England states to allow peddlers to sell their wares in the area, but the states' established merchants complained. The backlash resulted in a number of new state licensing laws, including the Massachusetts Hawkers and Peddlers Act of 1846, which "established a graded level of licenses based on 'morals and citizenship,'" extending from "town licenses for general merchandise peddlers . . . to state licenses for wholesale peddlers."[43]

Distrust of strangers and peddlers predated the arrival of large numbers of Jewish immigrants, and it transcended ethnicity or religious affiliation. As Paul E. Johnson's study of Rochester, New York, demonstrates, the appearance in towns of drifters, consisting largely of unmarried males looking for work, alarmed community leaders and contributed to the singular fury of the religious revivals that occurred in the region during the 1820s. Don Doyle's study of Jacksonville, Illinois, uncovered a similar uneasiness among the town's longtime residents regarding the large floating population. In 1835, several years before Jews began arriving in larger numbers to the United States, the established merchants of Ludlow, Massachusetts, declared that their town was "overrun with Hawkers and Pedlars," who were "carrying on a temporary and irregular business in towns and neighborhoods, where they are unknown, and to which they never expect to return." The Ludlow merchants argued that, unlike themselves, peddlers were outsiders who had no interest in the community's welfare. They "give no aid in the concentration of trade or encouragement of that enterprise which builds our smiling villages, cultivates our soil, and fills our workshops and the whole State."[44]

Other sources upheld these views. Several insurance companies in the early 1850s warned their agents against insuring Jews and itinerant peddlers.[45] In 1869 the business writer Samuel Terry advised retailers to be careful about extending credit to certain types of individuals. In addition to speculators, criminals, and drunks, Terry listed the following as high-risk debtors: "Men without families, whose attachments to any one locality are not firm, and who find no trouble in making a change of location, when even small obligations become pressing . . . Strangers either with or without families, who drop down into a community without any one being able to learn who they are, what they are, what they have done or are doing, or what are their resources for a livelihood."[46] Inevitably, Terry's warning encompassed the ambitious Jewish merchants, whose patterns of geographic mobility often prevented them from participating in the social life of communities and who were therefore regarded as lying outside of these communities' collective scrutiny.

Competition: A Mitigating Force

As their language makes all too clear, the credit reports participated in the widely held prejudices of the larger culture. Yet they also demonstrate that these prejudices were modified or reinforced according to the behaviors exhibited by individual merchants and observed by community members who were in a position to communicate their judgment to credit reporters and other agents. Negative comments were balanced by positive, even glowing, appraisals; sometimes the same individual would be disparaged in one instance and then praised in another. The often contradictory nature of the reports indicate that creditors and reporters, in common with the larger culture of the nineteenth century, perceived situations and individuals as contingent and fluid, not fixed. Judgments reflected the best available information as well as prevailing prejudices, but they were frequently reversed by the discovery of new information or by a change in individuals' circumstances.

Inclusion patterns in the ledgers of R. G. Dun provide one indication that there was little if any systematic discrimination that excluded Jewish businesses from being appraised. Instead, the proportion of Jewish establishments reported on and the kinds of businesses most likely to be covered were not significantly different from the inclusion patterns that characterized the distribution sector as a whole. Mostov's study of Cincinnati found that the Dun agency reported on 43 percent of all Jewish businesses in 1850, when there were 349 of them, and 45 percent in 1860, when the number had increased substantially to 582. These figures can be compared with a study done of Poughkeepsie, which found that the Dun agency covered only 37 percent of all the grocery establishments in that city during the 1850s.[47]

As was true of the distribution sector as a whole, large Jewish wholesalers, who were most likely to buy on credit, were almost always included in the credit reports. Larger retailers also tended to be well covered in the reports, their smaller counterparts less so, and peddlers least of all. In the case of Cincinnati, the Dun agency reported on nearly all of the Jewish wholesalers, one-half of the retailers, and one-fourth of the peddlers in the period from 1841 to 1875.[48] The large number of Jewish establishments in the Dun agency records suggests that these businesses were seen as potential customers by native-owned manufacturers and wholesalers looking for additional outlets for their goods. Although the existence of Jewish networks is indisputable, bankruptcy records confirm that Jews bought a portion of their stock from non-Jews.[49]

Dun's inclusive attitude did not stem solely or even primarily from a progressive ideology. Rather, it resulted from the competitive pressures imposed by the dynamic American market. On one level, the large number of reports on Jewish owners simply reflected the numerical importance of these individuals within specific trades, especially clothing and dry goods. But just as important, the immensely increased competition that was already a reality in the older commercial centers during the 1840s and 1850s and widespread by the 1870s encouraged the credit-reporting agencies to include more marginal businesses, many of them owned by women or members of minority ethnic groups. Business mortality data for the nineteenth century are sketchy, but several studies indicate that a large proportion of businesses lasted no longer than a few years. Suppliers who simply wished to maintain the same number of customers therefore needed continually to replace the ones that went under or, failing that, had to sell considerably more to their remaining customers, all of whom were courted by rival suppliers.

Moreover, wholesaling and retailing split along ethnic lines, with Jews being perhaps the only immigrant group active in both areas from an early date. The more capital-intensive wholesaling sector was dominated by native whites along with a few Jews, all of them male; in contrast, retailing remained much more open to diverse immigrants as well as to women. As a result, the relationship between established and newer groups became one of "complementarity" rather than competition. In such a situation, writes sociologist Roger Waldinger, "rather than attempting to quell business growth among the newcomers, the established groups, which benefit from their patronage, will be more likely to respond in an adaptive way."[50] The Dun agency's extensive reports on ethnic and female retailers suggest that native-owned wholesalers were open-minded about taking on these more marginal businesses as customers. The high closure rates within their customer base strongly argue that suppliers may have had no choice.

There was, too, another incentive for enlarging the number of businesses included in the Dun agency's reports: Dun itself felt threatened by the smaller credit-reporting firms that sprang up to serve specific market niches or smaller geographical regions. Faced with intensified rivalry from these start-ups, the agency responded by increasing the scope of its coverage, arguing that doing so gave its subscribers more value for their money.

Credit records reveal the mixed assessments of Jews throughout this period. Jews were described as "honorable" and "reliable." Good standing within the community was frequently noted. At times positive comments were expressed in a backhanded way, as when individuals were labeled as being of good character even though they were members of "the tribe." As was true of all of its reports, the agency seldom hesitated to convey negative impressions, and in the case of the Jewish business owners, such assessments sometimes took on an anti-Semitic cast. Credit reports expressed the widely held opinion that Jews were "mean," "grasping," and "closefisted."[51]

Tracing the experiences of individuals over time is more revealing, however. Doing otherwise tends to result in a static portrait of a dynamic market and an imperfect understanding of its flexibility. It also conceals the role that community standing played in the construction of creditworthiness. In common with the general business population, some Jewish merchants rose in the estimation of reporters, while others fell; a few rose and fell repeatedly, reflecting their fluctuating business fortunes. Credit reports made careful note of these changes, often over long periods. Jewish merchants who advertised in local newspapers and participated in community life received more positive reviews than merchants who remained aloof.[52]

The lack of systematic discrimination against Jews reflected the ambivalent attitude of the larger society, one that was shaped both by the prejudices of other recent European immigrants and the absence of institutional and legal constraints on Jewish life. Unlike Europe, the United States never had an established church that organized a movement against Jews, nor were they ever legally barred in the United States from participating in any branch of business or from settling wherever they chose. Even census takers and immigration officials did not treat Jews as a separate ethnic group but instead, to the considerable frustration of future researchers, lumped them in with German, Austrian, Russian, Czech, and other central and eastern European immigrants.[53] Neither officially anti-Semitic nor wholly enthusiastic about Jewish (or any other non-Protestant) culture, the United States produced images of Jews that were highly contradictory. A study of the Jewish image in American culture found that during the nineteenth century the "very same publication that vigorously opposed anti-Semitic manifestations . . . might engage in casual anti-Semitism, or even occasionally publish overtly anti-Semitic articles." Writers and editors juxtaposed positive and negative images of Jews, all the while apparently unaware of the mixed signals they were sending.[54]

American Jews themselves helped to shape the way they were received and perceived within the larger American culture, itself still fluid and expanding. Although long accustomed to living as a separate people, Jews in the United States did not shun local politics. In the 1840s and 1850s, Democratic party leaders in New York City felt compelled to attend Jewish social events to gain votes. Anti-Semitism was less prevalent in small towns, and a number of western communities had Jewish mayors. Their political and social participation in some communities was slight, as appears to have been the case among the two or three hundred Jews who lived in Buffalo during the 1850s. In New Orleans, however, a few Jews became members of the Boston and Pickwick clubs, two of the city's most exclusive establishments.

The focus of Jewish social activities in some small towns was not the synagogue but the lodge, and American Jews were active in the Masons, Odd Fellows, and a number of other fraternal organizations. Some 12 percent of the San Francisco Masons' one thousand members were Jews, in a city where they made up only 7 to 8 percent of the overall population.[55] In 1843 twelve New York City Jewish retailers, some of them members of the Masons or Odd fellows, organized B'nai B'rith ("Sons of the Covenant"). With its secret passwords, rituals, and insignia, the new organization exhibited its founders' experiences in and knowledge of American fraternal organizations.[56]

The nature of American Judaism also helped to ease the assimilation of Jews into the larger culture. For most ordinary Jews of this period, writes Hasia Diner, "Judaism as a formal body of knowledge, a vast corpus of law, and a tradition of textual analysis and commentary played little or no role." Diner points out that few rabbis emigrated to the United States, and they arrived later than did the mass of ordinary Jews, who "did not defer to them, asserting that rabbinic status did not confer the right to structure communal life." David Gerber writes that the Jewish tradition of a "decentralized congregational life meshed well with the pluralist and voluntarist pattern of much of American Protestant religious life." From the Protestant elite's point of view, the Jewish way was far preferable to that of either Roman Catholics or Mormons, whose "patterns of hierarchical organization and centralized, authoritarian leadership . . . led them to be branded enemies of republican government."[57]

Most telling of all was the fact that American Jews achieved a higher level of economic mobility than did almost any other immigrant group, attainments that were due largely to their collective success in business. In 1864 only 28 percent of all Columbus, Ohio, taxpayers had more than $1,000 in taxable income, compared to over 50 percent of the town's Jewish residents. Studies of Poughkeepsie, San Francisco, and Atlanta show similar attainments in the period up to 1880. A Bureau of the Census study of ten thousand Jewish families conducted in 1889 found that 40 percent of Jewish households had one servant, 20 percent had two, and 10 percent had at least three.[58] During the last decades of the nineteenth century, even as anti-Semitism (and antiforeign feeling in general) reached a new intensity with the mass arrival of immigrants from eastern Europe,

Jewish entrepreneurs became among the country's leading bankers, wholesalers, and retailers.[59]

The experiences of American Jewish merchants provide several insights into the evolving business culture of the United States. First, despite the obvious advantages of closed networks (including a greater capacity to maintain stability during economic downturns), credit reporters and their clients showed scant tolerance of such practices. Instead, they insisted that American Jews conform to the conventions of the country's large commercial centers, including making their business and financial structures more visible to credit reporters. The market's dynamism and competitiveness, combined with problematic bankruptcy laws that tended to work against the interests of out-of-state creditors, encouraged most American creditors to insist that all businesses become more transparent.

The role that communities played in an increasingly national market is a second facet of the business culture that the American Jewish experience places in stark relief. In a speculative environment that was characterized by high failure rates, communities provided the local knowledge that bolstered the confidence of outside creditors. Despite their impulse to boost their towns to outsiders, locals appear to have provided fairly accurate information on their resident merchants; indeed, credit-reporting firms could hardly have prospered if creditors had not deemed their locally gathered information to be mostly reliable. Credit manuals published at the beginning of the twentieth century reveal that the role of communities in determining individuals' creditworthiness became deeply entrenched in American business culture. One typical manual advised mercantile creditors from out of state to contact local attorneys for information on individual business owners. Attorneys, the manual explained, were "frequently acquainted with the personal and family history of local merchants from the time of their youth; and what the attorney does not know from this acquaintance, he knows from the gossip of other members of the community."[60]

The economic functions that communities came to assume worked to the disadvantage of many Jewish merchants, especially those who spent substantial amounts of time peddling away from home or whose business strategy was to migrate to progressively larger towns. Although praised for their orderliness and business success, the behavior of Jewish merchants provoked concern about their commitment to the prosperity and well-being of their communities. At a time when towns competed energetically for migrants, capital, and transportation facilities and when residents felt threatened by the large number of "strangers" within their midst, the migratory and aloof behavior that came to be associated with Jewish merchants caused resentment and distrust.

David Gerber writes that the image of Shylock was widespread in American culture during this period.[61] If that is true, the broad inclusion of Jews and the careful scrutiny of their businesses in the credit reports seem even more intriguing. The disapproval that Jewish business practices provoked did not result in rigid or systematic discrimination; in general Jews continued to be judged according to criteria that applied to all potential borrowers. These included not only the appraisal of these merchants' resources and assets but also of their willingness to provide information on their businesses' ownership and financial structures. The criteria involved, too, a specific set of character traits, including the borrower's perceived honesty, punctuality, economy, temperance, and energy, as determined by individuals in his community.

Judgments were colored by the perception, long widespread in Europe before migrating to America, that Jews were closefisted, secretive, and prone to dishonest dealings. But prejudices were contingent upon new information, reflecting a dynamic and ongoing reassessment of individuals and their particular circumstances rather than an inflexible attitude based solely on widely held stereotypes. Competitive pressures and the complementarity that developed between the wholesale and retail sectors made creditors receptive to the information: it made no sense to ignore potential customers solely because they were Jewish, especially in cases where these individuals' own communities vouched for their creditworthiness.

The credit reports on American Jewish merchants reveal that constructing and assessing the reputations of individual merchants involved a process of continual negotiation among the subjects of the reports, their communities, suppliers, and the credit-reporting agencies. Ultimately, however, it was the agencies and the large creditors they served who dictated which business behaviors were legitimate and deserving of support.

5

Growth, Competition, Legitimacy: Credit Reporting in the Late Nineteenth Century

The Civil War placed intense pressure on the credit-reporting industry. John Bradstreet died during the war, and his son Milton assumed management of the agency. Already struggling, the company was hit hard by its founder's death. R. G. Dun, too, saw its profits slide precipitously.

After the war, both firms participated in the nation's general business recovery and steadily increased their dominance of the industry. By around 1880, R. G. Dun and the Bradstreet agency were a clear duopoly in the field of national (as opposed to local or trade-specific) credit reporting. Throughout the postwar decades, the credit-reporting industry as a whole prospered. Perceived opportunities attracted dozens of new agencies, most only local in scope or targeted at particular lines of business. At the same time, all agency managers confronted intense criticism about the quality of the services they provided. They also continued to be challenged by subscribers, the subjects of their reports, and the press about the propriety and fairness of their methods.

General Trends

Mercantile credit changed in several ways during the postwar period. For one, terms became shorter across the board. Prior to the war, six to twelve months' credit had been common for nearly all goods. Yet the notion that shorter terms were less risky and potentially more profitable was already well understood. In the 1850s, Edwin Freedley had noted that shorter terms allowed merchants to offer their goods at a cheaper price, leading to faster sales.[1]

Only after the war, however, did better transportation and communications accelerate the shortening of credit terms. As with the economy generally, the terms became more specialized: slower-moving items such as jewelry

139

were sold on longer time than canned goods, which in turn commanded more time than perishable items such as fresh fruits and vegetables.[2] The monetary disturbance caused by the war accelerated the trend. When Congress suspended specie payments from 1862 to 1879, sellers tried to compensate for the fluctuating value of the currency by drastically shortening the credit period, sometimes to thirty or fewer days. Even after Congress resumed specie payment in 1879, the generally shorter terms continued, and 30 to 160 days became the norm for many lines of goods. There were exceptions: areas that were primarily agricultural and buyers of agricultural machinery continued to receive longer terms. So did merchants in the undeveloped areas of the West, where credit terms of one year could still be found as late as the 1890s.[3]

Wholesaler trade associations embraced the trend. At its very first meeting in 1876, the Western Wholesale Drug Association passed a resolution urging that "all credit be shortened as soon and as much as practicable" and that the least-profitable goods "be, as a rule, sold on the shortest time." From 1860 to 1901, terms in the wholesale drug trade shrank from as long as one year to only sixty days. Greater availability of bank loans also allowed merchants to take better advantage of cash discounts. Wholesale druggists, for example, could take a 1.5 percent discount for cash payments made within ten days.[4]

Credit transactions became more formalized by the use of instruments such as single-name paper, bank drafts, and trade acceptances. Single-name paper, an unsecured promise to pay backed by the issuer's reputation for financial soundness, was already popular with large buyers by 1860. After the war, note brokers sprang up to market the financial instrument to banks and other financial intermediaries.[5] Some suppliers began requiring their largest customers to deposit drafts at a bank, to be collected by the seller on the day payment was due—somewhat like a postdated check. The practice of issuing a note (later called a trade acceptance) rather than simply notating the transaction in the creditors' books also became more widespread among manufacturers and large middlemen. The notes circulated, subject to a discount, allowing sellers to release the value tied up in their accounts receivable. These instruments—single-name paper, bank drafts, and trade acceptances—generally were not used by smaller businesses, nearly all of which continued to rely on book credit (as did many large merchants).[6]

The enlargement of trade, shortening of credit terms, and greater formality of credit practices should not lead us to overstate the extent to which trade and credit became depersonalized. Constant negotiation still characterized the transactions between mercantile debtors and creditors, and trade continued to be conducted in a highly personalized language that drew on older notions of honor and trust. Requests for payment or financial statements were worded so as not to cause "offense." Longtime customers expected leniency and flexibility during times of general economic distress and were piqued when these were not forthcoming. Ideas about character as the best guide to creditworthiness also persisted and with it the importance of reputation. A formal, contractual order did not replace one based on personal relationships. Nor did quantitative measures, such as a debtor's capital strength, completely replace the older reliance on qualities such as honesty, thrift, and sobriety.

Credit as a Competitive Weapon

Shortening credit terms to reduce risk became a generally accepted goal. Yet merchants and manufacturers were driven by a simultaneous and contrary impulse: to be generous with credit and flexible about payments to attract and keep customers. It was the search for customers, after all, which had driven wholesalers' representatives into the country's newly settled regions.[7] After the Civil War, northern wholesalers eagerly sought to reestablish relationships with their southern customers by offering terms of six months to one year.[8] To a large extent, older norms persisted because competitive pressures made sellers much more willing to negotiate terms, a reality that buyers were only too willing to exploit.

By the last decades of the nineteenth century, the physical obstacles to reaching customers had been largely overcome, but they were replaced by the equally serious problems of greater competition and a deflationary economy. The 6 billion dollars' worth of goods and services the United States produced in the late 1860s expanded fivefold by the end of the century, to 30 billion in constant dollars. The population, meanwhile, grew much more slowly, about doubling between 1870 and 1900. More goods were chasing fewer customers, and the wholesale price index for all commodities behaved predictably: it fell—by nearly half in real terms, from one hundred in 1870 to only fifty-four by 1896.[9]

Nor was competition restricted to firms alone. Localities, too, intensified their attempts to attract trade. By 1860 suppliers in New York, Boston, Philadelphia, and New Orleans saw their customers switch to rival wholesalers in the newer commercial centers of Cincinnati, Chicago, Saint Louis, and Louisville. Smaller centers like Kansas City, Minneapolis/Saint Paul, and Milwaukee also joined the fray. Eastern cities responded by offering more attractive credit terms. (One reason auctions declined so dramatically was that they were conducted primarily on a cash basis.) Wholesalers' representatives hit the road in unprecedented numbers; from only one thousand in 1860, the new army of salesmen totaled nearly sixty thousand by 1890, a number that most historians believe is an underestimate. Towns that passed laws against traveling salesmen rescinded them when their own merchants began sending out drummers. Aggressive salesmen undersold the competition in a brutal contest to win and hold customers.[10]

As the market tipped in favor of buyers, business manuals counseled merchants to shop for the lowest price. "Be tied to no house nor man," advised one. "Buy of the man who offers you the cheapest goods, and guarantees the quality to be equal to the others."[11] Large buyers, in particular, were able to extract cheaper prices and longer credit terms from suppliers anxious to obtain their business.[12]

Competition also intensified on the retail level, where the total value of goods exploded, from $3.6 billion in 1869 to $13.2 billion by 1909.[13] Ready-made clothing in particular experienced a boom, expanding sixfold in retail value.[14] Ease of entry allowed an expanding number of small stores to spring up all over the country; in many instances, the competition among them was tied directly to the rivalry among new towns and localities. "As fast as a town or village is located," observed credit man Peter Earling, "two stores are ready to start where only one is really needed . . . Every new town is always going to be *the* town, and in the expectation that it will outstrip every other, more stores are generally started than can find profitable remuneration."[15] (The glaring exception was the cotton South. There, storekeepers managed to establish monopoly positions within their local areas and charged high rates for credit.)[16]

On the other end of the retail scale, new and much larger outlets appeared, including department stores, mail-order houses, and chain stores. Department stores typically evolved from large antebellum dry goods and wholesaling firms such as A. T. Stewart, Macy's, and Wanamaker's.[17] Their large size allowed them to buy merchandise at cheaper rates directly from manufacturers and to sell quickly for lower prices—what merchants described as "pursuing a nimble sixpence [rather than] a slow shilling."[18] Although the department stores sometimes lost these advantages due to high labor and rental costs, they continued to set the trends for fashion in urban areas. People began to see them not only as suppliers of goods but as exciting places to shop.

Mail-order houses, which competed with wholesalers, began appearing in the 1870s, their growth aided by a population that was highly literate and by the existence of an extensive and reliable mail delivery system. Montgomery Ward, founded in 1872, and Sears, founded in 1884, were the pioneers in this sector, and they quickly achieved sales volumes that surpassed even those of department stores. Chain stores, including the Great Atlantic and Pacific Tea Company (A&P), established in 1859, and Woolworth's, founded in 1879, were able to standardize their operations and manage their stock more efficiently across a large number of outlets.[19] All of these new retailers began offering or extending warranties and guarantees, and the one-price policy became more common.[20]

As might be expected in a growing economy, the absolute number of wholesalers and retailers rose; they also became more specialized by line of goods. Simultaneously, however, manufacturers learned how to exploit the power of brands. Brand management would reach the status of a near science in the twentieth century. In the late nineteenth century, the practice was still in its infancy; but even so, Kodak, Heinz, Coca-Cola, and other manufacturers of consumer goods learned to set up their own selling organizations to reach consumers directly, and they assumed many of the functions of traditional middlemen. The jobbers, factors, auctioneers, and commission merchants who had dominated the economy earlier in the century lost ground. They lagged behind manufacturers in developing their own brands and paid little attention to advertising; instead, they relied on their traveling salesmen to develop relationships with customers. (Marshall Field was one notable exception. The firm, which in this period ran a large wholesaling operation, developed its own brand and even handled some of the manufacturing facilities.) Small producers, especially those in glass, salt, drugs, meat, cordage, and petroleum products, as well as farmers and retailers, also chipped away at the power of middlemen by banding together into associations and buying directly from manufacturers.[21]

So although the absolute number of wholesalers increased, the proportion of manufactured goods they handled (some 70 percent in 1879) fell.[22] Of course, middlemen also formed associations to avoid competitive abuses and unify against common problems. Among these were the National Wholesale Druggists Association (1862), the Western Wholesale Drug Association (1876), the Wholesale Grocers' Association of New York City (1888), and the National Hardware Association (1895).[23]

These developments benefited consumers, but stagnating prices throughout the supply chain lowered the gross profit margins of large manufacturers and small retailers alike. Some responded by speculating. They bought much larger amounts of stock to take advantage of lower prices, which raised the risk of being stuck with unsold goods at the end of the season. James W. Kimball, the owner of a credit-reporting and collection agency, noted the irony of a situation in which the public "denounce speculation in one breath, and in the next clamor for goods at low prices." This "force[d] the jobber into large stores, and large sales at small profits, as the indispensable condition of his very existence." Kimball summed up the prevailing sentiment among this generation of merchants: "The question is no longer, How large a profit can I get? but, How small a profit shall I accept?"[24]

Sellers tried to turn merchandise more quickly in the hope of making up for the lower profit margins. (The success manual written by William Maher recommended that they try to turn their stock every four weeks, for "the nimble sixpence is the coin that fills the pocket quickest.") Those who sold on credit had to collect their debts more frequently. But mercantile creditors continued to be stymied by older commercial norms, which considered the too-strenuous pursuit of payments from regular customers as cause for offense. Maher conveyed the delicate negotiations that often accompanied credit sales. If a letter requesting payment were sent to eighty customers, only "forty or fifty will respond with tolerable promptness, while the balance will take their time to do it." Inevitably, "some one or two of the eighty will have had their feelings wounded; they don't like being dunned three times in a month; when they traded with So-and-so, they never were treated so, etc., etc." Offended, the customer "takes his valuable trade to another place."[25] Two decades later, a credit man spoke of how the "demands of business struggle" forced sellers "to make allowances of various kinds, to meet the prices and terms of . . . competitors." Gentle requests for cash payments, he reported, were met by "language more forcible than polite," as buyers tersely informed suppliers that goods could be obtained elsewhere, on credit. As a result, long credit, originally employed "to stimulate and steady production," was "now one of the most abused features of business life." Competitive pressures also forced suppliers to take personal checks from country merchants, despite the annoyance, delay, and cost.[26]

Business manuals attempted to restore some power to mercantile creditors by urging them to be less indulgent of late payers. Peter Earling, author of the first manual for credit men, argued that large suppliers had the power to educate and instill good business practices simply by insisting on punctual payments. But he also acknowledged that custom and usage worked against the creditor, for "mercantile bills or open accounts are not looked upon like an obligation to a bank that must be paid on a certain day and by a certain hour." Some buyers unilaterally granted themselves ten to twenty days' grace period on book credit, and it was not unusual for them to take three days' grace even on notes.[27] Decades of flexibility on the part of mercantile creditors, combined with intensified competition, had accustomed buyers to such privileges. Wholesalers tolerated the behaviors for the sake of maintaining friendly relations.

Strongly capitalized firms were best able to use credit to bind their customers more closely, usually by renewing short-term credit so that it effectively functioned as long-term credit. One department store executive recalled that his father was able to open the family business in 1874 only because Chicago wholesalers Carson, Pirie, Scott, and Company were willing to extend him credit in this way.[28] Chicago-based Marshall Field and the Claflin Company of New York were known for helping to finance new stores by extending long-term credit.[29] Earling recognized that the practice had value but warned that it could be employed only by the well-capitalized wholesaler, who, in effect, "turns banker every three or six months." By doing so, he "ties these men to him, and as long as they owe him and he wants their patronage, he need not fear competition. But this class of merchants are the exception."[30]

Small retailers, for their part, used credit to compete with both mail-order houses, which demanded cash on delivery (COD), and large chain stores like A&P, which had abolished credit. Although trade journals criticized retail credit as old-fashioned and dangerous, small-town and neighborhood retailers knew it was part of the complex relationship that bound them and their customers together. As one grocer put it, there was a "feeling of friendliness" within a credit relationship "that cannot be had from a floating cash trade." Granting credit, he said, allowed storeowners "to grow in the esteem of the community."[31] Like the wholesalers, retailers were bound by older norms that had remained entrenched due, in part, to competitive pressures.

Availability and Quality of Information

In keeping with the expanded scale of the economy, the number of full-time credit reporters increased, and in the larger cities, they began to specialize in certain lines of trade. But much information continued to come from resident correspondents, typically attorneys who worked for the agencies part time. They normally submitted reports two to four times a year, supplemented by items such as failures, the formation of new businesses, changes in ownership, and other urgent information.[32] New state laws required some incorporated firms to file an annual statement of the amount and nature of their paid-in capital and the extent of their liabilities.[33] But the laws covered only a small minority of all businesses, so reporters and correspondents continued to rely heavily on sources such as county records and newspapers. The latter proliferated in the decades after the war: by 1900 every urban center had an average of 4.1 dailies, compared with only 2.5 in 1870.[34] Editors realized that people liked to see their names and those of their loved ones in print. Obituaries grew longer, and marriage notices began to include more details, including the histories and present state of businesses to which these individuals and families were connected.[35]

So despite dramatic changes in the structure of the American economy, the criteria and sources for determining creditworthiness did not change radically. Instead, creditors and credit-reporting firms refined the techniques developed earlier in the century.[36]

Circulars issued by credit-reporting agencies, as well as sample and actual credit reports, indicate which items of information creditors could reasonably expect to obtain. In 1869 Charles F. Clark of the Bradstreet agency instructed the firm's reporters and correspondents to provide the following:

(1) Length of time in business. (2) Amount of capital in business. (3) Amount of net worth, after deducting all liabilities of every nature. (4) Of what is estimated wealth composed? (Viz.: Real estate less incumbrances, capital in business, personal property, which includes bonds and mortgages, stocks, notes, etc., etc.) (5) Character? good, fair, poor. (6) Habits? good, medium, poor. (7) Business Qualifications? very good, good, medium, poor. (8) Prospects of success? good, fair, medium, poor. (9) Succeeded whom? if any person or firm, state whom. (10) Give individual names of partners, with age.[37]

Like banks, credit-reporting firms began distributing printed forms requesting itemized information on borrowers' financial worth. R. G. Dun's ledgers for this period reveal that the firm obtained more information on accounts receivable, which often represented a considerable portion of a business's assets and (along with cash and securities) were considered liquid.[38] The firm's reports also contained more information on chattel mortgages on borrowers' property. Laws differed among states, but in general these mortgages were merchandise-backed securities given to particular lenders, in effect making them preferred creditors. Knowing about these liabilities was valuable because the holder of a chattel mortgage could foreclose at any time, to the disadvantage of other lenders who did not hold any security at all.[39]

The following sample report by Peter Earling is based on an actual report he reviewed in the course of his work as a credit man for a large firm. It indicates that by the 1880s significantly more financial information had become available to creditors:

G. A. Frank & Co., Northern Wisconsin
Wholesale Grocers
(June 10, 1887)

This firm commenced business here three years ago, and is composed of G. A. Frank and L. A. J. _____. The former is a married man, about thirty-five years of age, who, we believe, failed once some time ago, but is spoken of in favorable terms. Just prior to entering in this business, was engaged in shipping fruits to towns in this region, and not understood to have any means of his own. His partner, J _____, was an explorer, and understood to have a few thousand dollars. They started out with a *stock of about $3,000,* which they claimed was all paid for. They have been doing a large business from the start, and making some money, but their *capital is rather inadequate* for the trade they do, although there is no complaint regarding payments, and we understand they confine the bulk of their purchases to one house. About one year ago, a representative of a house called on them and received the following statement of their condition:

Stock, $10,000; outstandings, $6,000; cash, and in bank, $200; liabilities, about $9,000; on open accounts, about $500 past due, but not pressing, and $1,500 due the bank. J. _____ had homestead worth about $800. Merchandise sales for first six months of the year, $27,000, of which a little over one-fourth was cash.

This statement was considered a candid one, but showed that they credit quite freely for a house with so light active capital; but claimed to scrutinize closely. They are regarded strictly honest, and we understand they are given what little bank accommodations they need. They appear to have credit for the demands of their business, but it is probably reasonable to suppose that their account is allowed to run along. They do an immense business for their *capital,* which would be, *nominally, $4,000 or $5,000,* but thus far seem to be able to turn themselves without any apparent inconvenience. Are very fair business-men, steady and attentive, but it is advisable to use some caution in handling the account, as their business is crowding so rapidly that they are apt to overreach themselves.[40]

This 1887 report contained details that had been unavailable some two decades earlier. The business clearly had provided a statement (although it was now about a year old) that gave potential creditors information on its liquid assets. These consisted of the amount of cash the firm had on hand ($200) and the amount due from customers ("outstandings, $6,000"). The statement listed the firm's most immediate debts: of the "open accounts," $500 was "past due, but not pressing," and $1,500 was due to the bank. Unlike earlier reports, this one provided information on sales: G. A. Frank sold $27,000 worth of merchandise in the first six months of the year, one-quarter for cash, and the rest on credit.

In the 1890s, the Bradstreet agency's Portland, Oregon, office sent out the following form. Although it is doubtful that the majority of businesses was willing or able to provide all of the items requested, the form indicates what kind of information credit-reporting firms believed might reasonably be expected from buyer-borrowers:

FIRM NAME
Business [i.e., what line of business]
Name of city of village, county, street and number, state
Partners' names
   Age
   Married/single
Statement made by
Former occupation of each partner
Previous location of each partner
Commenced present business when
Succeeding whom
What capital did you start with, and how and by whom contributed, $
Has business been successful

Have you any branches or other business investments. If so, where
and under what style
Have you ever failed. If so, when and where.
What was amount of liabilities, $. How settled.

ASSETS
Estimated value of merchandise on hand
Notes and accounts receivable. Actually worth.
Cash on hand
Value of personal property, and of what composed.
Value of all Real Estate owned
Deduct Homestead (exempt by law)
In whose name does Homestead stand
In whose name does other Real Estate stand
Total assets

LIABILITIES
Bills payable (or debts closed by note)
Open Accounts payable
 How much due
 How much past due
 How much not due
Amount mortgages on Real Estate
Deduct mortgage on Homestead
Amount chattel mortgage on Merchandise
Amount cash borrowed
How are lenders secured
When payable
Total Liabilities
Total resources or *net worth* as basis for credit
Annual business
Do you endorse
With whom do you Bank

PLEASE GIVE NAMES OF PRINCIPAL CREDITORS.
Name, Location, Amount

Other references

Insurance on stock. Total
Insurance on Real Estate. Total.

What rent do you pay for business premises per month
When does lease of business premises expire
REMARKS (Is your Real Estate town or farming property? Where is
    it located? Add any further remarks that you may desire.)

PLEASE SIGN HERE.[41]

Sources hostile to the agencies confirm that they had become more demanding. William Chinn's *The Mercantile Agencies against Commerce*,
published in 1896, complained that "the printed form of statement which
the mercantile agencies furnish . . . is very minute in questioning."[42]

Other testimony, however, suggests that good financial information remained elusive. Earling reported that information on wholesalers and retailers was often "very vague and meager."[43] The extent of the problem can
be gauged by looking at the situation prevailing among publicly listed
firms. Some corporations such as railroads, insurance companies, and utilities prepared detailed (though unaudited) statements, but many other public firms did not. In 1900 the government issued a report noting that the
directors of publicly traded companies "practically never make reports to
the individual shareholders for periods." Many companies continued to use
the "private ledger," an account book equipped with a lock and key and
containing accounting information the firm wished to keep confidential.
Access to the data was confined to partners and one or two trusted employees.[44] The problem of inadequate reporting was naturally worse for private firms. Moreover, norms that had been in place for more than a century
accustomed business owners to believe that requests for financial statements impugned their honesty. They frequently refused to provide any
statements, even to suppliers from whom they were requesting credit.[45]

Financial statements, if submitted at all, were likely to contain serious
inaccuracies; this was especially true of smaller businesses. In his manual
for retailers, Samuel Terry decried the "universal" ignorance surrounding
double-entry bookkeeping. He estimated that one-half of all retailers had
only a vague idea of how much they owed their creditors because of the
"loose habit" with which they treated invoices and their "inattention to a
proper system of receiving goods."[46] (In the 1880s, John Patterson's National Cash Register helped to standardize receipts, which may have improved matters somewhat.)[47]

Terry himself exhibited a sophisticated understanding of what a later
generation would call "profit margins," or gross or net profits divided by

sales, and "inventory turnover," or the total cost of the inventory sold during the year divided by the value of the inventory the business had at a particular time. (This ratio measures how fast a firm's merchandise is moving.) Terry's manual was remarkably modern in its analytical approach, even suggesting that retailers try to ascertain, once a month, the profit made on each of their product lines. But Terry was significantly ahead of his time; very few, if any, retailers succeeded in being so meticulous.[48] Given the state of accounting practices and disclosure among large public companies, it is hardly surprising that small businesses were even less inclined, and less able, to furnish accurate and detailed statements.[49]

Because accurate financial information was so hard to come by, local trade gossip and the impressions of credit reporters continued to be vitally important. George Osmond, an R. G. Dun reporter based in Saint Louis, recalled that in the 1870s he visited storekeepers and officials in county seats to gather "gossip," in addition to examining assessment rolls for property descriptions. In a lawsuit involving R. G. Dun, a deputy auditor for Hamilton County, Ohio, testified that it was common for reporters to "ask me whether I know certain parties and sometimes when there is a person whose name is not in the directory, being perhaps new in the business, they ask me whether I know that he is engaged in that business."[50] Credit manuals acknowledged that a good reporter's instincts constituted an important skill. One manual writer stated, "The reporters give an account of what may be called their impressions—that is, it may seem to them that a business is retrograding; that the owner or manager is growing careless; that the stock is being allowed to degenerate, or some man may tell them that his firm has put in a new line, increased its capital or made some other change."[51] Despite the greater volume of publicly available information, most credit reporting actually consisted of educated guesswork on the part of correspondents and reporters, and they were given wide latitude to use their own judgment.

Court testimonies suggest that reporters and correspondents relied heavily on the opinions of local merchants and officials. Edward Paul, a traveling reporter for R. G. Dun, testified in *McLean v. R. G. Dun*, a case tried at the Toronto (Canada) Fall Assizes of 1875. Paul stated that he asked the subject of his report about "the amount of his stock; he told me he was dealing altogether with American houses; he said business had been very good; the store looked nice; there were numbers of boxes with shoes standing outside of them; he appeared candid . . . I never spoke to him afterwards . . . I got no statement in writing; I never saw his books; he told

me he had a stock of $10,000." Paul estimated that he spent twenty min-
utes interviewing the subject at his store. He then made inquiries among
the city's wholesalers to verify the merchant's statement. "The only kind
of corroboration I got was that some person said upon my saying he
claimed to have $10,000 stock, that perhaps he had." Nevertheless, Paul
appeared to believe that this "corroboration" was sufficient: "I never make
a report without corroboration . . . I know I got the whole report corroborated, because I got all my reports corroborated . . . we are always very
particular in getting our information corroborated by persons in the
trade."[52]

Credit-reporting firms tried to obtain financial statements, but they remained skeptical about the statements' value. According to Bradstreet,
"the given statement of the directly interested parties too often cannot be
relied upon in making up reports." Thus, "verification and substantiation,
by means of further information and observation," was necessary. In other
words, the opinions of local merchants regarding a business owner's worth
was often more reliable than a self-reported statement.[53] Some rival credit-
reporting agencies tried to differentiate their services from Bradstreet's
and Dun's by making no capital ratings at all, claiming that the system of
ratings was misleading and unreliable.[54]

Testimony in *Gibson v. R. G. Dun* reveals how much the agency relied
on the opinions of locals and the trade at large for "verification and substantiation" and how Dun did not necessarily check public records carefully during the course of an investigation. William and John B. Gibson,
subscribers to Dun's service, claimed to have lost money because they relied on erroneous information that Dun provided on a merchant. Specifically, the plaintiffs charged that the agency made no examination of the
record of mortgages on the subjects' property and were therefore guilty of
gross negligence. Dun replied that it was not the firm's custom to do so
unless the subscriber asked specifically for this information and that the
agency charged an extra fee for this service. "The defendants are not an association of attorneys," argued Dun's counsel. "A report as to the amount
and number of mortgages upon a party's property would avail nothing
unless a thorough examination of title was made, and the true condition
and value thereof reported." The agency's contract with subscribers "im-
plie[d] no agreement to examine records" but merely stipulated that Dun
would provide information on *"the reputation of the person in the community in which he resides."*[55]

The judge concurred and in his opinion gave a definition of what constituted mercantile "credit": "Mercantile standing and credit is the reputation of a house in the business community in which it stands. This is ascertained, not by an inspection of its books but by inquiring among men of business." This was, the judge concluded, all that the agency contracted to do. Such a contract was typical for the credit-reporting industry, and Dun's practices did not deviate from those of its competitors. Therefore, the firm had shown proper diligence and was not guilty of gross negligence.[56]

Character and Narrative

As testimony in the *Gibson* case suggests, creditworthiness continued to be based largely on reputation, including the reputed financial worth of individuals and businesses. The narrative of an individual's business life also constituted an important element; as Earling phrased it, "The applicant for credit favors, if he has ever failed, or whatever his past life may have been, has left a biography of himself that must be carefully read."[57] The agencies' published reference books were easy to use, which ensured their popularity with time-pressed creditors. Yet even as the agencies pushed aggressively to sell these products, they also urged subscribers to refer to the full reports. A typical advertisement by R. G. Dun stated that the firm "constantly reiterate[s] to our subscribers the necessity of applying to the office for reports, and not relying upon the Book where transactions of any moment are contemplated." Neither should subscribers, the agency cautioned, rely exclusively on the weekly notification sheets containing names of parties whose business affairs had experienced significant alterations.[58] In a long letter to the National Association of Credit Men, Charles Clark stated in 1899, "That capital is the legitimate foundation of credit is undeniable, but many qualifying circumstances may prevent success even when capital is employed; this is constantly demonstrated by our service."[59]

Most credit-reporting firms made a clear distinction between capital and character by separating their reference book ratings into two categories: capital strength and creditworthiness. "Men with ample Capital," explained R. G. Dun, "but lacking Integrity or Capacity, have a Credit far weaker than others with less means, whose Antecedents, Character and Ability, beget a general confidence." Its rating key distinguished among "gradations in Credit as compared with Capital" so as to better convey "shades of meaning" to creditors.[60] A rival firm, known simply as the Credit Bureau, went so far as to disregard capital in its published credit ratings entirely, instead relying on "honesty, business ability, nature and extent of business, (hazardous or otherwise,) [and] manner of paying bills,—promptness being the first consideration." The firm announced that it rated small concerns "doing a careful snug business" more highly than did other credit-reporting firms.[61] Apparently, the Credit Bureau believed it was hewing more closely to the attitude of creditors, who regarded the qualitative attributes of a borrower, along with his or her payment record, as more dependable indicators of creditworthiness.

The continuing emphasis by creditors and business writers on the specific set of character traits outlined in Chapter 3 should be distinguished from the larger discourse about character that took place during the later decades of the nineteenth century, a process traced by Karen Haltunnen and Judith Hilkey in their examination of success manuals. Some 80 percent of all such books—nearly all written by, and directed to, northern, small-town, white Protestant readers—appeared after the Civil War.[62] These later advice books placed much greater emphasis on the manipulation of outward appearance, as opposed to inner character.[63] Horatio Alger's books, now ensconced in American popular culture as fables about poor boys growing rich through hard work, in fact relied on "the cynical gambits of the smooth-talking 'confidence man' to advance their boy-heroes' fortunes," according to Hilkey. The stories embodied "the transition from a nineteenth-century focus on character to a twentieth-century emphasis on personality and the salesmen ethic of a consumer society, where ability to persuade would become more important than the authentic self implicit in the concept of character." Yet the idea of "character" was not on the wane; instead, millions of small-town and rural men consumed popular books and manuals that looked to character as the key to success. Hilkey interprets this seeming paradox as an attempt by writers of success manuals to legitimize the new corporate social order by demonstrating that individual virtue had a place within it. At the same time, by looking to the past for moral guidance, the manuals "implied a critique of the haste, greed, materialism, and intemperance" of contemporary life.[64]

For credit reporters, however, the term "character" retained the meaning it acquired earlier in the century: the willingness (as opposed to the mere ability) to repay debts when they came due. Business writers continued to insist on character as a useful indicator of creditworthiness, many even arguing that it was more important than capital: "A man without a dollar might be a perfectly safe man to trust, if he were honest, economical, and understood his trade perfectly," according to one typical declaration, "while another worth hundreds of dollars, but tricky, speculative, or neglectful of business, might be a very unsafe man to have on one's books."[65] The more scientifically oriented manuals on mercantile credit published toward the end of the century also asserted this sentiment. Their authors, members of the nascent credit profession, emphasized the importance of personal integrity and almost universally listed character and habits as the most important criteria for lending. "Our security as creditors," wrote Earling, "depends on these factors more largely than on any other two. No applicant for credit is entitled to it unless his record for both honesty and sobriety is above reproach."[66]

In his exposé of the credit-reporting system, Thomas Meagher, a disgruntled former employee of the R. G. Dun agency, claimed that the firms used an arbitrary set of criteria for determining creditworthiness, including church standing and participation in religious activities.[67] However, there is little evidence from the R. G. Dun ledgers, sample credit reports, or credit manuals that the agencies scrutinized individuals' religious activities or noted their membership in political parties and social clubs. Instead, the set of character traits that mattered remained specific: honesty, punctuality, thrift, energy, focus, and experience.

A borrower's "honesty"—his proven willingness to pay—mattered for a number of reasons. First, financial statements were often old—the sample provided by Earling earlier in this chapter was one year old—and the information they contained was frequently "vague and meager." Second, although the published reference books included real estate in their assessment of capital strength, this asset was seldom available to creditors in the case of default. Continuing a trend that had begun prior to the war, state laws exempted homesteads (which could include stores used as dwellings) and ever greater amounts of personal property from the reach of creditors. Exemptions became more generous the further west one traveled. Earling warned, "In the Territories . . . we find that a man of moderate circumstances may claim as exempt, nearly all he possesses." The generosity of state exemption laws was sobering. The debtor was entitled to and allowed to select "personal and miscellaneous property to the extent of $1,500 . . . which may mean twice the amount in fact." He was further entitled "to a homestead not exceeding 160 acres of land, or one acre in town, without limitation of value of buildings and improvements thereon."[68]

Earling further warned that debtors in the southern and western states were harder to collect from because courts did not meet as often. Those in the newer states and territories had a habit of protecting their residents against distant creditors. The impulse was understandable because new countries and territories were forced to offer compensation for the hardships and risks endured by settlers and pioneers. The result, however, was to give debtors all the advantage: "For the creditor there exists no legal jurisprudence," said Earling. Therefore, crucially, "he is more dependent on the honor and honesty of his customers than he is on the exercise of any legal rights that he ought justly be allowed to claim." Businesses capitalized at only $1,000 to $5,000 were another class for whom character traits were all-important, as were businesses on which chattel mortgages and other liens had been placed.[69]

The emphasis that creditors placed on honesty can be seen in the prejudice against corporations. Because honesty was thought to reside in individuals alone, joint-stock companies and corporations were disadvantaged when seeking credit. Limited liability, it was widely believed, tempted firms and individuals with tainted business reputations to trade under cover of a corporate name; if the business failed, they could claim simply to be unfortunate investors in the enterprise. Simmons Hardware Company of Saint Louis was one of the first hardware distributors to incorporate, in 1874. (Hardware manufacturers, though, had begun incorporating earlier.) By Simmons's own account years later, creditors looked with suspicion on the "experiment," believing that incorporation was a sign that the firm's owners were preparing for a fraudulent failure.[70] Small businesses that incorporated were even more subject to suspicion.

Many creditors believed, moreover, that corporate entities were profligate because shareholders did not behave as though their own money were being spent. According to Earling, banks and mercantile creditors therefore preferred to deal with individuals: "Credit is given to individuals, up to the limit of their probability to pay, character, experience, and reputation for honesty considered. Credit to companies is given to the extent of their paid-up capital." Different motivations led to dramatically different outcomes: "The former is bound to us during his life-time to pay his obligations; the latter, in case of failure, is 'wiped out of existence,' and with it all the creditors."[71] In sole proprietorships and partnerships, according to another credit manual, family honor and pride motivated debtors to avoid turning to the bankruptcy courts.[72]

As the practice of incorporation spread, however, and as the capital pools of these giant enterprises grew ever larger, the basis for credit ratings had to be rethought. Local correspondents, unexposed to giant firms, frequently gave their hometown businesses the same ratings as much larger New York concerns. R. G. Dun began instructing branch managers to "keep the credit markings in close relation to the capital marking." Local correspondents, Dun observed, "are apt to think the men in their locality quite entitled to the highest markings they give them relative to each other, not relative to the rest of the world; thus a good trader worth $40,000, they will not hesitate to call A1, forgetting that this is the only marking we can give A. T. Stewart and Company, who is worth half as many millions."[73]

In time, the balance tipped in favor of these well-capitalized entities, as the stigma of the limited liability provision fell away. Even then, however, character traits and business experience continued to play an important role in determining the creditworthiness of sole proprietorships and partnerships.[74]

The Effects of Competition on the Credit-Reporting Industry

The intensified competition that characterized the economy after the Civil War also plagued the credit-reporting industry. In the absence of government initiatives and regulation, competition became the most critical force shaping the evolution of the largest firms and the industry as a whole. Although first-movers R. G. Dun and the Bradstreet agency clearly were beginning to dominate, the industry remained dynamic, in part because no firm could patent its products and processes. Low barriers to entry allowed competitors to set up shop simply by issuing "change sheets," lists of businesses that had recently failed or undergone changes. These could be compiled by combing through newspaper notices, prompting one R. G. Dun Company manager to grouse that "any Agency could publish one . . . as there are plenty of traders selling out and dying off to furnish the names."[75]

Demand for credit-reporting services clearly was strong, as evidenced by the numerous new entrants into the field. Nearly all concentrated on specific geographical areas or lines of trade. The 1885 *New England Business Directory and Gazetteer,* for example, listed a number of smaller credit-reporting and collection firms in Boston specializing in the shoe and leather trade, an industry New England continued to dominate.[76] A number of firms calling themselves commercial or mercantile agencies were in fact primarily in the collection business. In addition to providing collection services, some issued blacklists of bad debtors and charged for the information.[77] (The R. G. Dun Company also engaged in collections, and this part of the business accounted for a quarter of its profits by 1900.)

Credit-reporting firms became so numerous that one New York publication declared in 1878 that there were too many; forty had been listed in New York alone during the previous five years. In Philadelphia, according to the branch manager for R. G. Dun in that city, some "12 or 15" firms were in business in the late 1870s.[78] The start-ups were a continuing source of irritation, and Dun's branch offices and correspondents regularly alerted one another about these new firms' advertisements and circulars. In some cases, Dun even had competitors investigated, as was the case in 1876, when Bradstreet filed for incorporation. In 1879 Dun hired Fuller's New York Private Detective Bureau to file a report on the American Mercantile Agency Company, which had incorporated a year earlier.

As the economy grew larger and more national, scale became a clear advantage. Firms providing wider coverage and a broader array of services could argue that they gave the best value for subscribers' money. Yet achieving wide, let alone national, coverage was difficult. It required a hefty capital investment, which largely explains why so many start-ups went out of business so quickly. After the Civil War, only four firms succeeded in being national; of these, R. G. Dun was by far the largest. In the late 1870s it had more branches than the next two competitors combined, and Robert Dun himself conservatively estimated that the firm's income was more than triple the total of all its major competitors'.[79]

The Bradstreet agency survived the difficult war years, but the death of John Bradstreet in 1863 left the firm in the less capable hands of his son, Milton. The firm passed out of the family when Charles F. Clark acquired control in 1876, the year the company was (ironically) in danger of insolvency. Bradstreet settled with its largest creditors by giving them stock in the newly incorporated firm. Clark was an experienced manager, having established the Detroit office in 1860; later he had managed the firm's Philadelphia and Boston offices. Clark restored Bradstreet's competitive edge, and he remained president until his death in 1904.[80] Thus, R. G. Dun and Bradstreet, the two firms that came to dominate the field, were run by talented, aggressive men whose decades-long tenures ensured continuity.

The other two national players were the Commercial Agency, founded in 1844 and reorganized several times before becoming McKillop and Sprague in 1872 and failing in 1879, and L. Ballard and Company, which sold out to McKillop and Sprague in 1872.[81] Neither, however, was as innovative as Bradstreet or Dun. By 1890 these two firms provided by far the widest geographical coverage in the industry. To compete on the basis of coverage, Bradstreet and Dun reported on an increasing number of small western communities, even when many still lay beyond the reach of railroads. Their branch offices varied widely in size and resources. Some of R. G. Dun's minor offices west of the Mississippi operated at a loss, yet Robert Dun remained committed to maintaining national coverage.[82] When faced with the prospect of closing minor or unprofitable offices during the Civil War, Dun opted to cut salaries in the most prosperous branches to bolster the ones struggling to survive.[83]

George Osmond was a traveling reporter assigned by Dun to cover the newer regions. In 1885 he was transferred to the Salt Lake City office, which had jurisdiction over Utah, part of Wyoming, Idaho, and Montana. Osmond later recalled that he traveled on "railroads when it was possible to do so, but as a rule" he rode "through the bottoms and over mountains upon the mail hack." The manager of the branch office covering West Virginia reportedly spent much of his time out in the field, traveling from fifty to one hundred miles in mountainous terrain to report on country merchants. When snow and ice made the roads almost impassable, the young man covered the territory on horseback.[84]

Gathering sensitive information from business owners required tact, discretion, and ingenuity on the part of reporters. Unlike salesmen, who wrote memoirs with titles like *Only a Drummer* (and whose iconic status in American culture was later captured in Arthur Miller's *Death of a Salesman*), credit reporters left very few personal accounts of their experiences. Yet the reporters clearly shared with traveling salesmen a preference for being independent and untied to an office, and they enjoyed recounting the raw conditions they encountered. According to one western credit reporter, the boom in mining around Denver from 1880 to 1890 attracted "merchants, traders, and shifty adventurers," who "came from all parts of the country, started in business, and immediately sought credit." He described Leadville, Colorado, as a town where men "would walk down the main street . . . swinging their revolvers by a chain attached to their wrists, ready for use on the slightest provocation. Shooting scrapes in a gambling 'joint' next to our office were regular occurrences." Yet credit reporters were present in Leadville even in its earliest days.[85]

Robert Dun's clear priority was expansion in the United States, but his company followed the international thrust of American business to some extent. In 1867 the firm had three international offices, in London, Montreal, and Toronto. The London branch reported only on importers and exporters trading between Britain and the United States, but British creditors soon began requesting reports on British as well as American traders. Both William Morrison, head of the London office, and Benjamin Douglass, the retired owner of the agency, favored expanding Dun's reporting services to include foreign traders. Robert Dun, however, balked at the costs involved. Significantly, he also had grave doubts about the ability of American credit-reporting agencies to transfer their practices to areas outside the United States, and he feared the hostile legislation and regulation that might result. Thus, of the Dun agency's foreign branches, only the Canadian offices reported on native merchants rather than confining themselves to American merchants operating on their soil.[86]

At the end of Dun's tenure in 1900, the agency had grown to 135 offices, including nine that were outside of the United States and Canada, in London, Glasgow, Paris, Melbourne, Sydney, Mexico City, Guadalajara, Havana, and Cape Town. International coverage accelerated after Robert Dun left the firm. From 1891 to 1916, 83 of the 115 new offices opened were located outside of the United States, including offices in Latin America and the Caribbean. Bradstreet also expanded abroad but at a slower rate.[87]

Competition drove the large agencies to become more inclusive in their reporting.[88] Instructions to correspondents expressed the goal of covering as many businesses as possible, whatever their size. A Bradstreet circular requested that correspondents provide full information on "all Merchants, Manufacturers, Bankers, Brokers, Grocers, Saddlers, Millers, Blacksmiths, Boot and Shoe Makers, Wagon Makers, Dentists, Milliners, Printers, Publishers, Insurance Agents, Lumber and Grain Dealers, etc., etc., doing business in your place . . . in fact, every person who does any kind of business, no matter how small."[89] McKillop and Sprague declared that "in addition to the Banks, Bankers, Merchants, and Manufacturers, we desire to include the Grocers, Druggists, Tanners, Hotels, Tailors, Shoemakers, Undertakers, Blacksmiths, Wagon-makers, Dentists, Physicians, Printers, Painters, Millers, Lumber Dealers, Artisans, Milliners, Dressmakers, in fact EVERY ONE engaged in the manufacture, making up, or selling of goods."[90] Inevitably, their drive for wider coverage placed within the agencies' purview the numerous small concerns owned by women and ethnic minorities, even when these businesses were not likely to request much credit. An internal analysis by the Bradstreet Company in 1899 found that some 85 percent of the businesses reported on were worth only between $500 and $5,000.[91]

The number of businesses and individuals covered by R. G. Dun grew from some twenty thousand in 1859 to over four hundred thousand in 1870 and nearly 1.3 million by 1900. Those figures, moreover, were net numbers; the reference volumes appeared between two and four times per year, and names were added and dropped between each edition. By the mid-1870s, Dun's reference book for the entire country underwent an average of over one thousand changes per day.[92] From March to July 1874, for example, almost fifty-four thousand new businesses were added and more than thirty-six thousand dropped; in addition, nearly seventeen thousand businesses had changed their names.[93] The firm also offered a notification service for subscribers wishing to be alerted immediately about changes in the condition of parties in whom they were interested.[94]

Number of ratings in R. G. Dun Reference volumes, 1859–1900

Year	Number of Ratings
1859	20,268
1865	123,000
1870	430,573
1875	641,239
1880	764,000
1885	982,993
1890	1,176,988
1895	1,298,169
1900	1,285,816

Source: Edward Vose, *Seventy-Five Years of the Mercantile Agency: R. G. Dun & Co., 1841–1916* (New York: R. G. Dun, 1916), p. 98.

Bradstreet reported in 1897 that its reference book contained about the same number of names (1.25 million) and that over 740,000 changes were made in the volume over the previous twelve months.[95]

The number of employees and subscribers grew as well. By the 1870s, Dun employed some ten thousand correspondents and reporters in the United States, to meet a demand that averaged five thousand requests for information per day. The firm continued to expand its subscriber base beyond merchants, manufacturers, and bankers to include promising industries, such as insurance.[96] According to the *Chicago Times*, in the 1870s Dun had twenty thousand subscribers to its reference book.[97] By the mid-1880s, the list had doubled, to about forty thousand.[98]

The need to circulate information to multiple parties drove R. G. Dun to experiment with new technology. The company first used carbon paper (initially a crude device using shoe blacking on yellow foolscap) but soon turned to the new typewriter technology. Dun was one of the first major American corporations to use the typewriter extensively, in the 1870s; most firms did not adopt the technology until two decades later.[99] All branch managers received a manual instructing them "to make, by aid of the typewriter and manifold paper, as many copies of every report as will be required by the various offices interested therein, and transmitting the same simultaneously to them."[100] For the first time, aided by court decisions that protected credit-reporting firms from charges of libel, Dun provided subscribers with typed reports on specific businesses rather than requiring them to obtain the information orally from the firm's offices.[101] (Sensitive information, however, continued to be transmitted orally.) Dun changed its subscription pricing to reflect the new efficiencies the typewriter allowed.

Of all their products and services, published reference books became the most important for Bradstreet and Dun after the war, and the key to their success. Bradstreet had pioneered the new method for putting information into subscribers' hands, and R. G. Dun copied, expanded, and refined the technique beginning in 1859. The books remained a distinctive product of the larger agencies; most smaller firms did not have the means to produce them on a regular basis.[102] The reference books became a critical companion to (or, for many subscribers, substitutes for) the full reports. Beginning in 1866, Dun issued its books semiannually, and then, beginning in 1873, quarterly.[103] Later, both Bradstreet and Dun expanded the reference books by including population estimates for major cities and listing the post offices and railways that served them.[104] Traveling salesmen constituted a promising new market, and both firms began producing for salesmen's use the "pocket edition," which focused on individual states.[105] Subscribers began using the volumes as the basis for mass mailings, a practice the agencies encouraged.

The success of the reference books drove R. G. Dun and the Bradstreet agency into the printing business, and both firms established presses at their New York City headquarters.[106] Sizeable investment in printing equipment in turn led the firms to expand into other areas of business information. Robert Dun and Charles Clark exploited the growing name recognition of their firms by attaching the brands to other information products. Business directories were R. G. Dun's first line extension; the firm launched its initial volume in 1867. (The directory did not succeed and was discontinued.) In 1877 the firm began publishing the *Mercantile Agency Annual,* containing information on legal, business, and other subjects of interest to businessmen. Two years later, it issued *A Synopsis of the Laws Relating to Assignments, Insolvency &etc. in the Various States of the Union.*[107] In 1893 the firm began publishing *Dun's Review,* a weekly journal that summarized business conditions and provided tables on the country's commercial and industrial business failures.

Bradstreet engaged in similar work. *Bradstreet's Weekly,* begun as a newsletter, became a full-fledged journal in 1879. In 1895 the firm began publishing a monthly wholesale commodity price index, continuing until 1937, by which time it had become the country's oldest continually published index of wholesale prices. Dun established a similar index and began providing periodic data on prices, the volume of bank clearings and building permits, and economic surveys.[108]

Their wide coverage positioned Bradstreet and R. G. Dun to collect data on the number of business failures across the country, a phenomenon not even the federal government was equipped to measure. Dun first published its business failure statistics in 1857. Soon the firm was publishing the statistics weekly, then compiling them into quarterly reports, all the while assuring subscribers that they included every failure, however small. (Bradstreet countered by publishing its own statistics and trying to discredit the accuracy of Dun's information.) Keenly aware of the marketing possibilities, Robert Dun told his branch managers that the statistics "afford us opportunity for more frequently and acceptably placing the Agency before the public."[109] Only a few years later the New York office expressed pleasure at "the large amount of gratuitous advertising which we have got all over the country from the newspapers" that published the statistics.[110]

Burgeoning amounts of information and the expansion of the agencies made accuracy an even more pressing problem. Beginning in the 1870s, Dun dispatched clerks from its various branches "to investigate on the spot the condition of business men, and to submit the result in writing." The spot reports were compared to those of the local correspondents and the discrepancies checked. According to Dun's own circulars, contested information was "submitted to the judgment of new authorities whose friendly criticism is solicited." Presumably, these included bankers, county officials, and merchants who may have had dealings with the party in question.[111] Dun soon relied heavily on full-time traveling reporters for the semiannual revisions of its reference books.[112]

Bradstreet, for its part, imposed fines on clerks for errors in transcription and awarded prizes for accurate work.[113] In addition, both firms invited subscribers to inform them of inaccuracies. Errors, stated the preface to Bradstreet's reference books, "can better be effectually checked with the aid and co-operation of our patrons." Soliciting help from their own subscribers was a tactic used by many credit reporting firms. *The Credit Guide*, published by a rival agency, broadcasted its "repeatedly expressed desire" that subscribers "should *advise us direct* of any rating or report that does an injustice, to enable us to re-investigate and correct the same."[114] R. G. Dun, too, responded to subscribers' complaints and tried to incorporate their corrections. The firm urged its correspondents and branch managers to verify information, often at the request of subscribers or the subject of the reports themselves. Subscribers sometimes pointed out discrepancies between Dun's reports and those of competitors, or informed Dun that rival firms were quicker to respond to requests.

The tendency toward self-correction was prompted by self-interest and competition. The *Chicago Times* came to this conclusion, observing that "continued support of [Dun's] patrons depends, as is evident enough, upon their truthfulness and general correctness." The dynamic interchange of information among the agency, its subscribers, and subjects tended to minimize error, for "every holder of the Reference Book scans sharply the reports of those he is particularly acquainted with, and whenever anything appears differing materially from his own judgement, he at once calls attention to it, and a discussion ensues, which is pretty sure to correct any existing misapprehension." Constant criticism "by twenty thousand holders of the Reference Book . . . is the most effective safeguard against injurious errors—or, at any rate, against *continued* injury of the kind."[115]

The Continuing Quest for Legitimacy

Growing acceptance of credit-reporting firms became evident among the public at large. New firms actually began announcing their opening to the agencies, and testimonials about the agencies' usefulness began appearing regularly in business manuals and the press.[116] "I am sure I cannot imagine how our predecessors were able to get along without the aid of mercantile agencies," declared success manual author William H. Maher. "I know that they are a necessity among business men of to-day, and that they are invaluable." Maher gave the following matter-of-fact description of how merchants used the agencies' services:

A stranger comes into your store; announces himself as Smith, of Blue Lick; wants to buy a bill of goods; will pay part cash, and wants a little time on the balance. You don't know him, and know no one to whom you can refer. You can't say to him: 'Well, Mr. Smith, I will write to someone, somewhere, to enquire about you; and if the answer is satisfactory I will sell you. Come in two or three days and I will let you know.' You must decide at once. Your reference book is at hand. You turn to the State, then run your eye down Blue Lick. Here it is: A, B, C—ah! yes, here he is: Zerubabel Smith, General Store; worth from $2,000 to $5,000, and in good credit. While you have been looking at this you have been chatting with him about business, and he may know what your book is, and he may not. As you close it you say you are ready to sell him, and you proceed to show him your goods and take his order.

When you are through with him, you pick up a blank form left you by the agency, which you proceed to fill out. After you are through with it, it will read something like this:

"Give us in confidence, and *for our exclusive use and benefit in our business, viz.:* that of aiding us to determine the propriety of giving credit, whatever information you have respecting the standing, responsibility, &c. of [fill in the blanks] Name, Business, Town, County, State."

This your clerk carries to the office of the Agency, and in a few minutes returns with a detailed report, which may read as follows: After reciting that you are to use the information for your own exclusive benefit, it goes on to say that Z. Smith, of Blue Lick, is 40 years of age, married, honest, temperate, and economical; has been in business ten years, is making money, and is a safe man to trust for such bills as his business requires. Probably worth clear $4,000.[117]

The *Chicago Times* ran a long article on R. G. Dun, in which the author claimed to have begun his inquiry skeptical of the value of credit-reporting agencies. He concluded, however, that the system "as conducted by this powerful house, is doing a great service to business interests." Although by no means perfect, the system was "absolutely indispensable to merchants in the present condition of our commercial affairs." R. G. Dun even looked legitimate: "No one can look upon the vast array of clerks . . . and the earnest, business-like systematic air worn by the whole establishment, and not be impressed with the conviction that they *mean* to do something for the money they receive from their [subscribers]."[118] Similarly, the author of an early manual for credit men declared in 1896 that the credit-reporting agency "has now become interwove [sic] with the trade of the country." If the agencies disappeared, "uncertainty, confusion, and distrust would come at once. Credits would shrink, and the distribution of merchandise [would be] restricted."[119]

Yet resistance to the agencies continued along with the endorsements. In some small towns, prejudice against local correspondents persisted through the late 1890s. According to one credit man, "it is almost a matter of contempt to be known . . . as a reporter for either Dun or Bradstreet."[120] The two largest agencies argued that much of the resistance could be traced to the activities of incompetent or unscrupulous fly-by-night firms. According to Bradstreet, these had "produced a prejudice against the system in the minds of many business men and the public generally."[121] Similarly, Dun's counsel, Charles O'Conor, argued in court that "all those things in the nature of a Mercantile Agency which have been condemned by the courts—the preparation and publication of 'black lists,' the printing of papers for general circulation, containing information which should be confidential—have been the devices of small, trifling concerns, unregulated, and, comparatively speaking, uncompensated."[122] Notorious cases, such as the one involving Brock and Company, two brothers who bought a reputable Boston credit-reporting company and then absconded to Canada without compensating their subscribers, further tarnished the reputation of the industry. So, too, did the many failed start-ups. The very success of the large credit-reporting firms, the *Dry Goods Bulletin* surmised, "induced the establishment of a numerous brood of imitators; irresponsible parties, whose only care is to inveigle business men into subscriptions to worthless concerns."[123] Newspapers reported how disreputable agencies sometimes spread false rumors about healthy firms to increase sales of credit reports to panicked creditors.

Sporadic and often sensationalized, the resistance to credit reporting was typified by an article in the *Toronto Mail* in December, 1875. The newspaper reported on the suit brought by one Andrew McLean against Dun, Wiman and Company, R. G. Dun's Toronto office, for damages sustained as a consequence of relying on information he had obtained from the agency. The jury found for the plaintiff, determining that Dun, Wiman was negligent in giving a favorable report on a merchant to whom McLean sold goods on credit and who subsequently failed. The *Mail* harangued the credit-reporting firms for "dragooning" merchants into subscribing to their services. Referring specifically to the foreign nature of the institution, the Canadian editor remarked, "There is something un-British and repugnant to most right-thinking men in a system of espionage that has become a huge Mercantile Inquisition, by no means infallible, and, it now appears, not always very careful of the way in which it conducts its inquiries." Old ways of doing business, he argued, were fairer and safer: "The cases are few in which private inquiry will not discover all a merchant wants to know of a purchaser seeking credit . . . Old firms will tell you much safer business was done before this new-fangled system came into operation."[124]

American credit men recognized that their occupation was based on a fundamental irony: that in a supposedly free democratic republic, there should exist an institution that many perceived as "a system of espionage, a prying into the affairs of firms and individuals for selfish and unworthy purposes," in the words of one Bradstreet publication.[125] Earling captured the essence of the paradox (and gave support to the Canadian editors' observations) when he wrote that the "free citizen of the United States is the only one on the face of the earth who tolerates it. It is a purely American institution and flourishes only on American soil."[126]

In the United States, at least two book-length critiques—one published in 1876, the other in 1896—questioned the legitimacy of the agencies' methods and the accuracy of the information they provided. The earlier work, *The Commercial Agency "System" of the United States and Canada Exposed*, was written by Thomas Meagher—the pen name for Charles F. Maynard—who had first worked for R. G. Dun as a messenger boy in Montreal in 1862 before being promoted to copyist and then placed in charge of petty cash. He moved to New York in 1866 and continued to work intermittently for the agency as copyist and reader. In 1875 the agency dismissed him for "dishonesty, and for attempting to corrupt the fidelity of some of his fellow clerks," according to a circular issued after the book's publication.[127]

Meagher's complaint against the agencies centered on their negative reports, portrayed in his book as tantamount to a "black list." One of Meagher's stated objectives was to disclose in the book's appendix the initials of several thousand allegedly blacklisted merchants, along with their home towns and cities. Future editions, he promised, would contain more names.[128] Meagher's book could be dismissed as the rantings of a crank, but R. G. Dun took it seriously and issued a circular disputing Meagher's claims. In 1889 Joseph Pulitzer's *New York World* published a series of articles on credit-reporting agencies, essentially repeating Meagher's arguments.

The book repeated objections that had been voiced since the 1840s—in particular, that the agencies violated the privacy of individuals and their families. Meagher added new twists, such as claiming to know of instances where businesses had been robbed after disclosing their assets. He criticized the agencies' use of new contracts to reduce their liability and presented R. G. Dun's attempts to control its information as evidence of malicious intent; credit-reporting firms, Meagher charged, retained ownership of their reference books to prevent injured parties from using them as evidence in lawsuits. The firms' strenuous lobbying against unfriendly acts introduced in the state legislatures was additional proof of the system's conspiratorial bent.[129]

Meagher's book contained a number of more serious objections—for example, that the opinions of subscribers regarding other traders was given more credence than the opinions of nonsubscribers. Nonsubscribers, moreover, had no access to reports and so could not know what was being said of them. Whether these claims had merit, they did point to the inherent conflict of interest that occurred when businesses were both subscribers to and subjects of the agencies' reports. Meagher was on even firmer ground when he described the information provided by the agencies as vague and contradictory. Each of their rating keys covered so huge a spread ("worth $250K–$500K") as to be meaningless. Comparing the reports of different agencies showed how far apart were their estimates regarding the same merchants. The reports were old, and the notification sheets that supposedly kept subscribers up to date, inadequate. Meagher alleged that most correspondents and clerks were inexperienced, incompetent, untrustworthy men; they were underpaid—and worth no more than their meager compensation.[130]

In 1896 another full-length attack, *The Mercantile Agencies against Commerce*, was published by one William Chinn. Like Meagher, Chinn decried the agencies' attempt "to introduce the spy system in every department of affairs where the element of confidence enters." Credit reporting constituted one of "the most gigantic and thorough-going private systems . . . apart from and above the government, disclaiming responsibility, and recognizing no law but that of self-interest." Chinn compared the American system unfavorably with the trade protection societies of Britain, whose sole object was "to discover and blacklist the 'swindlers and sharpers.'" The British societies' blacklists were prepared by and for the exclusive use of members for the purpose of mutual protection, and "no pretense is made of reporting the standing of everybody." Members selected their officers, all expenses were met by a modest subscription, and—most important— the societies did not sell their reports to everyone willing to pay for the in- formation. American credit-reporting firms, by contrast, did not confine themselves to "sharpers" and "swindlers" but instead recognized "no limi- tations as to whom they report, nor in the number of customers, provided the price is paid."[131]

A rambling and bizarre work, *The Mercantile Agencies against Commerce* nevertheless voiced objections with which the legal system had grappled during the previous decades. Faced with criticisms from the press and threatened with lawsuits, credit-reporting agencies had repeatedly stated that they merely performed, for a fee, what subscribers would have done for themselves; that is, they merely acted as agents for their subscribers. Many wholesalers, the agencies pointed out, also tried to check borrowers' reputations in their hometowns, obtained information from other suppli- ers, and occasionally sent a clerk or traveling salesman to check the infor- mation.

Chinn pointed to the absurdity of this claim, which implied that sub- scribers were both "customers" of the agencies and "principals" (that is, di- rectly responsible for their "agents"). He compared this arrangement to the earlier work of Sheldon Church, who was hired by a group of mer- chants to obtain information on their behalf and who therefore was an agent in the proper sense of the term. Church's employers owned the in- formation, and he could not sell it to other parties. By contrast, subscribers to credit-reporting agencies did not own the information; it stayed with the agencies, who sold the findings to whomever they pleased. Neither the cor- respondents nor the information itself was under the direct control of sub- scribers; instead, both were under the control of the agencies alone. How, then, could credit-reporting firms claim merely to be the agents of their subscribers? If this were true, Chinn reasoned, "the anomaly would be pre- sented of principals soliciting themselves to buy what was their own."[132]

Like Meagher, Chinn addressed the quality of the agencies' informa- tion. He described how correspondents and reporters did their work:

The salaried reporter . . . collects the opinions of others, and hearsay which may be floating around; sometimes he interviews the party in- quired about, or asks him for a written or verbal statement of his pe- cuniary circumstances. What he may gather from the party in the way of a statement is, however, submitted to others for criticism before the report for circulation is written. Then, on the other hand, the party may be written to for his statement, which if made is submitted to 'authorities' in the same way . . . But the vast bulk of this commodity is procured from correspondents, who, upon the whole, practically give merely their opinions, or what they have heard, as also they pass upon the statements made by those who reside in their jurisdictions.[133]

Meant to convey the inadequacies of the system, Chinn's description in fact did not differ materially from those found in later textbooks on the subject. In the ensuing decades, the new credit professionals would acknowledge the credit-reporting agencies' usefulness but chide them for their shortcomings in this area. Earling, for one, echoed Meagher's allegations about the agencies' correspondents, still perceived as the weakest link in the system. Although Earling's opinion of the larger agencies and their paid, full-time reporters was guardedly favorable, he blasted their continued reliance on corresponding attorneys, warning that these individuals "perform their labors entirely gratis, and the reports from this source seldom furnish details, but simply offer opinions that parties are supposed to be good or otherwise—generally good."[134]

In the industry's struggle for legitimacy, the courts, rather than the legislatures, continued to play the most prominent role. During and after the Panic of 1873, several state legislatures introduced measures that would have made the agencies responsible for losses to subscribers resulting from inaccurate information. R. G. Dun mobilized its branch offices to lobby against bills in Ottawa (Canada), Missouri, and Pennsylvania—further proof, according to critics, of the agencies' conspiratorial and malicious nature. The flurry of measures that accompanied the Panic of 1873 soon subsided and was never repeated. Lawsuits, however, continued to be brought against the agencies. Fortunately for them, the courts increasingly broadened the definition of privileged communication. Sixteen years after *Beardsley* had determined that credit reports could not be so protected, *Ormsby v. Douglass* (1867) resulted in an important rethinking of the issue. Once again, a libel suit was brought against the Dun agency; but this time the court accepted the firm's arguments and stipulated only that the communication must be made "in good faith."[135]

Several decisions in the 1870s, including the *Gibson* case discussed earlier, established that the agencies needed only to be "reasonably diligent."[136] In most cases, the courts rejected the argument that agencies were liable for losses resulting from reliance on the information they provided. Courts also punished individuals who knowingly submitted erroneous financial statements. These decisions were lauded by the business press as progressive—"in keeping with the advanced ideas of the business community, which demands telegraphs, telephones, lightning express trains—in fact everything that will enable them to transact business securely and rapidly," gushed the *Cincinnati Commercial Gazette*.[137]

A survey of court decisions affecting the agencies reported no cases in which they were sued for sharing information with nonsubscribers.[138] Yet courts and jurists clearly were troubled by the wide distribution of potentially damaging information. In *The Commonwealth [of Pennsylvania] vs. Stacey* (1870), in which a criminal action for libel was brought against R. G. Dun's Philadelphia office, the plaintiff's attorney described credit-reporting agencies as one of the "mean methods of making money—some legal, and some contrary to law"—that had proliferated in the nineteenth century. He resurrected the argument that no organization could possibly "go into the secret recesses of the hearts of the merchants throughout the country, and gather information for the purpose of sending out communications or publishing a book—alleging that they can give the precise standing of every merchant in the land." Such methods, "absurd on the face of it," frequently ended up ruining innocent merchants.[139]

The court sided with Dun, stating that "a communication is privileged, even though it be defamatory." However, it added, "We cannot agree with the position taken by the defendant, that . . . he may communicate to every person who becomes a subscriber to his agency statements prejudicial to the business or moral standing of the merchants of the land, whether the persons to whom the information is sent have an interest in receiving it or not." As a safeguard, the court suggested that every subscriber furnish the agencies with the names of firms with whom they had credit relations so that the agencies could restrict the scope of their reporting to those firms alone.[140] (The suggestion was never implemented.)

Meanwhile, the agencies refined their contracts with subscribers to include disclaimers about the accuracy of the information provided (although, of course, the agencies could still be sued for normal negligence). Nearly all agencies that provided reference books specified that subscribers must return them, and subscription agreements increasingly made this requirement explicit.[141] Some contracts specified that the reference books could not be loaned out to others.[142] Dun continually reminded its branch managers to protect the confidentiality of all the information they handled. A circular sent out in 1874 warned that even improperly sealed envelopes could be cause for concern.[143] Another reassured subscribers that the notification sheet was not intended "to be hawked about by canvassers and distributed to non-subscribers as a means of influencing subscriptions . . . but is used for *legitimate purposes only*."[144] Dun quickly put a stop to one branch manager's practice of using the notification sheets as a ruse to draw subscribers to his office so that he could extort information from them. The "question of printing names on the Sheet has never been covered by a decision in the courts," warned the head office, and "vague suspicions and surmises do not justify the insertion of a name on the Sheet."[145] Problems with the notification sheets persisted until Dun finally decided to discontinue them entirely in 1908, explaining that the sheets had "been treated more like circulars of no special importance than as confidential communications."[146] At the same time, Dun's company manuals increasingly discouraged language that explicitly tied opinions about an individual's or firm's prospects to the agency or its reporters. The final decision to extend credit should be left to the creditor alone.

Methods for determining creditworthiness remained essentially unchanged in the period 1865–1900, despite the expansion of trade and the significant structural alterations that occurred within the distribution sector. Important features that had first emerged during the antebellum period continued, including the reliance on character traits as an indication of a debtor's ability and willingness to pay. Judith Hilkey argues that the continuing focus on character by the authors of success manuals was an attempt to legitimate the new corporate order. This is no doubt true, but it was also the case that business creditors continued to rely on character traits because they perceived them to be genuinely effective indicators of creditworthiness. All the new credit-granting manuals, published beginning in 1890 with Peter Earling's seminal *Whom To Trust*, devoted significant sections to the analysis of character traits.

After the Civil War, R. G. Dun and the Bradstreet agency clearly began to dominate the industry. Increased scale had obvious advantages, including an enhanced ability to compare requests for information on the same individual from different areas of the country, making the detection of fraud more likely.[147] Another advantage was the ability to leverage information-gathering abilities to develop line extensions—such as directories—to the agencies' core business. Some of these new products and services succeeded; others did not.

Competition drove the agencies' experimentation and growth, as numerous start-ups took advantage of the industry's relatively low barriers to entry. Few had staying power, but their existence proved a continuing source of annoyance and anxiety to the established agencies, which responded by trying to expand coverage and improve their services. As R. G. Dun's circulars and letter books confirm, competition also enhanced the quality of the information reported.

Notorious instances of fraud and the financial weakness of many start-ups undermined the public's trust in the institution of credit reporting. Gross errors in reporting prompted lawsuits for libel and negligence. Agency managers no doubt regarded the suits as impediments, but the legal challenges functioned as an important check, forcing the agencies to curb their worst impulses and continue improving the quality of their reports. Moreover, favorable court decisions affirmed the legitimacy of the agencies' activities. Debates in the press and the publication of at least two book-length attacks on the institution mitigated the lingering suspicions by bringing them out in the open for public discussion.

Resistance, unorganized and largely sensationalized, continued throughout the post–Civil War period, but the trend clearly was in the direction of acceptance. The reports' greater convenience and uniformity, increased protection from the courts, the successful lobbying of state legislatures by the agencies, and the sheer prevalence of their practices succeeded in embedding the credit-reporting agencies as permanent elements of the country's commercial infrastructure. Favorable court decisions and the industry's strong growth indicate that by the 1870s an important shift had occurred: the desire for transparency had by then trumped concerns about accuracy. However serious some of the agencies' reporting errors may have been, the courts declined to declare their methods invalid, and growing numbers of mercantile creditors began to view the agencies' services as essential.

Toward the end of the nineteenth century, the movement toward professionalization, along with the heightened emphasis on rationality, efficiency, and order, led to the formation of the National Association of Credit Men. The organization lobbied strenuously for greater financial transparency and further solidified the place of credit reporting in the eyes of the business community.

From Competition to Cooperation: The Birth of the Credit Man, 1890–1920

The birth of the "credit man" was intimately tied to the appearance of the modern business corporation. During the last two decades of the nineteenth century, these new organizations began to overshadow the traditional, single-unit firms that had dominated earlier. A new class of professionals—urban, middle class, technically oriented, and committed to the ideals of efficiency—emerged to take advantage of the opportunities corporations offered. Corporate managers assumed the function of allocating resources throughout the economy, a role that previously had been largely the reserve of market and price mechanisms. They made the critical decisions affecting the flows of capital, people, and goods among the corporation's units and imposed greater control and tighter standards on operations that had become much larger and more dispersed.[1]

The movement to professionalize grew from the impulse of this group to define their status within the new order. It grew, too, from the perceived excesses of the Gilded Age.[2] Accountants were among the first to be shaped by these forces: they were at the forefront of designing more sophisticated accounting systems for municipalities and the rate-regulated industries, actions that earned the approval and respect of private and public administrators. The earliest professional accounting organization in the United States, the Institute of Accounts [sic] of New York, was formed in April 1882. Five years later the American Association of Public Accountants (a group more influenced by emigrant British practitioners) was incorporated. New York passed the first CPA certification law in 1896, and the next generation of accountants lobbied to pass similar laws in other states.[3]

Like accounting, credit granting was profoundly affected by the drive toward greater efficiency and professionalism. Instruments that formalized book debts, such as the trade acceptance, gradually gained importance. Trade acceptances forced debtors to adhere more strictly to payment terms, and this in turn allowed the instruments to circulate and release the value that would otherwise have been tied up in creditors' accounts receivable. The Federal Reserve and the American Trade Acceptance Council strongly encouraged the use of this instrument, by launching educational campaigns to inform businessmen of its value.[4]

The development of more-sophisticated credit analysis was another attempt to promote efficiency and order. Pioneering work in this area first occurred among New York factors in the textile industry and in brokerages specializing in single-name paper and accounts receivable.[5] Large manufacturers and wholesalers in nearly all industries soon employed "credit men," whose sole responsibility was to appraise the creditworthiness of current and prospective customers. Credit work previously done by owner-managers or traveling salesmen evolved into a separate function, carried out by men eager to endow their specialized knowledge with greater prestige and recognition.

As they became more self-conscious of their role in the organization and in society at large, these individuals sought to place the art of credit assessment on a more "scientific" basis, to complement the heavy reliance on "personal intuition, impressions and the variations of personal feelings" that had characterized credit granting in the past.[6] They also began to emphasize the centrality of the credit man within the organization, particularly to help increase sales.[7] Aspiring credit professionals distinguished themselves from salesmen, who were driven solely by the desire to sell. In contrast, spokesmen for the new credit profession emphasized their ability to transform uncertainty into calculated risk. "Losses come in taking chances—so does volume of sales," stated one credit manual. "That credit man excels who, taking what looks like a long chance, by such mental means and systematic methods as he possesses shortens the chance and brings it to the point of safety."[8]

The National Association of Credit Men

The persistent and violent business cycles of the nineteenth century provided an impetus for the reform of credit practices, one that merged seamlessly with the drive toward professionalization. By the 1890s, creditors and credit men had banded together into local associations to deal with insolvents and improve the quality and sharing of information. It was the Panic of 1893, however, that spurred the formation of a national group, and a resolution to do so was proposed during the World Mercantile Congress sponsored by the

Chicago World's Fair that year. Participants later described the meeting as "poorly attended" and "disappointing." Nevertheless, it initiated the establishment of the National Association of Credit Men (NACM), formed three years later in Toledo, Ohio. Ten existing local associations formed its nucleus, and ambitious plans were made to organize many more.[9]

The new organization, incorporated in New York State in 1897, had an initial membership of six hundred (although fewer than one hundred actually attended the first convention). Credit-reporting firms and collection attorneys eyed the new organization with trepidation, fearing it would set up services to rival their own. Associations of retailers, who made up the bulk of mercantile debtors, also expressed concern that a national association of credit men might work to their disadvantage. Credit men themselves harbored doubts about the merit of a national group. Even so, membership in the NACM rose by more than threefold during the first year, to 1,746 organizations and 245 individuals. (By 1920 it would claim a membership of over thirty-three thousand, making the NACM one of the largest commercial organizations in the world.)[10]

The committees formed during the association's first meetings reveal the precise areas of concern to credit men: legislative; business literature; credit department methods; improvement of mercantile agency service; and investigation. Composed of members chosen from local associations, these committees became the critical mechanisms for articulating and implementing the NACM's reform agenda.

Some of the association's earliest concerns revolved around the reform of payment methods—for example, discouraging debtors' use of local checks to pay bills, a costly practice for their out-of-state creditors. The association also lobbied for state laws to help stop fraudulent "bulk goods" sales (a common method of defrauding creditors, whereby dishonest individuals bought goods on credit and sold them to an accomplice or an unwitting buyer before absconding), fought the repeal of the newly enacted national bankruptcy law, urged uniformity and fairness in state collection laws, and pushed to scale back state exemption laws. Improving the services provided by credit-reporting agencies quickly became part of the association's core mission. Although they expressed resentment over the organization's interference and criticism, neither R. G. Dun nor Bradstreet resisted the NACM's overtures, and reports on the agencies' progress became a regular feature of the annual conventions.[11]

Members of the NACM published the first manuals on credit management and shaped the understanding of that subject during the opening decades of the twentieth century. The first, *Whom To Trust* by Chicago credit man Peter R. Earling, was published in 1890. (Earling later helped set up the meeting in Chicago that called for the formation of the NACM.)[12] Credit manuals were part of a larger development that saw the publication of numerous business books on a wide variety of technical topics. Chicago businessman Arch W. Shaw, whose company produced a range of business books and a well-regarded business journal (*System*), was among the most influential publishers of the genre.[13] Another major publisher, the Alexander Hamilton Institute of New York, issued a series called "Modern Business" under editor in chief Joseph French Johnson, Dean of the New York University School of Commerce, Accounts, and Finance, one of the country's first modern business schools. In addition to a volume on the principles of credit assessment and collections (*Credit and the Credit Man*), the series included titles like *Plant Management, Marketing and Merchandising, Advertising Principles,* and *Salesmanship and Sales Management.* By World War I, members of the NACM were offering courses on credit granting through the Young Men's Christian Association and attempting to establish them in a number of colleges and universities.[14]

The appearance of technical manuals and the establishment of specialized courses were part of a distinct pattern that could be found wherever new, self-conscious groups of practitioners aspired to become professionals. Typically, these groups claimed special status for the technical skills and knowledge of members by demonstrating that their expertise was necessary for the well-being of society.[15] The National Association of Credit Men made regular, almost ritualistic declarations about its members' expert attempts to infuse business practices with a spirit of moral responsibility. In a typical statement, association president William Prendergast declared that the NACM "was the first body that ever successfully attempted to accomplish an improvement in the conditions surrounding credit based upon *ethical* and *educational* purposes."[16] Assertions such as these also appeared in the forewords of the new credit management textbooks and manuals, sometimes accompanied by "histories" that endowed the occupation with a kind of pedigree. Credit manuals frequently began by tracing the beginnings of mercantile credit in the ancient world and then followed its development through several thousand years before ending with the enlightened and progressive practices of the author's own era.

Spokesmen for the new profession portrayed themselves as the instrument of order within a society perpetually rocked by financial disorder. Credit men "occupy a unique position in industrial society," according to one manual, because "they either induce a healthy moral tone or else are responsible for practices which result in heavy losses."[17] Prendergast went further, stating that "commercial credit exerts a greater influence upon the tendencies of the people than almost any other phase of human activity. This influence manifests itself in the social as well as the economic departments of life."[18] By teaching proper credit methods to business owners, the NACM sought to fulfill its role as the guardian of both economic stability and the morals of American business. (To be sure, the NACM's assertion that its members had a central role in the economy was justified. From a scholarly standpoint, corporate credit men epitomized Alfred Chandler's "visible hand"—the professional administrators whose collective decisions allocated resources more purposefully than the market.)

The credit men's claims to professionalism became linked to the idea of transparency and the accompanying need for cooperation among practitioners. "Selfish" and "secret" practices were equated with the past and contrasted to more modern, "liberal" attitudes. Asserted repeatedly in the NACM's conventions, articles, and pamphlets, the twin goals of transparency and cooperation became the distinctive modernizing mission of the association.[19] Ironically, the cooperative model that was established in Britain during the late eighteenth century, well before the appearance of credit-reporting firms in the United States, came to epitomize the more "progressive" business practices of the new American profession.

In common with other newly professionalized groups, the NACM looked to the technical and moral education of members as the key to achieving its goals. The association resolved to compile statistics, by commercial center and line of business, on current payment methods and practices and to publicize the most effective and innovative practices among local associations. Findings were printed in pamphlet form for distribution to the local associations and the trade press. In 1898 a monthly newsletter, *Bulletin of the NACM,* was founded to improve communication among members.[20]

Reforming Financial Statements

The waves of corporate mergers during the late nineteenth and early twentieth centuries led to demands for greater "publicity" of corporate financial information. Responding to the new political climate, Congress in 1898 created the Industrial Commission to hold hearings on whether trusts were in restraint of trade and competition. The commission met regularly until 1902, and in 1900 it published a preliminary report that, among other recommendations, called for the establishment of an independent public accounting profession to prevent corporate abuses such as stock watering.

Two years later the commission recommended that trusts be required to publish annual audited reports detailing their profits and losses as well as assets and liabilities. Although some witnesses argued that dividend payments provided sufficient information for investors to make decisions, many who represented the trusts sided with the commission. Their support stemmed largely from a desire to counter the intense public skepticism triggered by the corporate scandals of the previous two decades. The Bureau of Corporations, set up in 1902 and lasting until the start of World War I, further promoted the "efficient publicity" of corporate financial statements.[21]

The NACM went beyond the relatively modest aims of the federal regulators. Its early meetings were devoted to the determined, if halting, attempts to impose transparency on all American businesses, not just the controversial corporations and trusts. In 1897 the NACM's Credit Department Methods Committee argued for the necessity of procuring signed statements from all businesses.[22] The NACM soon joined forces with the American Bankers Association, which in 1908 recommended that audited financial statements be made more widely available. (Many bankers became members of the NACM. In 1915, they formed their own subgroup, the Robert Morris Associates, named for the most important financier and banker of the American Revolution.) Together, the NACM and the American Bankers Association worked to pass in every state laws punishing debtors who submitted false statements, whether directly to creditors or indirectly to credit-reporting agencies. Congress passed a measure (U.S. Criminal Code, Section 215) making it illegal to send false financial statements through the mail. The new law was more stringent than existing state laws.[23] Passage of the first federal income tax code in 1913 further increased the demand for statements and encouraged improvements in their content.[24]

The NACM pushed for greater uniformity of financial statements, arguing that it would ease the decision-making process for investors and creditors by allowing them to compare businesses more easily. Uniformity was in keeping with the spirit of Progressive reform, which had begun with efforts to standardize municipal accounts. Federal officials grew enamored of the idea and tried to expand it into the private sector. (Accountants

were less enthusiastic, fearing that a system of uniform accounts would reduce the need for professional judgment and turn accountants into mere
clerks.)[25] To encourage standardization, the NACM developed and sold
"uniform statement blanks." By its fourth annual convention in 1899, the
NACM counted 133 firms using the forms.[26]

Greater availability and uniformity of financial information made possible
the development of more-sophisticated ratios to analyze business performance. Simple ratios, such as expenses as a percentage of sales, had been
understood since at least the mid-nineteenth century. In the late 1890s, the
current ratio, or current assets divided by current liabilities, became more
prevalent. ("Current assets" are cash and other assets—notes and accounts
receivable, inventory, and marketable securities—that are expected to be
converted into cash during a firm's operating cycle, normally within a year.
"Current liabilities" are payments that are due within the year.) Because the
current ratio directly related a firm's liquid assets to the payments immediately due to creditors, it marked a significant step in allowing creditors to
predict the likelihood that a firm would meet its payments. Banks began to
rely heavily on this ratio as the only proper foundation for loans. They began touting the "50 percent rule," which dictated that a borrower's current
liabilities should not exceed 50 percent of current assets.[27] The NACM's
Bulletin set out similar guidelines in 1902, and in 1905 James Graham
Cannon, president of the Fourth National Bank of New York and an early
president of the NACM, recommended a set of ratios in a paper to the New
Jersey Bankers Association.[28]

Even so, resistance to providing financial statements to mercantile creditors, especially among smaller retail establishments, persisted. Vigorous
competition among suppliers ensured that retailers were constantly wooed
by traveling salesmen, who feared that requests for financial statements
might jeopardize their sales. The salesmen applied pressure on their companies' credit departments to approve requests for credit quickly, prompting some credit men to ask for statements only when they had strong
suspicions about the applicant.[29] The form issued by the Bradstreet agency
in the 1890s demonstrates the depth of the reluctance to furnish statements. Bradstreet phrased its request for financial information carefully, re-
assuring business owners that it "arises from no unworthy or impertinent
motive, but is intended simply as an act of courtesy and justice to yourself."
Requests for information gave the debtor the opportunity to "speak in his
own behalf . . . and give such references as have knowledge of his pecuniary

responsibility, and thus correct any errors [caused by] prejudice or want of knowledge on the part of those applied to."[30] A voluntary statement, in other words, was the best defense against becoming a victim of inaccurate information provided by others. The NACM argued that complying with the request for a statement would make the applicant a better merchant because it obliged him to take an annual inventory and pay more careful attention to the financial condition of his business.[31]

Yet R. G. Dun and the Bradstreet agency were themselves skeptical of the value of statements, even though both intensified their efforts to obtain statements and distributed pamphlets explaining their benefits. Bradstreet president Charles Clark told the NACM that his agency began soliciting statements primarily "to correct an impression [among the business community] that our information was gathered from secret sources." The need to obtain more complete and detailed information was a consideration, but only a secondary one, because the agency regarded self-reported statements as frequently inaccurate or overoptimistic. Clark pointed out that even banks—which, unlike mercantile establishments, were required by federal law to prepare statements and were subject to government examination and supervision—often failed unexpectedly. Given this scenario, the value of a haphazardly prepared statement, especially by a small merchant unschooled in proper methods, was questionable at best.[32]

Statistics from the period confirm that the quality of self-reported financial information continued to be low. A survey of small manufacturers and traders conducted for the U.S. Bureau of the Census in 1900 found that the majority of businesses did not keep accurate accounts. As a result, they could not calculate the extent of their liabilities or assets nor determine whether their businesses were profitable.[33] Credit manuals warned against taking statements at face value. "Unfortunately, many a small merchant does not keep books in any real sense," according to one manual. "You will find in his store a couple of spindles, on one of which he puts the bills as they come in, while on the other he puts the bills as he pays them. He may also have a blotter in which he records the sales he makes on credit."[34] Another manual reported that many country traders did not even keep ledger accounts; instead, they just depended on the bills and statements they received to serve as records of their transactions: "The original bill is their book account, the statement is their reminder, and their own check or the draft retuned to them by their bank is their voucher receipt."[35]

Expenses like utilities, insurance, taxes, transportation, mailing, office supplies, and losses from bad debts and theft were not properly recorded. Neither was depreciation expense. Credit manual writer Peter Wahlstad warned that "in certain lines, especially those affected by fashion . . . goods may be worth only a fraction of their original value."[36] Robert H. Montgomery, president of the American Association of Public Accountants, told the NACM in 1913 that the bad debts incurred through borrowers' ignorance "are *tremendously greater* than are those based on fraudulent statements."[37] The problem was so widespread that the NACM's Credit Department Methods Committee recommended distributing a pamphlet to retailers outlining a simple method for keeping accurate accounts. Prizes were offered for the best essays on simple and effective methods of bookkeeping and accounting for retailers.[38]

Serious problems in obtaining accurate financial statements explain why "character" (indications of the willingness to pay) continued to be so important to credit assessment. Attempts to put the process on a more scientific basis floundered because of indifference, suspicion, and ignorance about the basics of bookkeeping among business owners. Whatever the supposed benefits of making a statement, most business owners believed that the very fact of having provided one was itself sensitive information. Both Bradstreet and R. G. Dun refused to comply with requests by the NACM that the agencies indicate which capital ratings in their reference books were based on a signed statement. That information, the agencies argued, had been "entrusted to us to use with discretion."[39]

Interchange of Debtors' Payment Records

Toward the end of the nineteenth century, a consensus began to emerge that creditors themselves were the best sources of information on debtors. Payment records, known as ledger or trade information, increasingly were seen as more objective indicators of creditworthiness than were character, past experience, or capital.[40] Peter Wahlstad became one of the most vocal supporters of credit information interchanges (or "bureaus"), arguing that they were superior to agency reports. "It is now pretty well recognized," he claimed, "that the record of a dealer's purchases and payments, provided it is sufficiently complete, affords more material for intelligent credit analysis than the combined testimony of agency ratings and reporters' opinions."[41]

Local attorneys, banks, and traveling salesmen also began to be seen as inferior sources of information, although there was disagreement about the relative merits of each.[42] Creditors had long relied on attorneys for information and debt collection, and directories of attorneys willing to provide these services continued to be widely available. Attorneys paid a yearly fee for inclusion, and the directories were distributed to wholesale houses, collection agencies, and other interested parties. Some attorneys charged for their services based on a schedule of fixed rates adopted by county bar associations. More typically, publishers of the directories used the same system as the credit-reporting agencies: they required participating attorneys to provide free credit reports in return for debt collection work. Publishers even sold inquiry forms for subscribers to send to the attorneys. Wahlstad claimed that the system was less extensively used than formerly, but a textbook on credit practices published until the mid-twentieth century endorsed the use of local attorneys. They were "frequently acquainted with the personal and family history of local merchants from the time of their youth," it explained, "and what the attorney does not know from this acquaintance, he knows from the gossip of other members of the community." Moreover, attorneys were usually adept at valuing the local property owned by their fellow townspeople.[43]

Similar disagreement arose over the merits of banks and traveling salesmen as sources of information.[44] Some credit men did not consider banks reliable allies because bankers were too fearful of violating client confidentiality.[45] Entrusting salesmen with the task of collecting information also was controversial. According to critics, the eagerness of salesmen to close sales compromised the caution that was necessary to good decision making. In 1859 the *Cyclopaedia of Commerce* commended the credit-reporting agencies precisely because of their greater objectivity compared to traveling salesmen.[46] Nearly three decades later the *Cincinnati Commercial Gazette* affirmed that "the efforts to secure trade by sending out travelers, who frequently solicit patronage without regard to the fitness of the subject for credit, have made mercantile agencies a necessity."[47] Yet salesmen were in close touch with customers, seeing them anywhere from once a month to every six months, depending on the type of goods sold.[48] The salesmen's intimate knowledge of their customers' businesses prompted many suppliers to rely on their judgment.[49] Manufacturers and wholesalers with ethnically diverse customer bases depended heavily on salesmen who belonged to the same ethnic groups as their customers.[50]

Compared to these problematic sources, ledger information appeared much more objective and reliable. Yet it was the single most difficult piece of information to obtain because creditors had little incentive to share their records with one another. The systematic interchange of customers' payment records increasingly became an important objective of the NACM. Its Credit Department Methods Committee produced a directory of members to stimulate the practice, and local associations were encouraged to appoint secretaries to administer the exchange of information.[51] In its first year, the NACM developed and circulated a standard trade inquiry form. A year later, over 170 mercantile businesses were using it.[52] Among them were the National Wholesale Saddlery Dealers Association and the Associated Trades Credit Exchange, which included lines such as wagons and carriages, and millinery.[53]

Even prior to the formation of the NACM, a few local associations had already established reporting bureaus for the exchange of ledger information among merchants in their area. The NACM built on the experiences of the locals by providing a forum for comparing differences in practice and approach. Denver, for example, charged all members $35 regardless of size, while other locals charged on a per-use basis.[54] Baltimore reported not only on late and fraudulent accounts but also on attorneys who gave unsatisfactory service and employees who ran afoul of their employers. Nashville's members could obtain information on how much a debtor owed in that city, to whom the debt was owed, how much was past due, whether the debtor had been sued, and whether claims were pending against him. Its system was reportedly so successful that local businesses were inspired to apply for membership.[55]

Nashville's experience illustrated how the establishment of a reporting and collections bureau could stimulate interest among merchants. But with few exceptions—such as New York and Philadelphia, which regularly corresponded with one another—the locals rarely exchanged information on a regular basis.[56] Establishing a national interchange system would correct the flaw, but practitioners' skepticism about its viability and usefulness had first to be overcome, a process that proved slow and halting.[57]

Compared to merchants in Britain and Germany, those in the United States were slow to establish mechanisms for sharing information. British merchants and shopkeepers had begun alerting one another about problematic debtors in the late eighteenth century (see Chapter 1). By the 1850s, the country's local trade protection societies had formed debt collection departments and established funds to provide legal help to members. Soon after, they formed a national reporting network. Trade protection societies became a powerful interest group, lobbying Parliament on issues such as the continuance of imprisonment for debt.[58] In Germany, the Union of Credit

Reform Associations was organized in 1882; it consisted of manufacturers, merchants, bankers, and other creditors. The association did not request statements from debtors but instead distributed confidential information, gathered from its members, on the standing of firms seeking credit. It also collected delinquent debts.[59] By the late 1890s, the German association reportedly consisted of six hundred local offices with correspondents all over the world. It helped locate absconding debtors, acted as arbitrator in doubtful cases, secured the services of lawyers at reduced fees, and published a newsletter. Membership totaled forty-seven thousand, and the association provided over two million answers to members' inquiries annually.[60]

In the United States, a few short-lived trade protection societies had been established earlier in the century, but more permanent ones did not appear until the late 1870s. Even then, they were local in scope or focused only on particular lines of trade. In Detroit, a Merchants' and Manufacturers' Exchange was set up in 1878. In the West Coast, boards of trade functioned as credit interchanges during the 1880s. Wholesale druggists exchanged information on a regional basis beginning in the 1890s, and by the end of the century, exchanges had been set up by national industry groups such as the Heavy Hardware Credit Bureau and the Clothiers Association.[61] During the 1910s the Iron and Steel Board of Trade, headquartered in New York, operated a trade credit interchange service, as did the jewelry, furniture, shoe and leather, stationery, crockery, lumber, glass, paints, fruits and produce, electric, and building trades, among others. By 1920 nearly all large manufacturers and distributors reportedly participated in some kind of interchange.[62]

Trade protection societies were already beginning to proliferate by the time the NACM was founded. Yet the association argued that far more information should be exchanged, and it criticized the credit-reporting agencies for their deficiency in collecting ledger information.[63] The idea of establishing its own national interchange occupied the NACM beginning in 1901, but concerns about the relationship between the national and local associations hampered the project. As with all federations, questions about how power, responsibility, and sovereignty would be divided and delineated occupied a great deal of the national board's deliberations. In the beginning, the NACM found itself relatively powerless, able to do little more than exhort and cajole the locals into implementing the national association's agenda.[64] When the New York local proposed that the NACM itself might establish a clearinghouse, questions immediately arose about the national association's responsibility over such a body.[65] Even the tame suggestion that a committee be appointed was tabled when an objection arose that turning the national association into an interchange would dilute its effectiveness in other areas.[66] Credit interchanges, the Chicago association argued, already existed in many lines of business, and merchants generally were not interested in lines outside their own. Members who were dissatisfied with the service might drop out of the NACM altogether.[67]

Persuading all creditors and credit men of the merits of a national interchange remained difficult. Supporters attempted to overcome the resistance of members by equating the willingness to cooperate with shrewdness: "Today he is considered a shrewd and successful credit man who will inspire confidence among even his competitors by throwing open his ledgers and his credit records if necessary." Smart credit men knew that they would receive "an equally true statement from that same competitor." Other supporters pointed out that manufacturers cooperated to maintain prices. Why should not creditors do the same to control and monitor credit?[68]

Skepticism arose because of the disincentives common to all such cooperative arrangements. For credit men, these included the possibility that unscrupulous creditors would give favorable recommendations to unload weak customers onto other suppliers or use the interchange to find out about and poach a competitor's good customers.[69] However exceptional such actions may have been, they gave rise to mutual suspicions. Reports reached the NACM that a number of trade associations, including the dry goods and boots and shoe dealers in Minneapolis, resisted sharing trade information with one another. Indianapolis creditors feared that being drawn into correspondence with other cities would result in more competition, without any offsetting benefits. Trade creditors also resented receiving inquiries from fellow suppliers who were simply updating their records.[70] In 1902 the NACM's Credit Department Methods Committee confirmed that the sentiment toward interchanges was generally unfavorable in large cities.[71]

Similar obstacles also were apparent at the local level. One NACM member recounted how a local business with eight thousand to ten thousand accounts found itself overrun with requests for information, mostly from small suppliers who had little to offer in return. The requests so overwhelmed the clerk in charge that the business had to withdraw from the bureau.[72] The Nashville association reported other problems. One of its members regularly requested information but refused to provide precise figures himself, and there was no way to force him to cooperate. Some city members refused to admit merchants from the surrounding countryside, despite the obvious benefits of an enlarged membership.[73] The problems were not easily overcome. "Each creditor has sat mute and isolated, hermit-like and dignified," complained one credit manual, "refusing to be drawn into a discussion of any account on his books."[74]

At least one entrepreneurial concern, Credit Clearing House (CCH), capitalized with some success on the mercantile agencies' shortcomings in reporting ledger information. Founded in Saint Paul, Minnesota, in 1888, Credit Clearing House was set up along the lines of a trade protection society, but it was run for profit, with members as stockholders. (The firm left no records, so it is not possible to determine exactly how it made profits. Some of its revenues appear to have come from ancillary services such as debt collection.) In 1892 the organization expanded into Chicago, and in subsequent years it opened branches in Saint Louis, Louisville, and Cincinnati. As of 1902, Credit Clearing House had offices in twenty-two cities, and by 1916 it covered a reported five hundred thousand retail merchants in some thirty lines of trade.[75]

Although run for profit, Credit Clearing House differed from the older credit-reporting agencies in a number of ways. Like the agencies, the firm tried to obtain financial statements from borrowers, but the bulk of its information came from creditors, the organization's stockholder-members.[76] Members were required to register the names of all customers and to alert the company whenever any came under investigation. The reports were then distributed to all interested members. Credit Clearing House also flagged slow payments and unusually high requests for new credit.[77] Unlike the existing credit interchange bureaus, which confined themselves to specific trades and localities, Credit Clearing House covered merchants and manufacturers in every line of trade, local and national.[78] It presented its findings in statistical form ("25 payment experiences, 40 per cent. slow"), further imbuing the information with an aura of scientific objectivity.[79]

Credit men were intrigued by the benefits offered by Credit Clearing House.[80] Problems with the service, however, prevented their unreserved endorsement. A number of NACM members noted that the service was expensive and slow, and the information was often incomplete or inaccurate. Credit Clearing House was not immune to the disincentives that plagued trade protection societies: its larger member-stockholders, in particular, felt they did not get a fair return for the information they supplied. Whatever their size, members frequently complained that responding to requests was cumbersome, and the forms required too much detail. Paradoxically, they also groused that Credit Clearing House lacked a sufficient number of subscribers, which limited the network's usefulness. Many credit men also were leery of opening their ledgers to an organization that they did not control.[81]

Credit Clearing House responded to the concerns and criticisms in the NACM's annual conventions and in the pages of the *Bulletin*. To the complaint that its fees were too steep, the firm answered that there were no economies of scale in an interchange system: expenses rose in proportion to the number of branch offices it established, so fees had to be raised and the number of inquiries per member limited.[82] Credit Clearing House readily admitted that its membership base was insufficient. As for complaints that responding to requests for information was cumbersome, the firm pointed out that there was no way to make an interchange system as "simple" as a general reporting system—presumably referring to the by then well-established credit-reporting agencies. Credit Clearing House could do little except urge members to answer requests more promptly, and point out that the average number of requests made upon each member was only three per day. (Larger businesses, though, undoubtedly received significantly more.)[83]

Not surprisingly, Credit Clearing House recommended against the NACM setting up its own interchange. The initial investment would be high; Credit Clearing House itself had spent some $300,000 between 1888 and 1902 to develop its infrastructure, an amount that the NACM would find difficult to match. Duplication, moreover, was inefficient: "There is room for but one," the firm argued, "because the information . . . contributed by the same house to two or more sources would not increase its value one iota." Instead, Credit Clearing House proposed that two members of the NACM join its directorate and that each local association establish an advisory committee to confer with the firm's branch office in their city.[84]

The reluctance to form interchanges highlighted an inherent paradox: interchanges must have a high rate of participation but cannot be so large as to make it impossible for individual members to answer all inquiries. Greater scale led not to economies but to increased usage per member. One credit man likened the interchange to telephone companies, which gave good service in small towns for a relatively low rate. In larger towns, however, the number of calls made per household "seems to increase in geometrical ratio," forcing telephone companies to raise prices substantially.[85]

Peter Wahlstad argued that a point would inevitably be reached at which the work demanded of each member would far surpass any perceived benefits. He believed, however, that the system naturally achieved equilibrium because membership would automatically be reduced to a point where interchange once more became workable. This "automatic limitation" meant that the system could not attain universal application and would function only when restricted to particular markets. One way to lighten the workload, Wahlstad suggested, was to restrict the reporting to "abnormal" experiences, such as requests for new credit, substantial jumps in request for credit, or slow payments. He estimated that eliminating the "normal" experiences would reduce the burden on credit departments by more than 95 percent.[86] Other manuals suggested that establishing a central bureau run by full-time administrators or clerks might also mitigate the problem, although the initial outlay and maintenance costs could be high.[87]

In 1904 the NACM again rejected the idea of a national interchange as too costly and unwieldy.[88] It formed the special Committee on Credit Cooperation the following year, but subsequent conventions continued to reject a national interchange because the cost was prohibitively high. Supporters continued to be disappointed by the low levels of cooperation among local associations. A survey conducted by the NACM in 1910 found that of the thirty locals that responded, seventeen conducted a credit bureau, but only thirteen indicated a willingness to share ledger information with other locals.[89]

The NACM struggled for years to persuade locals even to establish a bureau, let alone share ledger information with one another. In 1918 still only about 30 percent of the total membership participated in an interchange. With the end of the Great War imminent, E. E. Pratt, chief of the U.S. Bureau of Foreign and Domestic Commerce, recommended to the annual convention that the interchange of ledger information proceed on an international basis. A "movement is on foot among the firms interested in doing a permanent export trade, to exchange credit information concerning their customers in foreign countries," Pratt stated, adding that NACM members "will need to cooperate with each other, with your banks, with our merchant marine that is to be, and with your government."[90] American credit men were forced to acknowledge the superiority of European mechanisms and institutions for conducting international trade. Europeans routinely relied on trade acceptances, and they had established far-superior sources of information in regions like Latin America.[91]

At war's end, the prospect of increased foreign and domestic trade provided the NACM with the leverage to complete two projects that had been stymied for years. In September 1919, the association established the Foreign Credit Interchange Bureau (FCIB), a clearinghouse for American exporters who did large amounts of business with foreign firms. The new bureau handled over 5,500 requests for information in its first few months alone. Long a project of the NACM's Foreign Credits Committee, the establishment of the FCIB had been resisted as unnecessary by some members.[92] Considerable progress also was achieved in the domestic credit bureaus. In 1920 the NACM reported that more than 60 percent of the local associations had established them, a substantial increase from only two years previous.[93] The NACM's Credit Interchange Bureau System was finally made national in scope with the establishment of a Central Bureau in Saint Louis in 1919. It acted as a clearinghouse but left the actual production of reports to the local associations.[94]

As for Credit Clearing House—it did not succeed in overcoming the challenges of a for-profit interchange model. After about 1920, references to the company all but disappeared from the speeches and literature of the NACM.

Attempts to establish credit interchanges, the vast majority of them still restricted to particular localities or lines of trade, continued to accelerate.[95] In 1920 William Prendergast remarked on the interchanges' lack of uniformity, which came about because each "system has had to depend for its development upon the sporadic attempts of its followers to cultivate its popularity among credit men."[96] One credit manual, however, emphasized the progress made. Despite continuing disagreement, "the feeling on this broadminded practice, previously regarded with considerable prejudice, has now practically disappeared."[97]

Improving the Credit-Reporting Agencies

In speeches and reports, credit men typically referred to "both" credit-reporting agencies, indicating that R. G. Dun and the Bradstreet agency now dominated the field. Both firms also expanded rapidly abroad: of the 115 new offices R. G. Dun opened between 1891 and 1916, 83 were located outside the United States.[98] Observers believed that the size and reach of the two agencies were a barrier to competition. They "are now so large and so well-established," wrote Peter Wahlstad, "that it is more than doubtful that a rival institution could be established." Attempts to do so, even when backed with large capital, invariably failed.[99] Yet the large scale of the two agencies did not necessarily translate into a duopoly because Bradstreet and Dun faced competition from at least three sources: smaller, more specialized credit-reporting firms; credit interchanges; and special agents hired by larger banks and wholesale houses to conduct proprietary credit investigations.[100]

Even critics conceded that growing scale and accumulated experience had allowed Bradstreet and Dun to improve their services. In large commercial cities, reporters now specialized in particular trades, and some veterans could boast twenty, even thirty, years' experience. Paid representatives in major courthouses throughout the United States telegraphed data on suits, judgments, chattel mortgages, and liens of all kinds. The rapid transmission of these items was reflected in the agencies' published reference books: Bradstreet's volume for the first six months of 1903 underwent over 489,000 changes, or an average of 3,239 for each business day.[101]

Yet many of the agencies' methods and practices had remained essentially unchanged since the 1840s. Full-time reporters covered the more densely populated areas of the United States, but in localities where they made only periodic visits, the agencies still depended on local attorneys, postmasters, bank cashiers, and merchants for the bulk of their information. Despite the enthusiasm for more-objective items such as payment records, rumors and reporters' impressions continued to play an important role.[102] The agencies, moreover, continued to emphasize the narrative of a borrower's business life. When the NACM suggested that Dun and Bradstreet standardize their reports to make them quicker to read, both agencies declined, insisting that reports had to be read in their entirety and that reporters should retain the freedom to write up their findings as they saw fit.[103]

By the beginning of the twentieth century, nearly all manufacturers and wholesalers used the information furnished by the credit-reporting firms. The National Association of Credit Men estimated that some 70 percent of all orders were shipped based on agency reports. Trade, the NACM stated, was "largely dependent for its development, security, and perpetuity upon mercantile agencies," and dependence upon them "for full and accurate knowledge of a merchant's standing is the most practical and convenient method for both debtor and creditor."[104] Manuals regarded the agencies positively, and the NACM's *Bulletin* regularly featured letters from credit men expressing confidence in the general usefulness of the service.[105] Along with the usual admonitions not to rely solely on data provided by the agencies, manuals typically recommended that credit men use them to secure fresh special reports and urged credit men to provide the agencies with the names of businesses in which they had an ongoing interest. Moreover, the agencies allowed credit men to avoid asking customers directly for financial statements, which might cause offense.[106]

Even so, complaints abounded that the information provided by the agencies still lacked accuracy and freshness. Nor did the agencies try hard enough to obtain ledger information. "Their reports are not guaranteed correct," admitted F. G. Helmbold, a former manager of Bradstreet's Philadelphia office, "and should only be used to supplement the work of the credit man to arrive at conclusions." E. F. Morgan of the National Furniture Company of Atlanta, who was also the president of that city's NACM chapter, made an even more frank assessment: "No agency of which I have any knowledge, approaches a perfect or even satisfactory service to its patrons— not even the special agencies which have put in new features and have made some progress in that direction." Even the best service was "subject to criticisms for inaccuracies in ratings and special reports, so serious as to make the credit man feel constantly that he is taking great risks in extending credit on any such so-called information."[107] The agencies' methods struck some credit men as overly impressionistic, and they continued to question the competence and integrity of reporters and correspondents.[108] According to the NACM, the agencies did not expend enough effort researching public records, including confirming the ownership of real estate.[109] Reports were plagued by errors; one NACM report ventured that 30 percent of losses could be directly attributed to the agencies' inaccuracies.[110]

In hindsight, monitoring the agencies should have seemed an obvious part of the NACM's agenda. Yet it was apparently not until Ernst Troy of the Cincinnati association suggested it that a committee was formed, with Troy as its first chairman. Questions about the NACM's official relationship to credit-reporting firms once again brought up the issue of the association's perceived independence. Should a resolution be passed clearly stating that the NACM was not allied with any firms? Should credit-reporting agencies be able to sell their stock to members of the NACM, and should members be allowed to sit on the firms' boards?[111] Was it a responsibility of the association to apprise its membership about new agencies? Given the difficulty of obtaining good information on new agencies and services, some members believed that the NACM should function as a clearinghouse for such information. Others, however, worried that the mere mention of an agency compromised the association's strict neutrality.[112]

Initially, the NACM passed only a few modest resolutions: that the agencies be encouraged to price their reports according to the amount and quality of information contained in them; that they not assign a capital rating unless a merchant had submitted a signed statement within the previous year; and that the NACM keep records of R. G. Dun and the Bradstreet agency to determine which offered better services. (Credit men generally believed that the quality of service offered by the two firms was roughly the same, varying mainly with the competency of individual branch managers.) Although it was agreed that the agencies had not done enough to meet requests for improved services, the NACM opted to monitor and cooperate with them rather than insist too forcefully on reforms. For their part, Bradstreet and Dun had initially feared that the NACM would establish rival services, and they often responded testily to the association's recommendations. In general, however, both firms indicated a willingness to cooperate. Certainly, they had a strong financial incentive to do so: NACM members purchased some 1 million dollars' worth of credit reports from agencies every year. In 1897 the NACM invited the heads of Bradstreet and Dun to attend its annual convention. Although neither man accepted the invitation, both sent representatives to address the association's concerns.[113]

The NACM believed that the problems could be traced to the agencies' difficulties in obtaining financial statements. A sampling of agency reports analyzed by the NACM in 1897, revealed that only 10 percent contained information based on signed statements, and a further 8 percent had information based on verbal statements only. In other words, a full 82 percent of all reports were not based on any financial statements whatsoever. The agencies responded that statements from individuals such as blacksmiths, builders, physicians, and barbers were not worth procuring. "I have found not to exceed eighteen to twenty percent of the merchants throughout the country in a position to make a statement," a representative of the Bradstreet agency told the association, because they "keep no books." He recounted receiving a letter from a business owner who admitted that "he hadn't taken stock for twenty-six years and didn't know how to make a statement."[114]

An investigation conducted by the NACM five years later found some improvement: this time, 37.5 percent of the agency reports contained financial statement information less than one year old. But it was still not good enough, according to the association. The agencies again defended their record, asserting that business owners often responded to requests for updated statements by declaring that their financial position had not changed at all. "Some of them resented it as a reflection on themselves," according to the Dun representative, "and asked of the reporter whether their word could not be believed, and if not, would the signed statement?"[115] (The problem was shared by members of the NACM, who themselves were hard pressed to obtain statements, especially from small businesses.)[116] Bradstreet and Dun rejected the NACM's recommendation that they push harder for additional information, such as a firm's annual expenses. Doing so, the agencies believed, would further discourage business owners from submitting any statement at all.[117] Asking for statements in person and checking the real estate ownership records of every individual and firm once a year also were beyond the agencies' means.[118]

The NACM continued to insist on the critical importance of financial statements, even going so far as to recommend that the agencies withhold capital ratings from businesses that refused to submit them. The association offered to provide an official endorsement of such requests, to be printed by the agencies on their request forms.[119] Yet at times, ironically, credit men themselves were the problem because they refused to provide the agencies with information on their own companies.[120] A Bradstreet representative told the 1897 convention, "I don't believe that the agencies . . . receive from the houses represented by the men here fifty per cent of their statements signed, and a great many of them prefer not to give a statement because they don't want their competitor to see it." Credit men, he concluded, gave financial statements reluctantly, "and yet they expect it from the small men who keep no books."[121]

As emphasis on debtors' payment records intensified, credit men began to complain that the agencies did not systematically collect the information.[122] Aware of the criticisms, the agencies tried from time to time to improve this aspect of their service. Again, though, they were frequently stymied by members of the NACM itself. Although the association acknowledged that credit men must share information with the agencies—and regularly offered resolutions to that effect in its conventions—in reality, members disagreed about the wisdom of giving ledger information to any organization over which they had no direct control and for which they received no reciprocal benefits. "Why should we give an agency our inside ledger facts," demanded one credit man, "that they may sell it to the world to offer us competition [for] desirable [customers]?"[123] Some local associations refused to give information to anyone, including credit-reporting agencies, who were not bona fide members.[124] The irony was not lost on the agencies, who chided the NACM for demanding information its own members were loath to provide. "We have made application for statements . . . from some who have championed the desire and effort to obtain through us this class of information," reported R. G. Dun, "and we have met from these same parties, not only refusal, but in several cases indignation was expressed. To us, it looks very much like a case of 'do as I say, not as I do.'"[125]

Pointing out the agencies' errors and encouraging competition between them by publicly commending the better firm became the primary strategies employed by the NACM.[126] In 1902 it published an analysis comparing Dun and Bradstreet, which revealed that they were fairly close in certain performance measures:

Quality and Timeliness of Reports: Dun vs. Bradstreet		
	Dun	Bradstreet
No. of days between request and receipt of report	4.15	4.8
Age of [most recent] report	3.18 months	2.92 months
Reports with statements not more than one-year old	38.6%	35.5%
Reports without statements, or with statements older than one year	61.3%	65.4%

Source: Compiled from *Bulletin of the NACM* 2 (July 5, 1902), p. 35.

The NACM was careful to temper any criticism with expressions of mutual interests, and it encouraged the local associations to form closer relationships with the agencies' branch managers in their districts.[127] Cooperation was aided by many NACM members who had worked as reporters or correspondents for the credit-reporting firms, and who could therefore provide perspective on the reasonableness of the association's demands.[128] The largest agencies, for their part, dutifully responded to the NACM's questions and suggestions and became regular participants in the annual conventions. Tensions between the two institutions continued, but most NACM members and agency representatives recognized that they had more in common than not. As one agency representative reminded the association, "the Mercantile Agency business gave [birth] to your work. It made the question of credit a study and a science, and brought into existence enterprises such as yours."[129]

Bankrupt Estates and Fraud

Encouraging cooperation among the creditors of bankrupt estates constituted another area of interest for the NACM. State laws had long been known to be deficient in this area because they practically encouraged the first or most aggressive creditor on the scene to wring everything out of the debtor, leaving little or nothing for other creditors. Fearful of being preempted, creditors instigated action against an insolvent earlier than was strictly necessary. As one dry goods manual remarked, the state collection laws "are such as to put each jobber in fear of every other; a first attachment taking all the property, if the debt be large enough."[130] Insolvency frequently put into motion a series of events that, as described by credit manual authors R. T. Ettinger and D. E. Golieb, resembled a comic opera:

> If one creditor had suspicion that a debtor was about to fail, immediately such creditor would rush to court and levy an attachment or execution. Then would begin a mad race for precedence between executions, attachments, etc.,—between the sheriff, receiver, assignee and mortgagee—to see which one would get possession of the debtor's property first, the receiver frequently finding upon arrival that he was forestalled by the sheriff under a levy or by some preferred mortgagee or assignee placed in possession by the debtor . . . Each creditor was eyeing the others, ready at a moment's notice to rush in ahead of them. It was the unmitigated right of the "Survival of the Fittest."[131]

Working together would have made the process more equitable and given debtors a greater chance to recover, but there was little incentive for creditors to cooperate.[132]

By the late nineteenth century, "adjustment bureaus" had formed in nearly all major cities to apportion assets more equitably among creditors.[133] Among the oldest was the Merchants' Protective Union of Portland, Oregon, an association of jobbers established in 1878. Its "stockholders' agreement" stipulated that members "will not in any case resort to any act, device, secret understanding, connivance or collusion whereby we may obtain, claim or seek to obtain, any preference or advantage over each other." A board consisting of the secretary and three appointed members took charge of the insolvent's estate.[134]

The bureaus took many legal forms: some were incorporated, some were partnerships, and some focused exclusively on liquidations or collections, or a combination of the two, while also providing credit-reporting services.[135] Trade groups, including jewelry manufacturers and wholesalers, dealers of boots and shoes, crockery, stationery, furniture, hardware, carpet, clothing, and many other lines, operated boards of trade similar to adjustment bureaus.[136] The NACM strongly encouraged the formation of these bureaus by the local associations.[137] It promised to allow as much autonomy as possible and to appoint an assistant to the NACM national secretary to act as an advisor.[138]

Adjustment bureaus remained in use even after passage of the National Bankruptcy Act of 1898 because they were relatively cheap and efficient compared to bankruptcy proceedings. According to the president of the San Francisco Board of Trade, outside creditors requested the board's assistance because "they found it was better than turning [the cases] over to lawyers." He reported that the average recoveries in 1915 through the board of trade were 52 percent, compared to 16 percent in bankruptcy courts. Administrative expenses through the board averaged only 7 percent; in bankruptcy court, they were 45 percent. Many also believed that such associations, run "by the creditors for the creditors," prevented debtors from obtaining a too-easy discharge from bankruptcy courts, which had become "a refuge for perjurers and deadbeats."[139] Even in cases where bankruptcy proceedings were initiated, the bureaus often got involved to help ensure efficiency and fairness.

Yet even bankruptcies that were clearly fraudulent failed to inspire full cooperation among creditors. (Bradstreet's statistics, generally considered reliable, showed that between 10 and 12 percent of all failures were attributable to fraud.)[140] Strong disincentives prevented creditors from prosecuting to the full extent of the law, including the fear that such actions would destroy any chance of recovering at least a partial amount from the debtor.[141] Free-rider problems also were to blame: when one creditor took the initiative to uncover fraud, the other creditors usually withdrew. More often than not, the creditor trying to uncover the fraud concluded he was bearing a disproportionate amount of the enforcement costs and gave up the fight, allowing the debtor to escape. Fraud also occurred because debtors and creditors compromised too quickly, almost always to the benefit of the debtor.[142]

In its first meeting, the Board of Administration of the NACM resolved to select legal attorneys throughout the country to act in connection with a reputable detective agency to investigate suspicious failures. Officers of the local associations were urged to work with the NACM's Investigations Committee to bring fraudulent failures to light.[143] Article II of the association's constitution provided for the establishment of a national fund for prosecuting fraudulent failures. The fund was raised by subscription among the general membership, and local associations were urged to establish their own funds.[144] Cases of fraud that had been successfully prosecuted appeared as a regular feature in the NACM's monthly *Bulletin,* and members were encouraged to publicize fraudulent cases in the association's publications.[145]

The National Association of Credit Men promoted the controversial idea, first introduced by credit-reporting firms, that all business owners should make their financial standing and past business behaviors available for scrutiny. The NACM also sought to break down the distrust among credit men and to increase cooperation between them and the credit-reporting firms. These two ideas—transparency for all businesses and cooperation among creditors and the credit-reporting firms—became synonymous in the NACM literature with modernity and progress.

The minutes of the NACM's earliest meetings reveal that its agenda did not emerge fully formed. Members voiced disagreement over issues such as the precise relationship of the NACM with the local associations, the credit-reporting agencies, and new organizations like the Credit Clearing House. Credit men initially expressed doubts about the desirability of cooperating with one another, and they balked at sharing their debtors' payment records. Gradually, however, members reached a consensus on this issue, and the NACM grew to support the interchange of ledger information among creditors, even though many members continued to act contrary to NACM's pronouncements. (A controversial idea at the time, the reliance on debtors' payment histories today, forms the basis for nearly all consumer lending in the United States and is among the most important considerations in business credit reports.) Immediately after the end of World War I, the NACM set up the Foreign Credit Interchange Bureau and finally succeeded in establishing a national interchange office in Saint Louis. Based on cooperation rather than competition, credit interchange bureaus were similar to the trade protection societies that had first appeared in England a full century earlier. In the United States, these bureaus existed alongside the older, for-profit credit-reporting agencies.

Monitoring the agencies became a critical component of the NACM's mission. In its public utterances and in the manuals written by members, the National Association of Credit Men affirmed the usefulness of the agencies' services while simultaneously exhorting them to do better. Perhaps paradoxically, encouraging debate and soliciting complaints did not discredit the agencies. Instead, the NACM's actions enhanced the legitimacy of for-profit credit reporting and embedded the institution even more deeply into American business culture.

Although credit men worked to put credit granting on a more objective and scientific basis, character persisted as an important indication of creditworthiness. Few credit men believed that a purely statistical approach should supplant the ability to judge "human nature." Instead, the vast majority accepted that the two approaches were naturally intertwined, a belief encapsulated by the axiom that creditworthiness was determined by the "three C's": character, capacity, and capital. In common with their antebellum forebears, the newly professional credit men insisted that the character of a firm's owners superseded even the information found in its statements—or at the very least, that character was the foundation for the reliability of those statements.[146] A record of honest behavior mattered because numerous temptations and opportunities existed to falsify accounts. Transferring assets to spouses and other family members prior to failing continued to be an important issue, as did perceived abuses under the state exemption laws.[147] The National Bankruptcy Act of 1898, the first permanent law of its kind, was only partially successful at ending these practices.

The National Association of Credit Men endorsed the idea, already current during the antebellum period, that debtor and creditor were partners and that honest failures deserved lenient treatment. Most credit men agreed with marketing professor James Hagerty that "in event of failure [the lender] willingly accepts a cancellation of a portion of the debt, providing that there has been no fraudulent conversion of the assets . . . The debtor who failed honestly should be considered simply an unfortunate investor."[148] R. T. Ettinger and D. E. Golieb, authors of a popular credit textbook first published in 1917, alluded to "humanitarian motives," which "should prompt the credit man to act with the utmost care, even hesitancy, before resorting to any drastic action which would bring about the bankruptcy of an honest debtor." Business losses were inevitable, and honest failures were "entitled to the moral support and active assistance of their creditors, who, over the years, have made profits out of their business relations with the now unfortunate debtor."[149] The NACM's "Property Statement Blank" for the 1910s made the viability of this unique relationship contingent on financial transparency: "The giver of credit is the contributor of capital, and becomes, in a certain sense, a partner of the debtor, and, as such, has a perfect right to complete information of the debtor's condition at all times."[150]

Despite occasional dissent, by 1920 the preference for transparency was firmly established in American business culture. The Truth in Securities Act, passed in 1933 as part of the New Deal reform of the securities industry, is rightly seen as a watershed in the history of financial transparency and a boon to investors and regulators. For a century prior to its passage, however, a struggle to establish the creditor's "perfect right to complete information of the debtor's condition at all times" had occurred in the area of mercantile credit.

In the ensuing decades, more information on debtors became available to American mercantile and bank creditors. After the Cold War ended, the idea of business transparency assumed ideological force when powerful entities like the World Bank began to view credit reporting as an important institution for enhancing markets in the world's poorest countries. With the spread of freer markets, local entrepreneurs in countries like China and the former Soviet bloc began exploiting outsiders' need for information on potential trading partners, by establishing credit-reporting firms modeled after those in the developed world. In addition to legal and structural obstacles, these firms faced cultural resistance to an unfamiliar way of doing business.

Epilogue:
Business Credit Reporting in the Twenty-First Century

The use of trade credit in the United States continued on a massive scale: at the end of the twentieth century, it constituted the single largest source of business financing, exceeding even the volume of bank loans.[1] The growing magnitude of trade credit could be seen in the Federal Reserve's flow of funds report, which compiled aggregate statistics on trade payables (the amount owed by businesses to other businesses). As of the last quarter of 2005, receivables outstanding for nonfarm, nonfinancial corporate businesses was a torrential $2.0 trillion, only slightly smaller than the $2.2 trillion of household consumer debt outstanding for the period.[2]

The industry pioneers who struggled to establish the legitimacy of business credit reporting in the United States would have marveled at how the institution became so tightly woven into the fabric of the country's business culture. In 1933 R. G. Dun and the Bradstreet Company merged, becoming the undisputed worldwide leader of the industry. With 2000 revenues of some $1.4 billion, Dun and Bradstreet had become the world's largest provider of business credit information.[3] It operated wholly or majority-owned firms in dozens of countries and had minority interests in several more. The firm continued to serve as a major source of official data on national failure rates, and its proprietary numbering system for businesses, called the D-U-N-S, was used as a global standard by the United Nations, the federal government, and over fifty industry and trade associations worldwide. Dun and Bradstreet covered some 54 million businesses around the globe, about 26 million of them in the United States. The vast majority were privately held firms. (Only a minuscule fraction of the world's businesses is publicly listed: 0.16 percent of all registered firms in developing countries and 0.55 percent in industrial countries, according to one survey.) Many were tiny: in the United States, for example, nearly 40 percent of the firms covered had only twenty or fewer employees.[4] Size and longevity had at least one unanticipated drawback. In the late 1990s, Dun and Bradstreet acknowledged that the public perceived it to be "conventional" and "old fashioned," an unfortunate side effect of being one of the world's most trusted and recognized brand names.[5]

Credit professionals, too, became a fixture in American business, and the influence of the National Association of Credit Men grew accordingly. The association lobbied strenuously for the rights of mercantile creditors, especially in amendments to the national bankruptcy law, and pushed for more stringent antifraud legislation. In 1958 the National Association of Credit Men changed its name to the National Association of Credit Management (NACM), to "reflect the growing stature of the credit profession," according to an association brochure. (Gender concerns apparently did not figure into the name change, although women were becoming more active in the organization. By the early 1920s, Los Angeles, New York, Philadelphia, and Saint Louis had separate women's credit groups.)[6] At the end of the twentieth century, the NACM provided numerous credit, collection, bankruptcy, and educational services. Its Foreign Credit Interchange Bureau was renamed the Finance, Credit, and International Business subsidiary. Like the original FCIB, the new organization served exporters—to over thirty countries by the end of the twentieth century.[7]

In the United States, institutional arrangements for making credit decisions continued to be transformed by improvements in the availability and quality of information. Nearly all large commercial banks and finance companies now relied primarily on the financial statements of the large and midsized firms that were their main constituency. Associations formed for the sharing of customers' payment records became more prevalent, and both Dun and Bradstreet and the NACM hosted many of the industry groups formed for this purpose.[8]

Innovative technologies for gathering and disseminating information further altered credit practices. Credit-reporting firms began delivering data via the Internet. New software programs allowed them to tailor their services to the needs of their subscribers, who could now purchase individual data elements to put into their own programs. Academics and credit-reporting firms developed new scoring techniques to predict whether an applicant would likely pay bills on time, late, or not at all, allowing lenders to flag accounts that needed attention and identify customers who were candidates for bankruptcy. Much credit granting became standardized and automated, especially in the consumer loan sector, whose scoring methods were adapted to small business loans by some creditors. Far from making credit analysis obsolete, scoring freed creditors to concentrate on problematic cases requiring human judgment.

Dun and Bradstreet helped develop some of the industry's most important credit scoring models. Its subscribers, still consisting primarily of suppliers and factors, typically extended credit ranging from \$3,000 to \$100,000. (The amounts could be substantial but still too small to justify spending more on investigation.) Financial information on small firms was included if it was publicly available or if the business agreed to submit a statement. But, as had been the case throughout the previous 150 years, many did not voluntarily do so, and banks were reluctant to share information on their small business borrowers. The problem was particularly acute in highly fragmented industries like construction. As a result, Dun and Bradstreets reports on new or small firms often had very little information aside from basic items such as the owners' names, the company's address, its standard industrial classification (SIC) code, and the number of years it had been in business.

Due to the increased willingness of trade creditors to share their customers' payment records, Dun and Bradstreet was able to provide substantially more information in this area than was the case during the previous century. The firm developed a proprietary "Paydex" measure, a composite statistic that allowed creditors to compare borrowers' records with up to two years' worth of aggregated and weighted data on hundreds of other borrowers in the same industry. Dun and Bradstreet also accessed information on suits, liens, and judgments from the federal and state bankruptcy courts. Other sources included the offices of the states' attorneys general, insurance commissioners, and secretaries of state; daily newspapers, publications, and electronic news services; the U.S. Postal Service; and utility companies.[9]

The firm's long history and exceptional dominance of its industry made Dun and Bradstreet a unique case study of how scale efficiencies can work in the credit-reporting business. At the same time, its unmatched scale raised questions about the extent to which market power was concentrated. Evidence suggested that a number of factors restricted the power that Dun and Bradstreet, or any business-credit-reporting firm, could potentially wield.[10] For one, Dun and Bradstreet's position was continually challenged by smaller, local and industry-specific agencies and associations. Competition, particularly from local and regional firms and Internet start-ups, remained brisk; throughout the world, rivals sought to fill niches not adequately served by the large international credit-reporting firms.[11]

Dun and Bradstreet itself openly acknowledged the limits of its authority, a stance motivated by the threat of lawsuits. Despite the much-improved quantitative methods available, Dun and Bradstreet analysts regularly stressed that models must be supplemented by the judgment of creditors. The claim has been accepted by most credit practitioners; one practitioner has characterized the granting of trade credit as similar to medicine, in that it is an "inexact exact science."[12] The authority of credit-reporting firms was debated constantly and publicly by those who relied on their services. Inaccuracies were discussed in trade publications like *Business Credit,* and investigative journalists tested the value of reports simply by obtaining several different ones on the same company, comparing the information, and then reporting their findings.[13]

Beginning in the 1960s, regulatory developments began to check the power of trade creditors to a greater degree than previously. A series of federal laws was passed, aimed at the consumer rather than the business credit sector. (Consumer credit and consumer credit bureaus proliferated during the twentieth century, especially after World War II.)[14] Although the line separating consumer and business credit historically has been clearer in the United States than in other countries, that line could sometimes blur, particularly for small business borrowers. In 1990 the Equal Credit Opportunity Act (ECOA), originally enacted in 1974 to regulate consumer creditors, became mandatory for business creditors. (The ECOA was passed primarily to address gender concerns but subsequently was widened to include race, color, religion, national origin, and age.) The act stipulated that business creditors provide notice within thirty days to applicants who were denied credit and that applicants' records be kept for sixty days after notification. If the applicant requested in writing the reasons for the credit decision, the creditor was required to keep the records for at least twelve months.[15]

In 1997 Congress reauthorized the Fair Credit Reporting Act (FCRA, first passed in 1971), which was followed by the drafting of new regulations by the Federal Trade Commission. The FCRA limited the information contained in consumer credit reports to the following: the consumer's name, address, Social Security number, place of employment, and spouse's name; open credit lines, outstanding credit balances, credit limits, history of timeliness of payments, and amount of last payment; and bankruptcies, liens, and public judgments against the consumer. Reports could not include information about a person's lifestyle, religion, political affiliation, driving record, or medical history. Aimed at enhancing the protection of consumer credit borrowers, the new restrictions affected creditors' access to information on business borrowers, especially sole proprietors, because only those with a "permissible purpose" could purchase the reports. The National Association of Credit Managers objected to the new regulations, arguing that they should not apply to transactions between businesses (as opposed to those between businesses and consumers.)[16]

Although they had become more restrictive, American laws remained laxer than those of Europe, Australia, and many other countries. In Portugal, for example, credit bureaus needed to have a person's consent before they could collect or sell any credit data, and the permission could be withdrawn at any time. Australian bureaus reported only negative information; creditors did not have access to the files of individuals with positive records. These laws frequently resulted from lobbying not by consumer protection advocates but by lenders wishing to limit competition. Despite the more-stringent laws, businesses in the United States were left with the responsibility of developing their own privacy policies and communicating them to customers. Many businesses voluntarily refrained from using certain criteria—such as the geographic location of debtors—to determine credit-worthiness because they feared a public relations backlash. Like many other countries, the United States did not grant its citizens the right to access data in every public or private database, even though international guidelines increasingly considered this a fundamental right.[17]

Credit Reporting Worldwide

Credit-reporting agencies and bureaus became entrenched in the world's developed countries during the twentieth century; from the 1980s onward, they also began appearing in nearly every developing one. In these countries, trade credit was often used prior to other kinds of funding, such as debt and equity finance (that is, borrowing from banks or issuing shares in an enterprise).[18] Development organizations such as the World Bank began to place increased emphasis on the establishment of credit-reporting systems to enhance market activity. Such systems, World Bank economists argued, should strengthen borrower discipline and reduce moral hazard because borrowers who default in their payment to one institution will face sanctions from others. The wide availability of credit reports would allow poor borrowers to build reputation collateral, which can be particularly important among people who own few or no physical assets. Lenders benefit because reputation collateral provides an incentive for debtors to meet commitments in much the same way as does a pledge of physical collateral. Good borrowers, who typically do not have the resources to broadcast their good records, also would gain because lenders would compete for them. The bank hoped that credit reporting would help democratize the financial systems of developing countries, where assets tend to be more concentrated.[19]

Between 1999 and 2001 the World Bank conducted the first worldwide surveys of credit registries (or "bureaus.") It determined that at least forty-one countries operated public credit bureaus, and at least forty-four had private ones. In Latin America, approximately one-half of private credit bureaus began operating only since 1989. According to information available from Creditworthy, a private organization, credit-reporting agencies had been present in Central and South America for several decades but became more common in Asia and eastern Europe in the mid-1980s.[20] As was true in the United States, government initiatives did not play a direct role in establishing the private firms and bureaus. Instead, they were set up by entrepreneurs trying to exploit the growing demand for reliable information on local businesses.

A number of governments, however, encouraged the establishment of public credit bureaus, to supervise and monitor bank lending activity rather than trade credit. The institution originated in Europe, first in Germany (1934) and then in Finland (1961) and Italy (1964). During the 1990s, public credit bureaus expanded most rapidly in Latin America, with the exception of the small island economies in the Caribbean. Although members consisted of commercial banks rather than trade creditors, the bureaus operated somewhat like trade protection societies, in that their ethos was one of reciprocal sharing of information rather than profit making. They collected information on both business and consumer loans (although in Europe finance and credit card companies generally were not included).[21]

Public credit bureaus had several shortcomings, according to the World Bank. Because they were quasi-official entities, they did not face competitive pressure and had little incentive to respond to users. The biggest drawback, however, was that they did not collect information on trade credit. Some World Bank economists therefore cautioned that public credit bureaus should not be expected to substitute fully for private ones because their objectives varied too widely for significant overlap to occur.

Financial crises as well as market opportunities drove the spread of credit-reporting firms into developing countries. After the 1998 crisis in Asia, Dun and Bradstreet took advantage of the desire of Asia-based companies to appear more credible to lenders. Chinese business leaders sought Dun and Bradstreet's help to learn how to manage their credit departments, prompting the firm to enlarge significantly its databases on companies in China, Singapore, and Malaysia.[22] The financial crisis also inspired the formation of a large number of local start-ups. Some one hundred large and small credit-reporting agencies were operating in China in 2000, almost ten times the number of five years before.[23]

Yet the worldwide credit-reporting industry could not simply be characterized as one of unfettered competition; instead, it was a mixture of competition and cooperation. Increased cross-border trading compelled credit-reporting firms, whether large or small, international or local, to ally with one another to provide better coverage—circumstances that complicate attempts to gauge the degree of concentration within this industry. Networks included ALIAC (Latin American Business Credit Reporting Association), TCM Group International (headquartered in Australia), American Business Information Association (based in New York City), and Eurogate, among many others. Industry giants Dun and Bradstreet, Experian, and Equifax formed alliances with or bought information from foreign agencies, and they opened additional foreign branches.[24]

Credit-reporting firms in developing countries typically served both foreign and local business creditors. Clients included exporters and importers, insurance companies, banks and other financial institutions, lawyers, manufacturers, construction companies, consulates and trade organizations, collection agencies, chambers of commerce, embassies and foreign diplomatic missions, other credit-reporting agencies, and information resellers. Subscribers were offered services ranging from a simple company profile to a thorough investigation that might include personal interviews with a company's management. Some credit-reporting firms produced original reports; some simply gathered the information prepared by others. Generally, the agencies attempted to provide the kind of credit reports that the older, U.S.-based firms had made standard.[25] Firms in developing countries also offered services that took advantage of their local presence and ability to provide firsthand knowledge and information. These services included market and consumer research, real estate investigations and appraisals, and aid to outsiders searching for local business opportunities.[26]

Accessing the types of information that U.S. creditors take for granted was difficult for these firms. Official data sources existed but were often inadequate. Many countries limited access to particular kinds of data; for example, Latin American countries like Costa Rica, Ecuador, and Guatemala prevented banks from sharing information on their customers' accounts. Privacy laws further restricted the type of information that could be obtained and reported.[27] Irregular business practices, such as tax evasion and the lack of generally accepted accounting practices (GAAP), threw into question the reliability of financial statements.[28] The credit-reporting firms and bureaus used a variety of methods to correct for inaccurate information. These included requesting a review from the reporting institutions when data problems arose, suspending access to the data by institutions with recurrent data problems, and providing consumers with a free copy to encourage review of the data. The methods have not been systematically studied, so their effectiveness remains unknown.[29]

The globalization trend that began in the late twentieth century accelerated the establishment of public and private information-sharing mechanisms in nearly all parts of the world. Foreign investment and alliances by the largest U.S. and European private credit-reporting firms increased, as did local investment. New locally based firms and bureaus helped establish standards of transparency where they had not previously existed, in much the same way that R. G. Dun, the Bradstreet agency, and their competitors had transmitted the values of the large commercial centers of the United States throughout the rest of the country. Collectively, credit-reporting firms and bureaus helped bring about a globally consistent set of criteria for assessing creditworthiness.

Notes

Index

Notes

Introduction

1. These definitions are based on Glenn Porter and Harold Livesay, *Merchants and Manufacturers: Studies in the Changing Structure of Nineteenth-Century Marketing* (Baltimore: Johns Hopkins University Press, 1971) and Bill R. Moeckel, *The Development of the Wholesaler in the United States, 1860–1900* (New York: Garland Publishing, 1986).
2. By the 1850s, the use of mercantile agencies had become sufficiently widespread to merit attention in popular journals. See, for example, "The Telegraph, Part 2," *DeBow's Review* 16 (February 1854): 167–168.
3. Robert G. Albion, *The Rise of New York Port, 1815–1860* (Newton Abbott, U.K.: David and Charles, 1970 [1939]), pp. 59, 63.
4. See Richard John, "Recasting the Information Infrastructure for the Industrial Age," *A Nation Transformed by Information: How Information Has Shaped the United States from Colonial Times to the Present,* ed. Alfred D. Chandler Jr. and James W. Cortada (New York: Oxford University Press, 2000), pp. 80–86.
5. Albion, *The Rise of New York Port,* pp. 275, 280, 421–422. See also Walter A. Friedman, *Birth of a Salesman: The Transformation of Selling in America* (Cambridge, Mass.: Harvard University Press, 2004) and Timothy Spear, *100 Years on the Road: The Traveling Salesman in American Culture* (New Haven, Conn.: Yale University Press, 1995).
6. Reprinted in *Hunt's Merchants' Magazine* 34 (January 1856): 135–136.
7. *Hunt's Merchants' Magazine* 1 (September 1839): 227.
8. Dictionary.com, 2006. In current usage, "transparency" can be defined in both a financial and political sense. In finance, it refers to the availability and accessibility of information about markets and corporations. In politics and government, transparency refers to accountability in public institutions, to minimize the potential for corruption.
9. For an excellent study of how credit reporting violated nineteenth-century norms of privacy and confidentiality, see Scott A. Sandage, *Born Losers: A*

211

History of Failure in America (Cambridge, Mass.: Harvard University Press, 2005).

10. James E. Hagerty, *Mercantile Credit* (New York: Henry Holt, 1913), chapters 3 and 4.

11. Ibid., p. 16.

12. Lewis E. Atherton, "The Problem of Credit Rating in the Ante-Bellum South," *Journal of Southern History* 12 (November 1946): 534; Atherton, *The Frontier Merchant in Mid-America,* pp. 143–146, 150. The merchants of Jacksonville, Illinois, also tried and failed to implement cash sales. Don Doyle, *The Social Order of a Frontier Community: Jacksonville, Illinois, 1825–70* (Urbana: University of Illinois Press, 1978), pp. 89–90.

13. Naomi R. Lamoreaux, "Rethinking the Transition to Capitalism in the Early American Northeast," *Journal of American History* 90, no. 2 (September 2003): 442 and note 14; Bruce H. Mann, *Republic of Debtors: Bankruptcy in the Age of American Independence* (Cambridge, Mass.: Harvard University Press, 2002), pp. 10, 24. In the 1830s, one Midwestern store reported a policy of adding between 20 and 30 percent to the sales price to compensate for credit sales and bad debts. Lewis Atherton, *The Frontier Merchant in Mid-America* (Columbia: University of Missouri Press, 1971), pp. 143–145.

14. Joseph Angell, *A Practical Summary of the Law of Assignments in Trust for the Benefit of Creditors* (Boston: Hilliard, Gray, 1835), p. iii.

15. *Hunt's Merchants' Magazine* 35 (October 1856): 519–520.

16. John Stuart Mill, *Principles of Political Economy with Some of Their Applications to Social Philosophy* (London: Longmans, Green, 1909 [1848]), pp. 513–514, 521–522. Historians of Anglo-American trade during the seventeenth and eighteenth centuries have argued that mercantile credit allowed cash-poor merchants and traders to enlarge their businesses. See, in particular, Jacob Price, *Capital and Credit in British Overseas Trade: The View from the Chesapeake, 1700–1776* (Cambridge, Mass.: Harvard University Press, 1980), pp. 121–122; and Thomas M. Doerflinger, *A Vigorous Spirit of Enterprise: Merchants and Economic Development in Revolutionary Philadelphia* (Chapel Hill: University of North Carolina Press, 1986).

17. See for example, Samuel H. Terry, *The Retailer's Manual* (Newark, N.J.: Jennings Bros., 1869) and Edwin T. Freedley, *A Practical Treatise on Business* (Philadelphia: Lippincott, Grambo, 1853).

18. Lendol Calder likened his own recent investigation of consumer credit to mapping a dark continent. Lendol Calder, *Financing the American Dream: A Cultural History of Consumer Credit* (Princeton, N.J.: Princeton University Press, 1999).

19. Dun and Bradstreet declined to give permission to cite the sources in the R. G. Dun Collection for this book. However, D&B gave permission to two previous works: Rowena Olegario, "Credit and Business Culture: The American Experience in the Nineteenth Century," (unpublished disserta-

tion, Harvard University, 1998); and Rowena Olegario, "'That Mysterious People': Jewish Merchants, Transparency, and Community in Mid-Nineteenth Century America," *Business History Review* 73 (Summer 1999): 161–189. Readers are referred to these works, which contain the relevant citations. The author also consulted materials consisting largely of company circulars, contracts, and advertisements in the archives of Dun and Bradstreet, Murray Hill, N.J. In 2003, D&B donated these items to Baker Library, Harvard Business School. The collection was unprocessed at the time of this book's publication. They will henceforth be cited as the Dun and Bradstreet Collection.

1. Mercantile Credit in Britain and America, 1700–1860

1. Daniel Defoe, *The Complete English Tradesman,* vol. 1, 2nd ed. (London, 1727 [1726]); vol. 2, 1st ed. (London, 1727).
2. John Brewer, *The Sinews of Power: War, Money, and the English State* (New York: Alfred A. Knopf, 1989); Neil McKendrick, et al., *The Birth of a Consumer Society: The Commercialization of Eighteenth-Century England* (Bloomington: Indiana University Press, 1982); Scott B. MacDonald and Albert L. Gastmann, *A History of Credit and Power in the Western World* (New Brunswick, N.J.: Transaction Publishers, 2001), pp. 127–128, 130–133.
3. Defoe, *The Complete English Tradesman,* vol. 1, letter 24.
4. Paula Backscheider, *Daniel Defoe: His Life* (Baltimore: Johns Hopkins University Press, 1989), pp. 510–513; Defoe, *The Complete English Tradesman,* vol. 1, letter 23. The constellation of works includes *A Tour* (1724), *The Royal Progress* (1724), *A General History of Discoveries and Improvements* (1726), *Plan of the English Commerce* (1728), *Atlas Maritimus and Commercialis* (1728), *An Humble Proposal to the People of England for the Encrease of Their Trade, and Encouragement of their Manufactures* (1729), and *A Brief State of the Inland or Home Trade* (1730). See also Donald F. Dixon, "Changing Concepts of the Virtue of Merchants in Seventeenth-Century England," *Business and Economic History,* 2nd ser., 28, no. 2 (Fall 1999): 155–165.
5. Defoe, *The Complete English Tradesman,* vol. 1, letters 18 and 23.
6. Ibid., vol. 1, letter 24; vol. 2, chapter 1.
7. Backscheider, *Daniel Defoe: His Life,* pp. 55–56.
8. Henry C. Carey, *The Credit System in France, Great Britain, and the United States* (Philadelphia, 1838); Calvin Colton [pseud. Junius], *The Crisis of the Country* (n.p., 1840); Calvin Colton, "The Currency," May 1843, in *The Junius Tracts* (New York: Greeley and McElrath, 1844); Daniel Webster, *Webster on the Currency: Speech of Hon. Daniel Webster At the Merchants' Meeting in Wall Street . . . September 28, 1840,* reported in full by Arthur J. Stansbury (New York: E. French, 1840).
9. Works celebrating commerce, however, predate Defoe. These include the

eleventh-century text *The Beauties of Commerce,* by Abu al-Fadl of Damascus, and *On Commerce and the Perfect Merchant,* by Benedetto Cotrugli of Ragusa, written in Naples in the late fifteenth century. Excerpts of both, in translation, can be found in Robert S. Lopez and Irving W. Raymond, eds., *Medieval Trade in the Mediterranean World: Illustrative Documents* (New York: Columbia University Press, 2001 [1955]), chapter 24.

10. MacDonald and Gastmann, *A History of Credit and Power in the Western World,* pp. 44, 61; Edwin S. Hunt and James M. Murray, *A History of Business in Medieval Europe, 1200–1550* (Cambridge: Cambridge University Press, 1999), pp. 65–66, 212–213.

11. M. M. Postan, *Medieval Trade and Finance* (Cambridge: Cambridge University Press, 1973), pp. 6–7, 21–22, 40–42, 48–51, 54, 58–62; Pamela Nightingale, "Monetary Contraction and Mercantile Credit in Later Medieval England," *Economic History Review,* 2nd ser., 43, no. 4 (1990): 560; Hunt and Murray, *A History of Business in Medieval Europe, 1200–1550,* p. 163. See also J. Day, *The Medieval Market Economy* (Oxford: Oxford University Press, 1987); R. H. Britnell and B. M. S. Campbell, *A Commercialising Economy: England, 1086–1300* (Manchester U.K.: Manchester University Press, 1995).

12. Nightingale, "Monetary Contraction and Mercantile Credit in Later Medieval England," pp. 563–564, 569.

13. Hunt and Murray, *A History of Business in Medieval Europe, 1200–1550,* p. 138.

14. Nancy Cox, *The Complete Tradesman: A Study of Retailing, 1550–1820* (Burlington U.K.: Aldershot, 2000), p. 157 and chapter 5 generally; Craig Muldrew, *The Economy of Obligation: The Culture of Credit and Social Relations in Early Modern England* (Basingstoke, U.K.: McMillan Press, 1998). For consumer credit in medieval Europe, see Rosa-Maria Gelpi and Francois Julien-Labruyere, *The History of Consumer Credit: Doctrines and Practices,* trans. Liam Gavin (New York: St. Martin's Press, 2000).

15. Muldrew, *The Economy of Obligation,* pp. 115–116.

16. B. L. Anderson, "Money and the Structure of Credit in the Eighteenth Century," *Business History* 12 (1970): 95–96; Jacob M. Price, *Capital and Credit in British Overseas Trade: The View From the Chesapeake, 1700–1776* (Cambridge, Mass.: Harvard University Press, 1980), p. 142; Jacob M. Price, "What Did Merchants Do? Reflections on British Overseas Trade, 1660–1790," *Journal of Economic History* 2 (June 1989): 278–279; McKendrick, et al., *The Birth of a Consumer Society,* p. 209. Nancy Cox traces the recognition of retailers' book debt as separate from other types of debts to around 1609, when Parliament passed a law specifying that shop books could be recognized as evidence of debt for only one year, absent the existence of a "Bill of Debt," or promissory note. Cox, *The Complete Tradesman,* p. 147.

17. Price, "What Did Merchants Do?" pp. 278–279; Jacob M. Price, "The Bank

of England's Discount Activity and the Merchants of London, 1694–1773," in *Industry and Finance in Early Modern History: Essays Presented to George Hammersley on the Occasion of His 74th Birthday,* ed. I. Blanchard, A. Goodman, and J. Newman (Stuttgart: Franz Steiner Verlag, 1992), p. 113, reprinted in Jacob M. Price, *Overseas Trade and Traders: Essays on Some Commercial, Financial, and Political Challenges Facing British Atlantic Merchants, 1660–1775* (Aldershot, U.K.: Variorum, 1996).

18. McKendrick, et al., *The Birth of a Consumer Society,* pp. 208, 213. See also Anderson, "Money and the Structure of Credit," p. 100.

19. Jacob M. Price, "Credit in the Slave Trade and Plantation Economies," in *Slavery and the Rise of the Atlantic System,* ed. Barbara L. Solow (Cambridge: Cambridge University Press, 1991), p. 338; Anderson, "Money and the Structure of Credit," p. 100.

20. *London Journal,* July 11, 1730, quoted in Julian Hoppit, *Risk and Failure in English Business, 1700–1800* (Cambridge: Cambridge University Press), p. 163. See also McKendrick, et al., *The Birth of a Consumer Society,* pp. 206–207.

21. McKendrick, et al., *The Birth of a Consumer Society,* p. 208.

22. Price, "Credit in the Slave Trade and Plantation Economies," p. 338. The quotation is in Price, *Capital and Credit in British Overseas Trade,* pp. 118–119.

23. Kenneth Morgan, "Business Networks in the British Export Trade to North America, 1750–1800," in *The Early Modern Atlantic Economy,* ed. John J. McCusker and Kenneth Morgan (Cambridge: Cambridge University Press, 2000), especially pp. 52–55.

24. Price, *Capital and Credit in British Overseas Trade,* pp. 102–106, 109.

25. Defoe, *The Complete English Tradesman,* vol. 1, letter 24.

26. Morgan, "Business Networks," p. 36.

27. Stanley Chapman, *Merchant Enterprise in Britain: From the Industrial Revolution to World War I* (Cambridge: Cambridge University Press, 1992), pp. 5, 26–28.

28. Jacob M. Price, ed., *Joshua Johnson's Letterbook, 1771–1774: Letters from a Merchant in London to His Partners in Maryland* (London: London Record Society, 1979), pp. xi–xii.

29. Larry Neal, *The Rise of Financial Capitalism: International Capital Markets in the Age of Reason* (Cambridge: Cambridge University Press, 1990), pp. 5–7; Price, "What Did Merchants Do?" pp. 280–281.

30. Price, "Credit in the Slave Trade and Plantation Economies," p. 294; Hunt and Murray, *A History of Business in Medieval Europe,* p. 212; Neal, *The Rise of Financial Capitalism,* p. 17; Brewer, *The Sinews of Power,* p. 133.

31. Muldrew, *The Economy of Obligation,* pp. 110–111, 191–192; Defoe, *The Complete English Tradesman,* vol. 1, letter 25.

32. Muldrew, *The Economy of Obligation,* pp. 114–115.

33. Anderson, "Money and the Structure of Credit," p. 90.

34. See Price, "The Bank of England's Discounting Activity."
35. Price, "What Did Merchants Do?" pp. 280–281; Anderson, "Money and the Structure of Credit," p. 100. According to John Stuart Mill, in the 1840s "the circulating medium of Lancashire, for sums above five pounds, was almost entirely composed of such bills." John Stuart Mill, *Principles of Political Economy with Some of Their Applications to Social Philosophy* (London: Longmans, Green, 1909 [1848]), pp. 518–519.
36. McKendrick, et al., *The Birth of a Consumer Society*, p. 205; Joyce Ellis, "Risk, Capital, and Credit on Tyneside, *circa* 1690–1780," in *From Family Firms to Corporate Capitalism: Essays in Business and Industrial History in Honour of Peter Mathias*, ed. Kristine Bruland and Patrick O'Brien (Oxford: Clarendon Press, 1998), pp. 87–88.
37. For a taxonomy of British middlemen, see N. S. Buck, *The Development of the Organisation of Anglo-American Trade, 1800–1850* (Newton Abbot, U.K.: David and Charles, 1969 [first published New Haven, Conn.: Yale University Press, 1925]), chapter 2. For the eighteenth century, see Daniel Defoe, *A Brief State of the Inland or Home Trade, or England* (London, 1730), pp. 21–22, and *The Complete English Tradesman*, vol. 1, introduction. In addition to merchants and wholesalers, Julian Hoppit identified gentlemen and widows as sources for mercantile credit in Britain during the eighteenth century. Hoppit, *Risk and Failure in English Business, 1700–1800*, p. 179 and chapter 9.
38. Price, "What Did Merchants Do?" pp. 273–274; Anderson, "Money and the Structure of Credit," p. 97.
39. The forbearance of the large merchants may have had a cultural (as well as a strictly economic) dimension. In Britain and France, a tradition existed among large landowners to delay the collection of rents during financial crises. See B. A. Holderness, "Credit in a Rural Community, 1600–1800: Some Neglected Aspects of Probate Inventories," *Midland History* 3 (1975): 94–115; Laurence Fontaine, "Antonio and Shylock: Credit and Trust in France, c. 1680–c. 1780," trans. Vicki Whittaker, *Economic History Review* 54, 1 (2001): 39–57. The expectation that those with the "deepest pockets" should refrain from taking advantage of people with fewer resources may have transferred to the mercantile realm.
40. Bruce H. Mann, *Republic of Debtors: Bankruptcy in the Age of American Independence* (Cambridge, Mass.: Harvard University Press, 2002), p. 12.
41. Price, *Capital and Credit in British Overseas Trade*, pp. 99–100, 112–113, 132, 135; Jacob M. Price, "Joshua Johnson in London, 1771–1775: Credit and Commercial Organization in the British Chesapeake Trade," *Statesmen, Scholars and Merchants: Essays in Eighteenth-Century History Presented to Dame Lucy Sutherland*, ed. Anne Whitman, et al. (Oxford: Clarendon Press, 1973): 163, 167. Johnson was London partner of the Annapolis firm of Wallace, Davidson and Johnson. The records are from the years 1771–1777. The major part of Johnson's letters to his partners, 1771–1774, have been

published in Price, *Joshua Johnson's Letterbook*. See also Price, "Credit in the Slave Trade and Plantation Economies," p. 295.

42. Muldrew, *The Economy of Obligation*, p. 188.

43. Brewer, *The Sinews of Power*, chapter 7. According to Brewer, criticisms reached a high point during the early eighteenth century. By the Seven Years' War (1756–1763), defenders of the public debt were making much more cogent arguments, and public denunciations had moderated.

44. Julian Hoppit, "Attitudes to Credit in Britain, 1680–1790," *Historical Journal* 33 (June 1990): 315, 318; Anderson, "Money and the Structure of Credit," pp. 92–93.

45. Muldrew, *The Economy of Obligation*, p. 186.

46. Defoe, *The Complete English Tradesman*, vol. 1, letters 6 and 15.

47. Chapman, *Merchant Enterprise in Britain*, p. 4.

48. See Morgan, "Business Networks."

49. Price, "What Did Merchants Do?" pp. 283–284. See also Buck, *The Development of the Organisation of Anglo-American Trade, 1800–1850*, p. 4.

50. Price, *Capital and Credit in British Overseas Trade*, pp. 99–100, 112–113.

51. Price, "Joshua Johnson in London, 1771–1775," p. 162; Price, "Credit in the Slave Trade and Plantation Economies," pp. 325–326; Price, *Capital and Credit in British Overseas Trade*, appendix C, pp. 156–157. Attorneys working for American creditors appear to have charged less. William Samuel Johnson, a delegate to the Constitutional Convention, was a lawyer in Connecticut before the Revolution. He charged his clients in New York and Boston 2.5 percent of the amount collected plus costs. Mann, *Republic of Debtors*, p. 18.

52. Local trade also frequently took the form of barter, sometimes of a quite complicated sort. Barter was much more common in the American colonies than in England. In America, transactions represented in journals and ledgers in money terms often involved no currency at all. Instead, the figure merely served as a convenient way to keep track of barter arrangements, which could involve several parties at once. William T. Baxter estimates that only one-third of debts were paid in cash; the remainder was settled by barter. W. T. Baxter, "Accounting in Colonial America," in *Studies in the History of Accounting*, ed. Ananias C. Littleton and Basil S. Yamey (New York: Arno Press, 1978), pp. 272–274. See also W. T. Baxter, "Credit, Bills, and Bookkeeping in a Simple Economy," *Accounting Review*, 21 (April 1946): 154–66.

53. Price, *Capital and Credit in British Overseas Trade*, pp. 17–18, 26, 120, 125–126.

54. Quoted in Price, *Capital and Credit in British Overseas Trade*, pp. 125–126.

55. Quoted in Hoppit, "Attitudes to Credit," p. 318; Anderson, "Money and the Structure of Credit," pp. 92–93.

56. Thomas M. Doerflinger, *A Vigorous Spirit of Enterprise* (Chapel Hill: University of North Carolina Press, 1986), pp. 52, 53–56, 68–69, 85–86, 88–90.

57. Price, "Joshua Johnson in London, 1771–1775," pp. 159–160. See Mor-

gan, "Business Networks," for examples of other American merchants who tried to master the credit terms of different goods bought from Britain.

58. Quoted in Gordon Wood, *The Radicalism of the American Revolution* (New York: Vintage Books, 1991), 248. See also pp. 249, 336–337. Philadelphia was one city where bank credit was fairly accessible. In the late 1790s artisans and retailers there could obtain loans from the Bank of North America for 6 percent interest on the security of promissory notes, drafts, or bills of exchange. Robert E. Wright, "Artisans, Banks, Credit, and the Election of 1800," *Pennsylvania Magazine of History and Biography* 122, no. 3 (July 1998): 211–239.

59. Bray Hammond, *Banks and Politics in America from the Revolution to the Civil War* (Princeton, N.J.: Princeton University Press, 1957); Harry L. Watson, *Liberty and Power: The Politics of Jacksonian America* (New York: Hill and Wang, 1990).

60. Price, *Capital and Credit in British Overseas Trade*, pp. 118–119. For statistics on the trade between the United States and Britain during this period, see Buck, *The Development of the Organisation of Anglo-American Trade, 1800–1850*, pp. 2–3. The French were much more conservative in their mercantile credit practices, and the Dutch were more interested in land speculation. Neither, therefore, replaced the British as a source of working capital for American traders. Peter J. Coleman, *Debtors and Creditors in America: Insolvency, Imprisonment for Debt, and Bankruptcy, 1607–1900* (Madison: State Historical Society of Wisconsin, 1974), p. 7.

61. Buck, *The Development of the Organisation of Anglo-American Trade, 1800–1850*, pp. 115–117.

62. Ibid., pp. 113–117, 134–135, and chapter 5, note 66.

63. Paul M. Angle, *"Here I Have Lived": A History of Lincoln's Springfield, 1821–1865* (Springfield, Ill.: Abraham Lincoln Association, 1935), p. 23.

64. Auctions diminished in importance except for textiles, large amounts of which continued to be sold at auction until the mid-nineteenth century. Buck, *The Development of the Organisation of Anglo-American Trade, 1800–1850*, pp. 149, 151.

65. Lewis E. Atherton, *The Frontier Merchant in Mid-America* (Columbia: University of Missouri Press, 1971), p. 147.

66. For the method of making payments, see Buck, *The Development of the Organisation of Anglo-American Trade, 1800–1850*, p. 155.

67. Chapman, *Merchant Enterprise in Britain*, pp. 69–71.

68. See Shelby D. Hunt and Jerry Goolsby, "The Rise and Fall of the Functional Approach to Marketing: A Paradigm Displacement Perspective," in *Historical Perspectives in Marketing: Essays in Honor of Stanley C. Hollander*, ed. Terence Nevett and Ronald A. Fullerton (Lexington, Mass.: D.C. Heath, 1988), pp. 35–51, especially the appendix.

69. For the structure of the distribution sector during the nineteenth century see Glenn Porter and Harold Livesay, *Merchants and Manufacturers: Stud-*

ies in the Changing Structure of Nineteenth-Century Marketing (Baltimore, Md.: Johns Hopkins University Press, 1971); Bill R. Moeckel, *The Development of the Wholesaler in the United States, 1860–1900* (New York: Garland Publishing, 1986); and Fred M. Jones, *Middlemen in the Domestic Trade of the United States, 1800–1860* (Urbana: University of Illinois, 1937).

70. Buck, *The Development of the Organisation of Anglo-American Trade, 1800–1850,* p. 160.

71. Atherton, *The Frontier Merchant in Mid-America,* p. 150.

72. Porter and Livesay, *Merchants and Manufacturers,* p. 69, note 24.

73. Buck, *The Development of the Organisation of Anglo-American Trade, 1800–1850,* p. 174.

74. Harry Resseguie, "A. T. Stewart and the Development of the Department Store, 1823–1876," *Business History Review* (Autumn 1965): 306–307.

75. Mercantile Agency circular, January 1858, reprinted in *Business History Review* 37, no. 4 (Winter 1963): 438–439.

76. Eighth Census of Manufacturers, 1860, p. lxxii, in Moeckel, *The Development of the Wholesaler,* p. 29.

77. James F. W. Johnston, *Notes on North America, Agricultural, Economical, and Social* (Boston: C. C. Little and J. Brown, 1851), p. 457.

78. *Hunt's Merchants' Magazine* 34 (1856): 522. See also Lewis Atherton, *The Southern Country Store, 1800–1860* (Baton Rouge: LSU Press, 1949), pp. 115–116.

79. Moeckel, *The Development of the Wholesaler,* p. 33.

80. Atherton, *The Frontier Merchant in Mid-America,* pp. 145–146.

81. Atherton, *The Southern Country Store,* pp. 36, 71, 74–75.

82. Lewis E. Atherton, "The Problem of Credit-Rating in the Antebellum South," *Journal of Southern History* 12 (November 1946): 534; Atherton, *The Frontier Merchant in Mid-America,* pp. 18, 143–146, 150; William Endicott, *Reminiscences of Seventy-Five Years,* quoted in Foulke, *The Sinews of American Commerce,* p. 154.

83. In 1860, for example, Illinois had seventy-four chartered banks. Of these, sixty-three showed no loan and discount activities, and fifty-two had no deposit liabilities. Thirteen had no specie reserves, and a further twenty-eight reported having only nominal amounts. Paul B. Trescott, *Financing American Enterprise: The Story of Commercial Banking* (New York: Harper and Row, 1963), p. 32. See also Donald R. Adams Jr., "The Role of Banks in the Economic Development of the Old Northwest," in *Essays in Nineteenth Century Economic History: The Old Northwest,* ed., David C. Klingaman and Richard K. Vedder (Athens: Ohio University Press, 1975), especially pp. 238–239.

84. Edward J. Balleisen, *Navigating Failure: Bankruptcy and Commercial Society in Antebellum America* (Chapel Hill: University of North Carolina Press, 2001), p. 30.

85. Atherton, *The Frontier Merchant in Mid-America,* p. 143.

86. *Illinois Daily Journal,* May 6, 1854.

87. Foulke, *The Sinews of American Commerce*, p. 153; Porter and Livesay, *Merchants and Manufacturers*, p. 31.
88. Atherton, *The Frontier Merchant in Mid-America*, p. 96.
89. Charles Cist, *Sketches and Statistics of Cincinnati in 1859*, quoted in Jones, *Middlemen in the Domestic Trade*, p. 53.
90. Moeckel, *The Development of the Wholesaler*, p. 74.
91. See Timothy R. Mahoney, *River Towns in the Great West: The Structure of Provincial Urbanization in the American Midwest, 1820–1870* (Cambridge: Cambridge University Press, 1989).
92. *Illinois Daily Journal*, June 8, 1849.
93. *Illinois Daily Journal*, Aug. 10, 1851.
94. William Smith, *Annual Statement of the Trade and Commerce of Cincinnati* (Cincinnati, Ohio, 1859), p. 18.
95. Mahoney, *River Towns in the Great West*, pp. 167–169.
96. Doerflinger, *A Vigorous Spirit of Enterprise*, pp. 142–143; Samuel H. Terry, *The Retailer's Manual* (Newark, N.J.: Jennings Bros., 1869), p. 348.
97. Atherton, *The Frontier Merchant in Mid-America*, pp. 145–146.
98. Foulke, *The Sinews of American Commerce*, p. 156.
99. *Illinois Daily Journal*, March 26, 1849.
100. John Mack Faragher, *Sugar Creek: Life on the Illinois Prairie* (New Haven, Conn.: Yale University Press, 1986), p. 104.
101. Angle, *"Here I Have Lived,"* p. 158. The local barter system continued until at least the 1870s and existed alongside the new national bank notes. In 1874 one general merchandise establishment in Christian County, Illinois, advertised that they took "all kinds of country produce in exchange for goods." *Illinois Register*, July 13, 1874.
102. Atherton, "The Problem of Credit Rating," p. 534; Atherton, *The Frontier Merchant in Mid-America*, p. 18; Christopher Clark, *The Roots of Rural Capitalism: Western Massachusetts, 1780–1860* (Ithaca, N.Y.: Cornell University Press, 1990), p. 164; Gerald Carson, *The Old Country Store* (New York: Oxford University Press, 1954), p. 67. See also Tony Freyer, *Producers Versus Capitalists: Constitutional Conflict in Antebellum America* (Charlottesville: University Press of Virginia, 1994).
103. *Illinois Daily Journal*, January 23, 1850.
104. Atherton, *The Frontier Merchant in Mid-America*, pp. 152–153.
105. Balleisen, *Navigating Failure*, pp. 80–81, 120.
106. George W. Hawes, *Ohio Gazeteer and Business Directory for 1860–61* (Indianapolis, Ind., 1860), pp. ii–iii.
107. William H. Maher, *On the Road to Riches: Practical Hints for Clerks and Young Business Men* (Chicago: J. Fred Waggoner, 1878), pp. 126–127, 196–199.
108. Balleisen, *Navigating Failure*, p. 12.
109. Mann, *Republic of Debtors*, p. 30.
110. Balleisen, *Navigating Failure*, p. 69 and chapter 3 generally.

111. Ibid., pp. 12–13.
112. Circular, Dun, Boyd & Co., New York, January 2, 1860, p. 2, in folder marked "Forms, Circulars, Letters," Dun and Bradstreet Collection, Baker Library, Harvard Business School.
113. See Peter Matthias, "Risk, Credit and Kinship in Modern Enterprise," in *The Early Modern Atlantic Economy*, ed. John J. McCusker and Kenneth Morgan (Cambridge: Cambridge University Press, 2000).
114. *A List of Members of the Society of Guardians for the Protection of Trade Against Swindlers and Sharpers* (London: G. Sidney, 1812).
115. C. McNeil Greig, *The Growth of Credit Information: A History of UAPT-Infolink plc.* (Oxford: Blackwell Publishers, 1992), pp. 12–14, 106.
116. Ibid., pp. 14–17, 21.
117. *Society of Guardians for the Protection of Trade against Swindlers and Sharpers* (Liverpool: J. Nevett, 1824).
118. Ibid., p. 12.
119. Margot C. Finn, *The Character of Credit: Personal Debt in English Culture, 1740–1914* (Cambridge: Cambridge University Press, 2003), pp. 290, 299. By 1939 some seventy societies were affiliated with the National Association of Trade Protection Societies (NATPS). However, the trade protection society movement declined dramatically after World War II, as the economy nationalized, and local-based societies became less useful. C. McNeil Greig argues that the societies' not-for-profit orientation contributed to their demise. Greig, *The Growth of Credit Information*, pp. 14–17, 19.
120. James Henry Dixon, *A Statement of Facts in Reference to the City of London Trade Protection Society* (London: Effingham Wilson, 1851).

2. A "System of Espionage"

1. Owen Sheffield, "The Mercantile Agency . . . A Private History," 4 vols., Dun and Bradstreet, unpublished manuscript, 1965, vol. 1, sec. 1, p. 3, Dun and Bradstreet Collection, Baker Library, Harvard Business School (hereafter cited as Dun and Bradstreet Collection).
2. Quoted in *Hunt's Merchants' Magazine* 26 (May 1852): 650. "Brother Jonathan" was a symbol of the new republic. It emerged during the Revolution but disappeared by the 1870s.
3. Reprinted in *Hunt's Merchants' Magazine* 17 (September 1847): 324–325.
4. Henry David Thoreau, *Walden: or, Life in the Woods* (New York: Dover Publications, 1995 [1854]), pp. 20–21.
5. Samuel H. Terry, *The Retailer's Manual* (Newark, N.J.: Jennings Bros., 1869), p. 17. Research by Clyde Griffen and Sally Griffen on Poughkeepsie businesses in the R. G. Dun ledgers reveals the complexity behind the phenomenon of failure, a subject that scholars have yet to plumb. Of the 371 recorded failures Griffen and Griffen studied, more than half "did not result in terminations of the business, 40 percent surviving for three years or more and

20 percent for ten years or more. Firms which went under more than once account for 6 percent of the total." Clyde Griffen and Sally Griffen, "Family and Business in a Small City: Poughkeepsie, New York, 1850–1880," *Journal of Urban History* 1 (1975): 322.

6. Roy A. Foulke, *The Sinews of American Commerce*. (New York: Dun and Bradstreet, 1941), pp. 333–334.

7. Ibid., pp. 329–330. See also Ralph Hidy, "Credit Rating Before Dun and Bradstreet," *Bulletin of the Business Historical Society* 13 (December 1939): 84–88.

8. Later, Church offered for sale a volume containing information on merchants in the West, South, and Southwest.

9. The form is headed "P. G. Berry & Co," 265 Washington St., New York, dated March 22, 1856, in possession of the author. The name of the recommending firm is illegible.

10. Lewis E. Atherton, "The Problem of Credit Rating in the Ante-Bellum South," *Journal of Southern History* 12 (November 1946): 536.

11. Daniel Defoe, *The Complete English Tradesman*, vol. 1, 2nd ed. (London: 1727 [1726]), letter 15.

12. James W. Kimball, *The Dry-Goods Jobbers* (Boston: The Commercial Agency, n.d. [1865–1880?] p. 23.

13. "The Telegraph, Part 2," *DeBow's Review* 16, no. 2 (February 1854): 167–168; Edward D. Page, *Trust Companies*, March 1914, pp. 206–207, excerpted in Foulke, *The Sinews of American Commerce*, p. 156.

14. Bertram Wyatt-Brown, *Lewis Tappan and the Evangelical War Against Slavery* (Cleveland, Ohio: Case Western Reserve University Press, 1969), p. 42.

15. Walter A. Friedman, *Birth of a Salesman: The Transformation of Selling in America* (Cambridge, Mass.: Harvard University Press, 2004), p. 85.

16. Edwin T. Freedley, *A Practical Treatise on Business* (Philadelphia: Lippincott, Grambo, 1853 [1852]), p. 131.

17. *Hunt's Merchants' Magazine* 24 (January 1851): 50.

18. Hidy, "Credit Rating Before Dun and Bradstreet," pp. 87–88.

19. See Thomas M. Doerflinger, *A Vigorous Spirit of Enterprise: Merchants and Economic Development in Revolutionary Philadelphia* (Chapel Hill: University of North Carolina Press, 1986).

20. Lewis E. Atherton, *The Frontier Merchant in Mid-America* (Columbia: University of Missouri Press, 1971), p. 76.

21. *Hunt's Merchants' Magazine* 1 (July 1839): 30.

22. Richard John writes that by the late 1820s the United States had seventy-four post offices per one hundred thousand inhabitants. In contrast, Great Britain had seventeen and France four. Apart from credit reporting, entities that benefited from the U.S. Post Office's extensive coverage and reliable service included life insurance companies and nationally oriented reform groups and parties. And the post office was by no means the sole distributor of mail; from 1839–1845, it faced competition from a number of private ex-

presses. Richard John, "Recasting the Information Infrastructure for the Industrial Age," in *A Nation Transformed by Information: How Information Has Shaped the United States from Colonial Times to the Present*, ed. Alfred D. Chandler Jr. and James W. Cortada (New York: Oxford University Press, 2000), pp. 60, 63, 70.

23. Sheffield, "The Mercantile Agency," vol. 1, sec. 2, p. 3.

24. Wyatt-Brown, *Lewis Tappan and the Evangelical War Against Slavery*, pp. viii, xiii, 72, 100, 250 262.

25. Ibid., pp. 177–180, 337–338. However, the Tappans never employed blacks as clerks in their wholesaling business, even when urged by a black minister to do so.

26. Edward N. Vose, *Seventy-Five Years of the Mercantile Agency: R. G. Dun & Co., 1841–1916* (New York: R. G. Dun, 1916), p. 12; Wyatt-Brown, *Lewis Tappan and the Evangelical War Against Slavery*, pp. 67, 671.

27. Arthur came to the cause later than Lewis. Arthur had supported the colonization movement, which sought to resettle freed slaves in Africa and the Caribbean, a movement that Lewis scorned. Wyatt-Brown, *Lewis Tappan and the Evangelical War Against Slavery*, pp. 84–87.

28. Ibid., pp. 152–153.

29. Ibid., pp. 152–156.

30. Ibid., p. 18.

31. Sheffield, "The Mercantile Agency," vol. 1, sec. 1, p. 39; Wyatt Brown, *Lewis Tappan and the Evangelical War Against Slavery*, p. 304.

32. Wyatt-Brown, *Lewis Tappan and the Evangelical War Against Slavery*, pp. 44–45.

33. Ibid., pp. 112, 169, 174–175, 226, 241.

34. Ibid., p. 229.

35. C. McNeil Greig, *The Growth of Credit Information: A History of UAPT-Infolink plc.* (Oxford: Blackwell Publishers, 1992), p. 19.

36. Wyatt-Brown, *Lewis Tappan and the Evangelical War Against Slavery*, p. 230.

37. Ibid., pp. 213–217.

38. Ibid., p. 232.

39. See Bray Hammond, *Banks and Politics in America From the Revolution to the Civil War* (Princeton, N.J.: Princeton University Press, 1957) and Harry L. Watson, *Liberty and Power: The Politics of Jacksonian America* (New York: Hill and Wang, 1990).

40. Lewis Tappan, *Is It Right to Be Rich?* (pamphlet), excerpted in Lewis Tappan, *The Life of Arthur Tappan* (London: Sampson, Low, Son, and Marston, 1870), p. 414.

41. Wyatt-Brown, *Lewis Tappan and the Evangelical War Against Slavery*, pp. 231, 237; James D. Norris, *R. G. Dun & Co., 1841–1900: The Development of Credit-Reporting in the Nineteenth Century* (Westport, Conn.: Greenwood Press, 1978), pp. 20–21. Norris's book was the first academic history

of R. G. Dun, and it remains the single best source on the firm during the nineteenth century. I have relied extensively on this work, in particular for the details on Dun's corporate structure and profits.

42. Mark Casson, *Entrepreneurship and Business Culture: Studies in the Economics of Trust,* vol. 1 (Aldershot, U.K.: Edward Elgar, 1995), pp. 202–204.

43. Edward E. Dunbar, *Statement of the Controversy Between Lewis Tappan and Edward E. Dunbar* (New York, 1846), p. 9; Norris, *R. G. Dun & Co.,* p. 20.

44. The Commercial Agency subsequently split into two firms: McKillop and Sprague Company served the eastern half of the country, and Tappan, McKillop and Company the West. The Tappan of the latter firm may have been related to Lewis. This firm failed in 1878. Joseph W. Errant, *The Law Relating to Mercantile Agencies, being the Johnson Prize Essay of the Union College of Law for the Year 1886* (Philadelphia: T. and J. W. Johnson, 1889), pp. 3–4.

45. Wyatt-Brown, *Lewis Tappan and the Evangelical War Against Slavery,* p. 238.

46. Dunbar, *Statement of the Controversy,* p. 70.

47. Norris, *R. G. Dun & Co.,* pp. 24, 29.

48. Wyatt-Brown, *Lewis Tappan and the Evangelical War Against Slavery,* pp. 145, 239.

49. W. A. Cleveland, circular, June 1844, Dun and Bradstreet Collection, in folder marked "Memorabilia, Miscellaneous."

50. Wyatt-Brown, *Lewis Tappan and the Evangelical War Against Slavery,* pp. 238–240; Norris, *R. G. Dun & Co,* pp. 28–29.

51. Atherton, "The Problem of Credit Rating in the Ante-Bellum South," pp. 536–37.

52. Griffin, Cleaveland & Campbell, circular, June 9, 1835, Dun and Bradstreet Collection, folder marked "Credit and Collection Agencies."

53. Wyatt-Brown, *Lewis Tappan and the Evangelical War Against Slavery,* p. 234.

54. Maxwell Bloomfield, *American Lawyers in a Changing Society, 1776–1876* (Cambridge, Mass.: Harvard University Press, 1976), pp. 154–155.

55. David Donald, *Lincoln* (New York: Simon and Schuster, 1995), p. 144.

56. Lewis Tappan, circular [1843?] in Sheffield, "The Mercantile Agency," vol. 1, sec. 2, p. 26–AA.

57. *Hunt's Merchants' Magazine* 24 (January 1851): 47–48. Emphasis in the original. One agency disagreed, arguing that there was a distinction between a merchant's reputation in his hometown versus in New York: "It is known that the standing of a merchant in New-York is often different from that at home. Many country merchants are better known in New-York than in their own town or neighborhood . . . We have made it our work to reflect, by numerals, the opinion at home; and Merchants using the book may add to, or to deduct from, as the opinion in New-York may justify." The Commercial Agency, McKillop & Co., New York, circular, January 15, 1863, Dun and Bradstreet Collection, in folder marked "Tappan Family."

58. Credit-rating book, 1861–1862, Jackson, Michigan, in Michigan Historical Collections, Bentley Library, University of Michigan. The book's format was identical to that of the Dun agency ledgers and suggests that the merchant may have worked as a correspondent for the agency or one of its competitors.

59. The implications for Jewish dealers are discussed in Chapter 4.

60. Credit-rating book, 1861–1862, Jackson, Michigan. The name of the merchant is illegible.

61. Letter from William Goodrich (partner in the Mercantile Agency's Philadelphia office) to David A. Smith, law partner of John Hardin, Jacksonville, Illinois, August 19, 1846, Hardin Papers, Chicago Historical Society, Box 17, July and August 1846. Emphasis added. Addicks, Van Dusen, and Smith soon contacted David A. Smith to collect overdue payments.

62. Lewis Tappan, circular, [1843?].

63. Letter to David A. Smith from Addicks, Van Dusen and Smith, Philadelphia, no date, Hardin Papers, Chicago Historical Society, Box 17, July and August 1846.

64. Atherton, "The Problem of Credit Rating in the Ante-Bellum South," pp. 536, 541–542, 544.

65. Lewis Tappan, circular [1843?].

66. Lewis Tappan, circular, December 20 [1842?], in Sheffield, "The Mercantile Agency," vol. 1, sec. 1, p. 5BB. See also W. A. Cleveland, circular dated June 1844, Dun and Bradstreet Collection, in folder marked "Memorabilia, Miscellaneous"; and John, "Recasting the Information Infrastructure for the Industrial Age," pp. 61–62, 65, 71.

67. Letter from Calvin DeWolf to Mason Brayman, August 23, 1845, Mason Brayman Papers, Chicago Historical Society, Folder 2. Emphasis added.

68. Letter from William Goodrich to David A. Smith, August 19, 1846.

69. Ibid.

70. The Commercial Agency, McKillop & Co., New York, circular, January 15, 1863; Errant, *The Law Relating to Mercantile Agencies*, p. 25.

71. Lewis Tappan, circular, December 20 [1842?]; Foulke, *The Sinews of American Commerce*, p. 309.

72. Wyatt-Brown, *Lewis Tappan and the Evangelical War Against Slavery*, p. 234.

73. Ibid.

74. Lewis Tappan, circular [1843?].

75. Lewis Tappan, circular, December 20 [1842?]. See also Atherton, "The Problem of Credit Rating in the Ante-Bellum South."

76. Lewis Tappan, circular, December 20 [1842?].

77. Sheffield, "The Mercantile Agency," vol. 1, sec. 2, p. 17.

78. Atherton, "The Problem of Credit Rating in the Ante-Bellum South," pp. 550–551.

79. Dunbar, *Statement of the Controversy* p. 9; Dun and Bradstreet, *The Mercantile Agency: The Story of Impartial Credit Reporting* (New York: Dun and Bradstreet, 1941), p. 23.

80. *Hunt's Merchants' Magazine* 15 (October 1846): 339–347.
81. J. Smith Homans and J. Homans Jr., *A Cyclopedia of Commerce and Commercial Navigation,* 2nd ed., vol. 2 (New York: Harper and Brothers, 1859), pp. 1344–1345.
82. Lewis Tappan, circular [1843?].
83. Lewis Tappan, circular, June 10, 1842, in Sheffield, "The Mercantile Agency," vol. 1, sec. 1, p. 5BB.
84. Letter from W. A. Cleveland to William G. Brown, February 21, 1845, Dun and Bradstreet Collection, in folder marked "Memorabilia, Miscellaneous."
85. Lewis Tappan, circular, June 10, 1842.
86. Wyatt-Brown, *Lewis Tappan and the Evangelical War Against Slavery,* pp. 232, 236.
87. [Dun, Barlow & Co.], *Reports of the Four Leading Cases against the Mercantile Agency for Slander and Libel* (New York: Dun, Barlow, 1873), pp. 14, 19, 21.
88. Sheffield, "The Mercantile Agency," vol. 1, sec. 2, p. 19; Norris, *R. G. Dun & Co.,* pp. 25–26.
89. Wyatt-Brown, *Lewis Tappan and the Evangelical War Against Slavery,* pp. 66–67, 233.
90. Norris, *R. G. Dun & Co.,* pp. 33, 36–37.
91. Ibid.
92. Wyatt-Brown, *Lewis Tappan and the Evangelical War Against Slavery,* pp. 241–242, 304; Norris, *R. G. Dun & Co.,* pp. 36, 40–41.
93. Norris, *R. G. Dun & Co.,* pp. 60–63, 66.
94. James D. Norris, "A Northern Businessman Opposes the Civil War: Excerpts from the Letters of R. G. Dun," *Ohio History* 71, no. 2 (July 1962): 140, 144.
95. Norris, *R. G. Dun & Co.,* p. 101–104.
96. Lewis Tappan, circular [1843?]; Wyatt-Brown, *Lewis Tappan and the Evangelical War Against Slavery,* pp. 237–238, 240–241.
97. Norris, *R. G. Dun & Co.,* pp. 43–44, 47–48, 71.
98. Ibid., p. 71.
99. Ibid., pp. 29, 43, 44, 46, 159; Sheffield, "The Mercantile Agency," vol. 1, sec. 1, pp. 28–29.
100. Mercantile Agency, circular, Cincinnati office, 1853, probably written by B. Douglass, Dun and Bradstreet Collection, in folder marked "Forms, Circulars, Letters."
101. Mercantile Agency, circular, New York office, 1855, Dun and Bradstreet Collection, in folder marked "Forms, Circulars, Letters."
102. American Collection Agency to Elijah Morgan, February 18, 1858, Morgan Family Papers, Michigan Historical Collections, Bentley Historical Library, University of Michigan (hereafter cited as Morgan Family Papers). See also Atherton, "The Problem of Credit Rating in the Ante-Bellum South," p. 545.
103. Mercantile Agency, circular, New York office, 1855.

104. Mercantile Agency, circular, New Orleans office, 1852, Dun and Bradstreet Collection, in folder marked "Forms, Circulars, Letters." Potter and Russell was the successor to W. A. Cleveland.
105. Mercantile Agency, circular, New York office, 1855; Norris, *R. G. Dun & Co.,* p. 49.
106. Atherton, "The Problem of Credit Rating in the Ante-Bellum South," pp. 544–545.
107. Elijah Morgan correspondence, Morgan Family Papers.
108. Griffin, Cleaveland & Campbell, circular, June 9, 1835.
109. Lewis Tappan, circular, December 20 [1842?].
110. J. M Bradstreet & Son, circular, 1864, Dun and Bradstreet Collection, in folder marked "Bradstreet Co.; Contracts, Letters, Miscellaneous."
111. R. T. Ettinger and D. E. Golieb, *Credits and Collections* (New York: Prentice-Hall, 1917), p. 100.
112. Sheffield, "The Mercantile Agency," vol. 2, sec. 7, p. 4; Dun & Bradstreet, *The Mercantile Agency,* p. 17.
113. James Norris speculates that the "decision to switch to symbolic ratings, which were more vague and generalized than detailed reports, may have been strongly influenced by fear of libel suits." Norris, *R. G. Dun & Co.,* p. 51.
114. Foulke, *The Sinews of American Commerce,* pp. 298, 366, 368.
115. Norris, *R. G. Dun & Co.,* p. 52.
116. *Taylor v. Church,* 1 E. D. *Smith's N.Y.R.,* 282–284, and Court of Appeals, 8 N.Y.R., 353; Mercantile Agency, circular, Pittsburgh office, 1855, Dun and Bradstreet Collection, in folder marked "Forms, Circulars, Letters."
117. Norris, *R. G. Dun & Co.,* pp. 53–54, 68–73, 84–94, 111–113, 142–147. Norris writes that the reference books replaced the descriptive reports, but it is clear that the latter continued to be important sources of information. Both the R. G. Dun and Bradstreet companies urged subscribers to obtain the full reports for smaller firms and for cases that were "doubtful," i.e., ambiguous. See James H. Madison, "The Evolution of Commercial Credit Reporting Agencies in Nineteenth Century America," *Business History Review* 48 (Summer 1974): 174, and B. H. Blanton, *Credit, Its Principles and Practice* (New York: Ronald Press, 1915), p. 82.
118. Foulke, *The Sinews of American Commerce,* pp. 297–298; Norris, *R. G. Dun & Co.,* pp. 56, 86.
119. Norris, *R. G. Dun & Co.,* pp. 25–26, 54–56, 68, 83–85.
120. Rowena Olegario, "Credit and Business Culture: The American Experience in the Nineteenth Century" (unpublished dissertation, Harvard University, 1998), pp. 175–176; Clyde Griffen and Sally Griffen, *Natives and Newcomers: The Ordering of Opportunity in Mid-Nineteenth Century Poughkeepsie* (Cambridge, Mass.: Harvard University Press, 1978), p. 104.
121. Atherton, "The Problem of Credit Rating in the Ante-Bellum South," p. 545; Terry, *The Retailer's Manual,* p. 84.
122. Madison, "The Evolution of Commercial Credit Reporting," p. 169.

123. Quoted in Atherton, "The Problem of Credit Rating in the Ante-Bellum South," p. 552.
124. *Hunt's Merchants' Magazine* 29 (January 1856): 51–52.
125. Freedley, *A Practical Treatise on Business,* pp. 130–131.
126. Mercantile Agency, circular, ca. 1850–1855, D&B Archives, in folder marked "Forms, Circulars, Letters."
127. Mercantile Agency, circular, New York office, 1852, Dun and Bradstreet Collection, in folder marked "Forms, Circulars, Letters." See also Lewis Tappan, circular [1843?].
128. Mercantile Agency circular, Charleston office, May 1853, Dun and Bradstreet Collection, in folder marked "Forms, Circulars, Letters."
129. Terry, *The Retailer's Manual,* p. 83.
130. For a history of court decisions and legislation involving the agencies, see Madison, "The Evolution of Commercial Credit Reporting Agencies"; and Errant, *The Law Relating to Mercantile Agencies.*
131. Errant, *The Law Relating to Mercantile Agencies,* pp. 13–15.
132. Ibid., pp. 16–18.
133. [Dun, Barlow & Co.], *Reports of the Four Leading Cases against the Mercantile Agency for Slander and Libel,* pp. 127–128. For an account of the *Beardsley* case which is deeply critical of the Mercantile Agency and of credit reporting generally, see Scott A. Sandage, *Born Losers: A History of Failure in America* (Cambridge, Mass.: Harvard University Press, 2005), chapter 6. Sandage found evidence that the correspondent, whom the Mercantile Agency refused to name, was at fault and argues that the agency should not have protected him.
134. Norris, *R. G. Dun & Co.,* p. 54; Dun and Bradstreet, *The Mercantile Agency,* p. 33.
135. *Hunt's Merchants' Magazine* 24 (January 1851): 47–52.
136. *Hunt's Merchants' Magazine* 35 (August 1856): 260.
137. Homans and Homans Jr., *A Cyclopedia of Commerce and Commercial Navigation,* pp. 1344–1345.
138. Vose, *Seventy-Five Years of the Mercantile Agency,* p. 130.
139. Until recently, there were no rigorous studies to counter the model presented by classical economics. This state of affairs began to change with the work of institutional economists George Akerlof, Michael Spence, and Joseph Stiglitz, who shared the Nobel Prize in Economics in 2001. Collectively, they and other researchers demonstrated that lack of good information is a serious obstacle to the effective allocation of credit, whether among moneylenders in rural India or within a large commercial bank operating in a developed economy. See George A. Akerlof, "The Market for Lemons," *Quarterly Journal of Economics* 84, no. 3 (1970): 488–500; Joseph Stiglitz and Andrew Weiss, "Credit Rationing in Markets with Imperfect Information," *American Economic Review* 71 (1981): 393–410; Joseph Stiglitz and

Andrew Weiss, "Banks as Social Accountants and Screening Devices for the Allocation of Credit" (working paper no. 2710, National Bureau of Economic Research, Cambridge, Mass., 1988).

140. Recent scholarship has highlighted the advantages possessed by closed networks, including their ability to provide superior access to information and effective enforcement of contracts. See, for example, Avner Greif, "Reputation and Coalitions in Medieval Trade: Evidence on the Maghribi Traders," *Journal of Economic History* 49, no. 4 (December 1989): 857–882; Andrew Godley and Duncan M. Ross, eds. *Banks, Networks, and Small Firm Finance* (London: Frank Cass, 1996), pp. 4–5; Alejandro Portes, ed., *The Economic Sociology of Immigration: Essays on Networks, Ethnicity, and Entrepreneurship* (New York: Russell Sage Foundation, 1995). Networks are invaluable in economies that have underdeveloped communications and transportation infrastructures or that lack effective enforcement institutions such as courts. Networks can also be effective in developed economies, where mutual protection societies can complement, rather than supplant, more formal arrangements. The International Bank for Reconstruction and Development/The World Bank, *World Development Report 2002: Building Institutions for Markets* (Oxford: Oxford University Press, 2001), pp. 174–179.

141. In Latin America during the twenty-first century, to take one counterexample, a competitive credit-reporting industry has had difficulty developing because people are less mobile and markets and industries more concentrated. Industry groups have set up their own credit information–sharing arrangements and restrict the sharing of information to insiders only. Margaret J. Miller, "Foreword" and "Introduction," in Margaret J. Miller, ed., *Credit Reporting Systems and the International Economy* (Cambridge, Mass.: MIT Press, 2003) pp. vii, 6; John M. Barron and Michael Staten, "The Value of Comprehensive Credit Reports: Lessons from the U.S. Experience," in Miller, *Credit Reporting Systems,* p. 277; Rafael del Villar, Alejandro Diaz de Leon, and Johanna Gil Hubert, "Regulation of Personal Data Protection and of Credit Reporting Firms: A Comparison of Selected Countries of Latin America, the United States, and the European Union," in Miller, *Credit Reporting Systems,* pp. 424–425.

142. A credit-reporting firm, Perry's (Perry's Original Bankrupt and Insolvent Registry Office for Protection against Fraud, Swindlers &c.) was established in London in 1810 and published *Perry's Bankrupt and Insolvent Weekly Gazette* from at least 1828. It left few if any records, and I have not been able to determine its size and scope, how it operated, or who were its clients. I have also not come across any references to it in the contemporary literature, indicating that it had a limited impact. See Finn, *The Character of Credit: Personal Debt and English Culture, 1740–1914* (Cambridge: Cambridge University Press, 2003), p. 306, note 86.

143. The trade protection societies also increasingly engaged in lobbying activities. See Finn, *The Character of Credit*, pp. 314–315, 325.

3. Character, Capacity, Capital

1. *Daily Illinois State Journal*, January 8, 1856.
2. James D. Norris, *R. G. Dun & Co., 1841–1900: The Development of Credit-Reporting in the Nineteenth Century* (Westport, Conn.: Greenwood Press, 1978), p. 24.
3. On the mercantile library associations, see Thomas Augst, *The Clerk's Tale: Young Men and Moral Life in Nineteenth-Century America* (Chicago: University of Chicago Press, 2003).
4. *Hunt's Merchants' Magazine* 17 (December 1847): 635–636.
5. *Hunt's Merchants' Magazine* 33 (September 1855): 390–391.
6. *Hunt's Merchants' Magazine* 13 (July 1845): 106.
7. See, for example, Stuart M. Blumin, *The Emergence of the Middle Class: Social Experience in the American City, 1760–1900* (Cambridge: Cambridge University Press, 1989); Mary Ryan, *Cradle of the Middle Class: The Family in Oneida County, New York, 1790–1865* (Cambridge: Cambridge University Press, 1981); Augst, *The Clerk's Tale*.
8. Karen Haltunnen, *Confidence Men and Painted Women: A Study of Middle-Class Culture in America, 1830–1870* (New Haven, Conn.: Yale University Press, 1982); Judith Hilkey, *Character Is Capital: Success Manuals and Manhood in Gilded Age America* (Chapel Hill: University of North Carolina Press, 1997). See also Nancy F. Cott, *The Bonds of Womanhood: "Woman's Sphere" in New England, 1780–1835* (New Haven, Conn.: Yale University Press, 1977) and Eric Foner, *Free Soil, Free Labor, Free Men: The Ideology of the Republican Party Before the Civil War* (New York: Oxford University Press, 1970). For the colonial period, see Bruce H. Mann, *Republic of Debtors: Bankruptcy in the Age of American Independence* (Cambridge, Mass.: Harvard University Press, 2002), pp. 260–261.
9. Naomi Lamoreaux, *Insider Lending: Banks, Personal Connections, and Economic Development in Industrial New England* (Cambridge: Cambridge University Press, 1994), pp. 74–75.
10. *Hazard's* 1., no. 1 (February 1839).
11. William D. Samson and Gary John Previts, "Reporting for Success: The Baltimore and Ohio Railroad and Management Information, 1827–1856," *Business and Economic History* 28 (Winter 1999): 235–248.
12. Gary J. Previts and Barbara D. Merino, *A History of Accounting in America: An Historical Interpretation of the Cultural Significance of Accounting* (New York: Wiley, 1979), pp. 61, 77–81, 94–95.
13. Previts and Merino, *A History of Accounting in America*, p. 45.
14. Naomi Lamoreaux, "Rethinking the Transition to Capitalism in the Early American Northeast," *Journal of American History* 90, no. 2 (September

2003): 443–444, note 21. The profit-and-loss statement was not treated as important by many accountants until well into the twentieth century.

15. Previts and Merino, *A History of Accounting in America*, p. 89.
16. Lamoreaux, "Rethinking the Transition to Capitalism," p. 445.
17. Previts and Merino, *A History of Accounting in America*, pp. 58–59.
18. Edwin T. Freedley, *A Practical Treatise on Business* (Philadelphia: Lippincott, Grambo, 1853 [1852]), p. 111.
19. Samuel H. Terry, *The Retailer's Manual* (Newark, N.J.: Jennings Bros., 1869), p. 217.
20. Mercantile Agency, circular, New York office, 1853, Dun and Bradstreet Collection, in folder marked "Forms, Circulars, Letters," Baker Library, Harvard Business School (hereafter cited as Dun and Bradstreet Collection).
21. Lewis Tappan, circular, December 20 [1842?], in Owen Sheffield, "The Mercantile Agency . . . A Private History," 4 vols., Dun and Bradstreet, unpublished manuscript, 1965, Dun and Bradstreet Collection, vol. 1, sec. 1, p. 5BB.
22. Lewis E. Atherton, *The Frontier Merchant in Mid-America* (Columbia: University of Missouri Press, 1971), p. 157.
23. Town maps often detailed the precise locations of businesses and dwellings. See, for example, "Map of the Business Portion of Chicago," prepared by Edwin Whitefield, 1862. The map contained a directory of Chicago businesses printed on its margins, and it indicated the positions of all businesses, by type, as well as dwellings and government offices. The map hangs in the Chicago Historical Society.
24. Freedley, *A Practical Treatise on Business*, pp. 113–114.
25. Griffin, Cleveland & Campbell, sample reports, New York, June 9, 1835, Dun and Bradstreet Collection, in folder marked "Credit and Collection Agencies."
26. See W. A. Cleveland, circular, New York, July 1, 1846, Dun and Bradstreet Collection, in folder marked "Contracts, Letters, Miscellaneous."
27. [B. Douglass?], circular, Cincinnati, 1853, Dun and Bradstreet Collection, in folder marked "Forms, Circulars, Letters."
28. Elijah W. Morgan, correspondence with American Collecting Agency [1850s?], Morgan Family Papers, ca. 1830–1900, Box 1, Michigan Historical Collections, Bentley Historical Collections, University of Michigan (hereafter cited as Morgan Family Papers).
29. For an example of an actual report, see Rowena Olegario, "Credit and Business Culture: The American Experience in the Nineteenth Century" (unpublished dissertation, Harvard University, 1998), p. 190.
30. Elijah W. Morgan, correspondence with American Collecting Agency [1850s?].
31. According to jurist Seymour D. Thompson, exemption laws were of Spanish origin. A remnant of feudalism, they were introduced into the United States through the Republic of Texas in 1839. Thompson, *A Treatise on Homestead and Exemption Laws* (Saint Louis, Mo.: F. H. Thomas, 1878), pp. 1–9, 119–126, 164–184, 604–605, 613–623.

32. Terry, *The Retailer's Manual,* p. 196.
33. Griffin, Cleaveland & Campbell, circular, New York, June 9, 1835, Dun and Bradstreet Collection, folder marked "Credit and Collection Agencies."
34. W. A. Cleveland, circular, Dorr's, New York, June 1844, Dun and Bradstreet Collection, in folder marked ".viemorabilia, Miscellaneous."
35. [B. Douglass?], circular, Cincinnati, 1853.
36. Julian Hoppit, *Risk and Failure in English Business, 1700–1800* (Cambridge: Cambridge University Press, 1987), p. 164.
37. Ralph W. Hidy, "Credit Rating Before Dun and Bradstreet," *Bulletin of the Business Historical Society* 13 (December 1939): 82.
38. Ibid., 85, 86–87.
39. The consumer credit bureaus that began forming in the early twentieth century appear to have focused more explicitly on race, church affiliation, and membership in fraternal organizations. See, in particular, C. O. Hanes, *The Retail Credit and Adjustment Bureaus: Their Organization and Their Conduct* (Columbia, Mo.: C. O. Hanes, 1915), pp. 15, 23, 29.
40. Hoppit, *Risk and Failure in English Business, 1700–1800,* chapter 2; *Hunt's Merchants' Magazine* 6, no. 3 (March 1842): 253–254.
41. Edward J. Balleisen, *Navigating Failure: Bankruptcy and Commercial Society in Antebellum America* (Chapel Hill: University of North Carolina Press, 2001), p. 176.
42. Norris, *R. G. Dun & Co., 1841–1900,* p. 46. See also Freedley, *A Practical Treatise on Business,* p. 237.
43. Reprinted from the *New York Journal of Commerce* in the *Illinois Daily Journal,* October 11, 1854.
44. Sheffield, "The Mercantile Agency . . . A Private History," vol. 1, sec. 1, p. 38.
45. *Hunt's Merchants' Magazine* 24 (January 1851): 51.
46. *Hunt's Merchants' Magazine* 7 (August 1842): 182.
47. Daniel Defoe, *The Complete English Tradesman,* vol. 1, 2nd ed. (London, 1727 [1726], letter 7. See also letter 13 wherein Defoe urges creditors to be lenient with honest insolvents.
48. See, for example, Cee & Turner, Coldwater, Michigan, account book/ledger, 1836, Michigan Historical Collections, Bentley Library, University of Michigan.
49. Tony A. Freyer, *Producers Versus Capitalists: Constitutional Conflict in Antebellum America* (Charlottesville: University Press of Virginia, 1994), pp. 86–88.
50. Balleisen, *Navigating Failure,* pp. 89, 91, 102–103.
51. *Hunt's Merchants' Magazine* 1, no. 5 (November 1839): 385.
52. Freyer, *Producers Versus Capitalists,* pp. 86–88.
53. *Hunt's Merchants' Magazine* 7 (December 1842): 528–529.
54. Charles Francis Adams, "The Principles of Credit" *Hunt's Merchants' Magazine* 2 (March 1840): 191–192; Robert Hare, *Proof that Credit as Money,*

in a Truly Free Country, Is to a Great Extent Preferable to Coin, rev. ed. (Philadelphia: John C. Clark, 1834 [1810]), p. 6.

55. *Hunt's Merchants' Magazine* 16 (May 1847): 511.
56. *Hunt's Merchants' Magazine* 28 (May 1853): 650–651.
57. Mann, *Republic of Debtors,* pp. 40–43.
58. The great English legal commentator William Blackstone wrote in the mid-eighteenth century that "at present the laws of bankruptcy are considered as laws calculated for the benefit of trade, and founded on the principles of humanity as well as justice; and to that end they confer some privileges, not only on the creditors, but also on the bankrupt or debtor himself." W. Blackstone, *Commentaries on the laws of England,* 4 vols. (Oxford, 1766), vol. 2, p. 472.
59. *Hunt's Merchants' Magazine* 34 (January 1856): 61.
60. *Hunt's Merchants' Magazine* 6 (March 1842): 253–254.
61. Defoe, *The Complete English Tradesman,* vol. 1, letter 13. The sentiment was expressed even earlier (1665) by a French writer, Savary, in *Le parfait négociant:* "One should not make too much of debtors who are unable to pay their debts because their business has failed; this is a time when one should treat them gently so as not to force them into banckruptcy." The quote, in translation, appears in Laurence Fontaine, "Antonio and Shylock: Credit and Trust in France, c. 1680–c. 1780," trans. Vicki Whittaker, *Economic History Review* 54, no. 1 (2001): 54.
62. *Hunt's Merchants' Magazine* 6 (March 1842): 253–254.
63. *Hunt's Merchants' Magazine* 7 (August 1842): 180.
64. *Hunt's Merchants' Magazine* 35 (September 1856): 385, 390–391.
65. James W. Kimball, *The Dry-Goods Jobbers* (Boston: The Commercial Agency, n.d. [1865–1880?]), p. 26.
66. Defoe, *The Complete English Tradesman,* vol. 1, letters 13, 25.
67. Terry, *The Retailer's Manual,* pp. 189, 211.
68. Mercantile Agency, circular, January 1858, reprinted in *Business History Review* 37, no. 4 (Winter 1963): 439. In her study of British credit practices, Margo Finn points out that the language used in the correspondence between creditors and debtors was highly personalized: creditors apologized for having to ask for payment, and debtors often expressed themselves as offended at being asked. The character of the language—personal rather than legalistic—indicates the continuity of traditional modes of operating and thinking, even within a rapidly modernizing economy. Margo Finn, *The Character of Credit: Personal Debt and English Culture, 1740–1914* (Cambridge: Cambridge University Press, 2003), p. 302.
69. *Hunt's Merchants' Magazine* 35 (September 1856): 385, 390–391.
70. Dun, Boyd & Co., circular, New York, January 2, 1860, Dun and Bradstreet Collection, in folder marked "Forms, Circulars, Letters."
71. Mercantile Agency, circular, January 1858.
72. Terry, *The Retailer's Manual,* pp. 150–151.

73. Freedley, *A Practical Treatise on Business,* p. 55. Emphasis in the original.
74. Terry, *The Retailer's Manual,* p. 274.
75. Freedley, *A Practical Treatise on Business,* p. 115.
76. *Hunt's Merchants' Magazine* 15 (September 1846): 261–263.
77. Reprinted in *Hunt's Merchants' Magazine* 21 (August 1849): 249–250.
78. Balleisen, *Navigating Failure,* p. 216.
79. *Illinois Daily Journal,* Aug. 16, 1850.
80. Reprinted in *Hunt's Merchants' Magazine* 32 (May 1855): 649.
81. Reprinted in *Hunt's Merchants' Magazine* 21 (August 1849): 249–250.
82. *Illinois Daily State Journal,* July 23, 1868.
83. See Olegario, "Credit and Business Culture," p. 218, for example in the R. G. Dun reports.
84. Ibid.
85. My discussion of drinking and temperance relies heavily on W. J. Rorabaugh, *The Alcoholic Republic: An American Tradition* (New York: Oxford University Press, 1979), pp. 10, 61, 90, 96–97, 202.
86. See Paul E. Johnson, *A Shopkeeper's Millennium: Society and Revivals in Rochester, New York, 1815–1837* (New York: Hill and Wang, 1978).
87. *Hunt's Merchants' Magazine* 35 (September 1856): 390–391.
88. Excerpted in *Hunt's Merchants' Magazine* 30 (June 1854): 775.
89. Hoppit, *Risk and Failure in English Business, 1700–1800,* p. 12. Joan Scott makes the important point that the designation "entrepreneur" is inherently political. One could, with justification, refer to the owners of very small enterprises as self-employed, even "proletarianized," artisans. Joan Scott, "Comment: Conceptualizing Gender in American Business History," *Business History Review* 72 (Summer 1998): 242–249.
90. Thomas M. Doerflinger, *A Vigorous Spirit of Enterprise: Merchants and Economic Development in Revolutionary Philadelphia* (Chapel Hill: University of North Carolina Press, 1986), p. 164.
91. Clyde Griffen and Sally Griffen, *Natives and Newcomers: The Ordering of Opportunity in Mid-Nineteenth Century Poughkeepsie* (Cambridge, Mass.: Harvard University Press, 1978), pp. 34–35.
92. Olegario, "Credit and Business Culture," p. 221.
93. Edward N. Vose, *Seventy-Five Years of the Mercantile Agency: R. G. Dun & Co., 1841–1916* (New York: R. G. Dun, 1916), p. 84. The separate markings for importers, manufacturers, and jobbers were not sustained in later editions of the reference book.
94. On the pressure put on white men to be "energetic," see Scott Sandage, *Born Losers: A History of Failure in America* (Cambridge, Mass.: Harvard University Press, 2005), especially chapter 3.
95. *Hunt's Merchants' Magazine* 29 (December 1853): 775.
96. *Hunt's Merchants' Magazine* 44 (February 1861): 268–269.
97. J. Christopher Schnell and Katherine B. Clinton, "The New West: Themes

in Nineteenth Century Urban Promotion," *Bulletin of the Missouri Histori-cal Society* 30 (January 1974): 82.

98. *Illinois Daily Journal,* Aug. 10, 1851.

99. Balleisen, *Navigating Failure,* p. 211.

100. Sandage, *Born Losers,* pp. 232–233.

101. Balleisen, *Navigating Failure,* p. 53.

102. Bertram Wyatt-Brown, *Lewis Tappan and the Evangelical War Against Slavery* (Cleveland, Ohio: Case Western Reserve University Press, 1969), p. 237; Nor-ris, *R. G. Dun & Co.,* pp. 104, 117. See also Sandage, *Born Losers,* p. 142.

103. See, for example, Terry, *The Retailer's Manual,* p. 289.

104. *Hunt's Merchants' Magazine* 33 (September 1855): 394.

105. Lewis Atherton, cited in Laurence A. Johnson, *Over the Counter and on the Shelf: Country Storekeeping in America, 1620–1920* (Rutland, VT.: C. E. Tuttle, 1961), p. 35.

106. Blumin, *The Emergence of the Middle Class,* pp. 66–137; Naomi Lamoreaux, "Constructing Firms: Partnerships and Alternative Contractual Arrange-ments in Early Nineteenth-Century American Business," *Business and Eco-nomic History* 24 (Winter 1995): 64.

107. *Daily Illinois State Journal,* June 2, 1856.

108. *Hunt's Merchants' Magazine* 20 (May 1849): 570.

109. *Hunt's Merchants' Magazine* 24 (January 1851): 50–51.

110. *Hunt's Merchants' Magazine* 18 (January 1848): 118.

111. *Hunt's Merchants' Magazine* 18 (April 1848): 453.

112. Benjamin R. Haynes and Harry P. Jackson, *A History of Business Education in the United States* (Cincinnati, Ohio: South-Western Publishing, 1935), pp. 14, 24–26.

113. Freedley, *A Practical Treatise on Business,* pp. 37–38.

114. Previts and Merino, *A History of Accounting in America,* p. 151.

115. [B. Douglass?], circular, Cincinnati, 1853.

116. Sandage, *Born Losers,* chapter 6.

117. *Hunt's Merchants' Magazine* 23 (November 1850): 524.

118. Clyde Griffen and Sally Griffen, "Family and Business in a Small City: Poughkeepsie, New York, 1850–1880," *Journal of Urban History* 1 (1975): 329–330.

119. Credit-rating book, 1861–1862, Jackson, Michigan, Michigan Historical Collections, Bentley Library, University of Michigan.

120. Griffen and Griffen, "Family and Business in a Small City," pp. 329–330.

121. Balleisen, *Navigating Failure,* p. 96.

122. Linda E. Speth, "The Married Women's Property Acts, 1839–1865: Re-form, Reaction, or Revolution?" in *Women and the Law,* vol. 2: *Property, Family and the Legal Profession,* ed. D. Kelly Weisberg (Cambridge, Mass.: Schenkman Publishing, 1982). Edith Sparks' research on San Francisco dur-ing the 1870s suggests that only about 20 percent of businesses that oper-

ated under a woman's name were actually run by a husband or male relative. Sparks, "Married Women and Economic Choice: Explaining Why Women Started Businesses in San Francisco Between 1890 and 1930," *Business and Economic History* 28 (Winter 1999): 295.

123. Studies of milliners in Boston and Iowa indicate that most of those women were unmarried, while a study of women who operated establishments in Illinois (the majority of whom were milliners) determined that half were widowed, separated, or never married. Susan Ingalls Lewis's study of successful women-owned businesses in Albany, New York (that is, businesses that lasted more than five years and had an estimated worth of at least $2,000) found that milliners were more likely to be unmarried, but that the majority of Lewis's overall sample were married for at least part of their business careers. Wendy Gamber's Boston study shows that married women's businesses lasted twice as long as those of single women, although it is unclear whether there was a causal link between marriage and enhanced business longevity. Susan Ingalls Lewis, "Female Entrepreneurs in Albany, 1840–1885," *Business and Economic History,* 2nd ser., 21 (1992), pp. 67–68; Wendy Gamber, "A Precarious Independence: Milliners and Dressmakers in Boston, 1880–1890," *Journal of Women's History* 4 (Spring 1992): 79–80. See also Christie Daily, "A Woman's Concern: Millinery in Central Iowa, 1870–1880," *Journal of the West* 21 (April 1982): p. 30; Lucy E. Murphy, "Her Own Boss: Businesswomen and Separate Spheres in the Midwest, 1850–1880," *Illinois Historical Journal* (Autumn 1987): 155–176; Lucy E. Murphy, "Business Ladies: Midwestern Women and Enterprise: 1850–1880" *Journal of Women's History* 3 (1991): 65–89. My own Springfield, Illinois, sample indicates that marriage did not necessarily enhance the creditworthiness of women. Olegario, "Credit and Business Culture," pp. 262–264.

124. The historical literature on women and blacks in business is relatively thin. For the reasons why these groups have been slighted in the historiography, see Robert E. Weems Jr., "Out of the Shadows: Business Enterprise and African American Historiography," *Business and Economic History* 26, no. 1 (Fall 1997): 200–212; Wendy Gamber, "A Gendered Enterprise: Placing Nineteenth-Century Businesswomen in History," *Business History Review* 72 (Summer 1998): 188–218. As with small businesses in general, the sources of loans for women and minorities were often informal. See, for example, Edith Sparks, "Terms of Endearment: Informal Borrowing Networks among Northern California Businesswomen, 1870–1920," *Business and Economic History On-Line,* vol. 2, 2004, www.thebhc.org/publications/BEHonline/2004/Sparks.pdf. Blacks attempted to form mutual aid societies, including formal rotating credit associations, to compensate for their lack of access to other forms of credit. Juliet E. K. Walker, *The History of Black Business in America* (New York: Macmillan Library Reference USA, 1998), pp. 85–86, 90.

125. A significant portion of the literature on women in business during this period concentrates on milliners. This is not surprising, for although hats were

an integral part of women's clothing, they were not mass-produced. As a result, milliners had a significant presence in large and small towns alike, and the growing business districts in new towns of at least five hundred people almost always included at least one millinery establishment. Because they tended to sell items at retail, milliners requested credit from suppliers and therefore appeared in the ledgers more often than did dressmakers. In Boston, according to Gamber, Dun reported on 58 percent of the milliners but only 3 percent of the dressmakers listed in that city's 1880 directory. Daily, "A Woman's Concern," p. 30; Wendy Gamber, "A Precarious Independence," pp. 61, 64.

126. According to Lucy E. Murphy, businesswomen of this region (totaling 26,240) were engaged primarily in artisanal activities. Of these, the skilled trades of millinery and dressmaking (19,234) and the semiskilled trade of seamstress (6,649) were the largest occupational categories. Murphy, "Her Own Boss," pp. 155–176; Gamber, "A Gendered Enterprise," p. 189.

127. R. G. Hutchinson, A. R. Hutchinson, and Mabel Newcomer, "A Study in Business Mortality: Length of Life of Business Enterprises in Poughkeepsie, New York, 1843–1936," *American Economic Review* 28 (September 1938): 497–514; Murphy, "Her Own Boss," p. 165. Gamber's study of Boston milliners and modistes found that one-third of these female-owned businesses lasted less than two years, and a full 60 percent lasted five years or fewer. A number of factors accounted for the volatility within the millinery and dressmaking trades. The customers of these predominantly female-owned businesses were largely dependent on husbands and fathers for their disposable income, and these customers' precarious financial position affected the cash flow of millinery and other female-oriented businesses. Moreover, the millinery trades were highly seasonal. Milliners worked long hours during the spring and fall, when the new fashions arrived. When the season ended in July and January, those who had inadequate savings to tide them over were obliged to turn to other pursuits for their income. The competitive pressures increased toward the end of the century, when these small female-owned shops were forced to operate alongside much larger dry goods and department stores. Wendy Gamber, *The Female Economy: The Millinery and Dressmaking Trades, 1860–1930* (Urbana: University of Illinois Press, 1997), p. 37 and chapter 7; Daily, "A Woman's Concern," p. 27.

128. Terry, *The Retailer's Manual*, pp. 382–383.

129. Edwin J. Perkins, "The Entrepreneurial Spirit in Colonial America: The Foundation of Modern Business History," *Business History Review* 63 (Spring 1989): 186; Mary A. Yeager, ed., *Women in Business,* vol. 1 (Cheltenham, U.K.: Edward Elgar, 1999), p. xvi.

130. Lewis's study of Albany, New York, found that even the most successful women-owned businesses rarely built up estates worth more than $20,000. Lewis, "Female Entrepreneurs in Albany, 1840–1885," p. 66.

131. Gamber, *The Female Economy,* pp. 12, 37.

132. Olegario, "Credit and Business Culture," pp. 233–234, 261. Gamber; *The Female Economy*, p. 159.
133. Gamber, "A Gendered Enterprise," p. 212.
134. Olegario, "Credit and Business Culture," pp. 262, 264.
135. Daily, "A Woman's Concern," p. 29.
136. See, for example, *Hunt's Merchants Magazine* 25 (August 1851): 262 and Matthew Hale Smith, *Successful Folks: How They Win: Illustrated in the Careers of Eight Hundred Eminent Men* (Hartford, Conn.: American Publishing, 1878), pp. 228–229.
137. Murphy, "Her Own Boss," pp. 174–176. Gamber makes the point that what constituted a "woman's" trade constantly shifted. Both women and men spent a great deal of energy articulating and defending gender distinctions that were essentially unstable. See Gamber, "A Gendered Enterprise."
138. See, for example, articles from a variety of journals reprinted in *Hunt's Merchants' Magazine* 11 (August 1844): 193; *Hunt's Merchants' Magazine* 23 (September 1850): 248; *Hunt's Merchants' Magazine* 25 (August 1851): 262; *Hunt's Merchants' Magazine* 33 (December 1855): 766.
139. Gamber, "A Precarious Independence," p. 71; and *The Female Economy*, p. 41. See also Murphy, "Business Ladies," pp. 81–82.
140. Susan Ingalls Lewis, "Beyond Horatia Alger: Breaking through Gendered Assumptions about Business 'Success' in Mid-Nineteenth-Century America," *Business and Economic History* 24, no. 1 (Fall 1995): 98–99. Gamber reports that in the nineteenth century, milliners were sometimes identified with prostitutes, which lent special urgency to the term "respectable." Gamber, "A Gendered Enterprise," pp. 211–212.
141. Peter R. Earling, *Whom To Trust: A Practical Treatise on Mercantile Credits* (Chicago: Rand, McNally, 1890), pp. 149–151. Lewis's investigation appears to confirm Earling's intuitive assertion. "If . . . one reserves the term entrepreneur for ventures that involved risk taking and gambling with financial resources, I have found no evidence that women in 19th century Albany could be considered entrepreneurial capitalists . . . There appears to be little risk taking—rather, a slow and steady return on a relatively small initial investment." Lewis, "Female Entrepreneurs in Albany, 1840–1885," p. 72. Edith Sparks reaches similar conclusions in her study of San Francisco business women. When other white-collar-wage jobs became more available in the early twentieth century, the proportion of women opting to go into business for themselves dropped. Edith Sparks, "Married Women and Economic Choice: Explaining Why Women Started Businesses in San Francisco between 1890 and 1930," *Business and Economic History* 28, no. 2 (Winter 1999): 287–300.
142. Lyle Dorsett, "Equality of Opportunity on the Urban Frontier: Access to Credit in Denver, Colorado Territory, 1858–1876," *Journal of the West* 18 (July 1979): 78. Dorsett speculates that the favorable reports on women may have been motivated by the desire of locals to retain morally upstanding women in the male-dominated territory.

143. Walker, *The History of Black Business in America*, p. 103. Walker calls slaves who hired out their time "businessmen" and argues that they should properly be considered entrepreneurs. See Juliet E. Walker, "Black Entrepreneurship: An Historical Inquiry," *Business and Economic History*, second series 12 (1983): 37–55.

144. For excerpts from court cases, see Walker, *The History of Black Business in America*, pp. 54, 58, 62–63, 67, 72. See also Daniel Horsmanden, *The New-York Conspiracy; or, A History of the Negro Plot . . . 1741–2* (New York: Negro Universities Press, 1969 [1744]) for evidence that many slaves in New York City were openly entrepreneurial and were granted a great deal of independence by their masters.

145. Walker, *The History of Black Business in America*, pp. xxiv, 126, 176–180. Walker argues that the rate of black entrepreneurship has not increased since the nineteenth century.

146. Walker, *The History of Black Business in America*, pp. 89, 93–94, 111, 112, 129, 148, 155, 156, 158, 159–60, 161, 162, 178.

147. Margaret J. Miller, "Credit Reporting Systems around the Globe: The State of the Art in Public Credit Registries and Private Credit Reporting Firms," in Margaret J. Miller, ed., *Credit Reporting Systems and the International Economy* (Cambridge, Mass.: MIT Press, 2003), p. 34.

148. In Britain, the signifiers of class (dress, personal appearance, and personal connections) played a much larger role than in the United States, particularly in consumer credit. Finn, *The Character of Credit*, pp. 292–293.

149. Max Weber, "The Protestant Sects and the Spirit of Capitalism," in *From Max Weber: Essays in Sociology*, trans. and ed. H. H. Gerth and C. Wright Mills (London: Routledge, 1991 [1948]), p. 303.

150. At least one early manual on consumer credit bureaus argued that having both positive and negative information was superior to one that confined itself to negative information only. See Hanes, *The Retail Credit and Adjustment Bureaus*, pp. 4–5, 10–11.

151. Margaret J. Miller, "Introduction," in Miller, *Credit Reporting Systems*, pp. 2, 8; Kevin Cowan and Jose De Gregorio, "Credit Information and Market Performance: The Case of Chile," in Miller, *Credit Reporting Systems*, p. 195; John M. Barron and Michael Staten, "The Value of Comprehensive Credit Reports: Lessons from the U.S. Experience," in Miller, *Credit Reporting Systems*, pp. 297, 304.

152 . Mercantile Agency, circular, Saint Louis office, 1851, Dun and Bradstreet Collection, in folder marked "Forms, Circulars, Letters." See also Sandage, *Born Losers*, p. 135.

153. Dun, Boyd & Co., circular, New York, January 2, 1860.

154. Alexander Armstrong, Manager, R. G. Dun & Co., circular, Chicago, June 1865, Dun and Bradstreet Collection, in folder marked "Forms, Circulars, Letters."

155. Dun, Boyd & Co., circular, New York, January 2, 1860.

156. Atherton, *The Frontier Merchant in Mid-America*, p. 40.
157. Bruce G. Carruthers and Wendy Nelson Espeland, "Accounting for Rationality: Double-Entry Bookkeeping and the Rhetoric of Economic Rationality," *American Journal of Sociology* 97, no. 1 (July 1991): 57–58.
158. Something of this idea was already present in the first known English text on bookkeeping, first published in 1543 and republished in 1588 as *A Breif Instruction and Maner how to Keepe Bookes of Accompts*. According to Craig Muldrew, the book asserts that riches were attained "not through the diligent recording of capital, but rather through the faithful observation of 'good fidelitie and credence faithfully observed and kept.' . . . Thus, the purpose of keeping good accounts was not to see how much 'capital' the merchant had at any one time, but rather to maintain his reputation for honesty and just dealing." Craig Muldrew, *The Economy of Obligation: The Culture of Credit and Social Relations in Early Modern England* (Basingstoke, U.K.: McMillan Press, 1998), p. 128.
159. Thomas Haskell, "Capitalism and the Origins of Humanitarian Sensibility," *American Historical Review* 90 (June 1985): 557–558.
160. Douglass C. North, *Institutions, Institutional Change, and Economic Performance* (New York: Cambridge University Press, 1990).

4. Jewish Merchants and the Struggle over Transparency

This chapter, with minor changes, is reprinted by permission of the *Business History Review*. Rowena Olegario, "That Mysterious People: Jewish Merchants, Transparency, and Community in Mid-Nineteenth Century America," *Business History Review* 73 (Summer 1999): 161–189. © 1999 by the President and Fellows of Harvard College.

1. Alice Kessler-Harris and others have urged business and economic historians to pay attention to the postmodern idea of the "other" as a way to better understand how apparently value-neutral economic ideas are in fact contested and constructed piecemeal, through imposition and accommodation. See "Ideologies and Innovation: Gender Dimensions of Business History," *Business and Economic History*, 2nd ser., 20 (1991): 48.
2. Leonard Dinnerstein argues that American anti-Semitism was founded not primarily on status anxiety or economic competition but on the hostility that Christians have historically felt towards Jews. See his *Anti-Semitism in America* (New York: Oxford University Press, 1994), p. xiii.
3. Stanley Chapman, *Merchant Enterprise in Britain: From the Industrial Revolution to World War I* (Cambridge: Cambridge University Press, 1992), pp. 45, 55–56.
4. In his study of anti-Semitism in American business, David A. Gerber looks at similar evidence but comes to different conclusions. See David A. Gerber, "Cutting Out Shylock: Elite Anti-Semitism and the Quest for Moral Order

in the Mid Nineteenth-Century American Market Place," *Journal of American History* 69 (December 1982): 615–637.

5. Howard M. Sachar, *A History of the Jews in America* (New York: Alfred A. Knopf, 1992), pp. 41, 42, 73; Bertram W. Korn, *American Jewry and the Civil War* (Philadelphia: Jewish Publication Society of America, 1951), pp. 1, 12; *Harvard Encyclopedia of American Ethnic Groups*, ed. Stephan Thernstrom (Cambridge, Mass.: Belknap Press, 1980), s.v. "Jews," p. 576; Steven Hertzberg, *Strangers within the Gate City: The Jews of Atlanta, 1845–1915* (Philadelphia: Jewish Publication Society of America, 1978), pp. 3, 16. For discussions of the problems that arise when using primary sources (such as the federal census) to study American Jews and some possible solutions, see Ira Rosenwaike, "Characteristics of Baltimore's Jewish Population in a Nineteenth-Century Census," *American Jewish History, Annual 1994* 82, nos. 1–4: 123–139; and Jonathan S. Mesinger, "Reconstructing the Social Geography of the Nineteenth-Century Jewish Community from Primary Statistical Sources," *American Jewish History* 72 (March 1983): 354–368.

6. Historians traditionally have depicted the Jewish migration to the United States as a three-stage process: the Iberian (Sephardic) Jews predominated from the colonial period to around 1820; the German Jews supplanted them from 1820 to around 1880; and then eastern European Jews came in mass numbers thereafter. Hasia Diner points out, however, that "German" has always been a problematic designation, because many so-called German Jews in fact had roots in eastern Europe. Diner argues that the Jewish migration from the 1820s through the 1920s can more accurately be considered "as a single movement that began in western Europe and moved gradually and unevenly to the east." Hasia R. Diner, *A Time for Gathering: The Second Migration, 1820–1880* (Baltimore, Md.: Johns Hopkins University Press, 1992), pp. 1–2, 49, 53, 232.

7. At the beginning of the nineteenth century, as much as 80 to 90 percent of all German Jewish families in Europe engaged in petty trade. Diner, *A Time for Gathering*, p. 11.

8. Marc L. Raphael, *Jews and Judaism in a Midwestern Community: Columbus, Ohio, 1840–1975* (Columbus: Ohio Historical Society, 1979), p. 10.

9. Diner, *A Time for Gathering*, p. 10; Bertram W. Korn, *American Jewry and the Civil War*, pp. 1, 12; *Harvard Encyclopedia of American Ethnic Groups*, p. 576; Louis J. Swichkow, "The Jewish Community of Milwaukee, Wisconsin, 1860–1870," *The Jewish Experience in America: Selected Studies from the Publications of the American Jewish Historical Society*, vol. 3: *The Emerging Community*, ed. Abraham J. Karp (New York: Ktav Publishing, 1969), p. 152; Lee S. Weissbach, "The Jewish Communities of the United States on the Eve of Mass Migration: Some Comments on Geography and Bibliography," *American Jewish History* 78 (September 1988): 83; Avraham Barkai, *Branching Out: German-Jewish Immigration to the United States, 1820–1914* (New York: Holmes and Meier, 1994), pp. 12–13.

10. Naomi W. Cohen, *Encounter With Emancipation: The German Jews in the United States, 1830–1914* (Philadelphia: Jewish Publication Society of America, 1984), p. 41; Weissbach, "The Jewish Communities of the United States on the Eve of Mass Migration," p. 89 .

11. Sachar, *A History of the Jews in America,* pp. 42, 86–87; *Harvard Encyclopedia of American Ethnic Groups,* pp. 576, 579.

12. Abram V. Goodman, "A Jewish Peddler's Diary," *Critical Studies in American Jewish History: Selected Articles from American Jewish Archives,* vol. 1 (New York: Ktav Publishing House, 1971), pp. 45–73.

13. Diner, *A Time for Gathering.* p. 56. Many Jews complained about the necessity of conducting trade on Saturday. Peddler Abraham Kohn found it difficult to observe the Jewish Sabbath and claimed that he was continually encouraged by well-meaning Gentiles to attend church on Sunday. Goodman, "A Jewish Peddler's Diary," pp. 70–71.

14. Elliott Ashkenazi, *The Business of Jews in Louisiana, 1840–1875* (Tuscaloosa: University of Alabama Press, 1988), p. 151. See also Gerald Tulchinsky, "'Said To Be A Very Honest Jew': The R. G. Dun Credit Reports and Jewish Business Activity in Mid-19th Century Montreal," *Urban History Review/Revue d'histoire urbaine* 18 (February 1990): 207; Clyde Griffen and Sally Griffen, *Natives and Newcomers: The Ordering of Opportunity in Mid-Nineteenth Century Poughkeepsie* (Cambridge, Mass.: Harvard University Press, 1978), pp. 122–123; Gerber, "Cutting Out Shylock," p. 631.

15. Olegario, "'That Mysterious People,'" pp. 168–169, contains examples from the R. G. Dun reports.

16. See, for example, *Hunt's Merchants' Magazine* 7 (August 1842): 182.

17. *Hunt's Merchants' Magazine* 26 (January 1852): 91–92.

18. Joseph Angell, *A Practical Summary of the Law of Assignments in Trust for the Benefit of Creditors* (Boston: Hilliard, Gray, 1835), p. 27; Tony A. Freyer, *Producers Versus Capitalists: Constitutional Conflict in Antebellum America* (Charlottesville: University Press of Virginia, 1994), pp. 20–21.

19. Paul Goodman, "The Emergence of Homestead Exemption in the United States: Accommodation and Resistance to the Market Revolution, 1840–1880," *Journal of American History* 80 (September 1993): 470–498; Linda E. Speth, "The Married Women's Property Acts, 1839–1865: Reform, Reaction, or Revolution?" in *Women and the Law,* vol. 2: *Property, Family and the Legal Profession,* ed. D. Kelly Weisberg (Cambridge, Mass.: Schenkman Publishing, 1982), pp. 69–91. For a history of the national bankruptcy laws, see Charles Warren, *Bankruptcy in United States History* (Cambridge, Mass.: Harvard University Press, 1935).

20. Stephen G. Mostov, "Dun and Bradstreet Reports as a Source of Jewish Economic History: Cincinnati, 1840–1875," *American Jewish History* 72 (March 1983): 350.

21. Ashkenazi, *The Business of Jews in Louisiana,* pp. 110–114.

22. Mostov, "Dun and Bradstreet Reports," 351–352.
23. Alejandro Portes, "Economic Sociology and the Sociology of Immigration: A Conceptual Overview," in *The Economic Sociology of Immigration: Essays on Networks, Ethnicity, and Entrepreneurship*, ed. Alejandro Portes (New York: Russell Sage Foundation, 1995), p. 29.
24. Rachel E. Kranton and Anand V. Swamy, "The Hazards of Piecemeal Reform: British Civil Courts and the Credit Market in Colonial India," *Journal of Development Economics* 58 (February 1999): 1–24.
25. Stanley Elkins and Eric McKitrick, "A Meaning for Turner's Frontier, Part I: Democracy in the Old Northwest," *Political Science Quarterly* 69 (September 1954): 341. There is a large literature on town building and boosterism during the nineteenth century. See especially Carl Abbott, *Boosters and Businessmen: Popular Economic Thought and Urban Growth in the Antebellum Middle West* (Westport, Conn.: Greenwood Press, 1981); Harry Scheiber, "Urban Rivalry and Internal Improvements in the Old Northwest, 1820–1860," *Ohio History* 71 (October 1962): 227–239; J. Schnell, J. Cristopher, and Katherine B. Clinton, "The New West: Themes in Nineteenth Century Urban Promotion," *Bulletin of the Missouri Historical Society* 30 (January 1974): 75–88; and David Hamer, *New Towns in the New World: Images and Perceptions of the Nineteenth-Century Urban Frontier* (New York: Columbia University Press, 1990).
26. Reprinted in *Hunt's Merchants' Magazine* 24 (May 1851): 648–649.
27. *Hunt's Merchants' Magazine* 24 (January 1851): 47–48. Emphasis in the original.
28. Lewis Tappan, quoted in James D. Norris, *R. G. Dun & Co., 1841–1900: The Development of Credit-Reporting in the Nineteenth Century* (Westport, Conn.: Greenwood Press, 1978), p. 22.
29. Olegario, "'That Mysterious People,'" p. 174, contains examples from the R. G. Dun reports.
30. Gerber, "Cutting Out Shylock," p. 624; John Higham, *Send These to Me: Immigrants in Urban America*, rev. ed. (Baltimore, Md.: Johns Hopkins University Press, 1984 [1975]), p. 158; Diner, *A Time for Gathering*, pp. 144–145, 149. See also Louise A. Mayo, *The Ambivalent Image: Nineteenth-Century America's Perception of the Jew* (Rutherford, N.J.: Fairleigh Dickinson University Press, 1988), pp. 112–113.
31. A typical example of this genre is John C. Power, *History of Springfield, Illinois: Its Attractions as a Home and Advantages for Business, Manufacturing, Etc.* (Springfield: Illinois State Journal Print, 1871).
32. *Harvard Encyclopedia of American Ethnic Groups*, p. 577; Mostov, "Dun and Bradstreet Reports," pp. 341–346.
33. Weissbach, "The Jewish Communities on the Eve of Mass Migration," pp. 83, 88–89; Griffen and Griffen, *Natives and Newcomers*, pp. 122–123; Peter R. Decker, "Jewish Merchants in San Francisco: Social Mobility on the Urban Frontier," *American Jewish History* 68 (June 1979): 405; Hertzberg,

Strangers within the Gate City, p. 143; Raphael, *Jews and Judaism in a Mid-western Community,* p. 48.

34. *Niles' Weekly Register* 7 (October 21, 1820): 114; Decker, "Jewish Merchants in San Francisco," p. 397; Diner, *A Time for Gathering,* p. 151.

35. Olegario, "'That Mysterious People,'" p. 174; Hertzberg, *Strangers within the Gate City,* p. 20. Hertzberg points out that the Southern Mutual Insurance Company's Atlanta agent, Adoph J. Brady, was Jewish.

36. Ashkenazi, *The Business of Jews in Louisiana,* pp. 62, 165.

37. Gerber, "Cutting Out Shylock," pp. 627–629.

38. Hertzberg, *Strangers within the Gate City,* p. 141. See also Ashkenazi, *The Business of Jews in Louisiana,* pp. 150–151.

39. Diner, *A Time for Gathering,* p. 47; Sachar, *A History of the Jews in America,* pp. 39–40; Hertzberg, *Strangers within the Gate City,* pp. 37–41.

40. David Jaffee, "Peddlers of Progress and the Transformation of the Rural North, 1760–1860," *Journal of American History* 78 (September 1991): 522; Diner, *A Time for Gathering,* p. 68; Higham, *Send These to Me,* p. 114; Oliver B. Pollak, "The Jewish Peddlers of Omaha," *Nebraska History* 63 (Winter 1982): 474–501.

41. Raphael, *Jews and Judaism in a Midwestern Community,* pp. 35–36; *Harvard Encyclopedia of American Ethnic Groups,* p. 576; Barkai, *Branching Out,* pp. 45, 56–57.

42. *Hunt's Merchants' Magazine* 26 (May 1852), p. 649.

43. Jaffee, "Peddlers of Progress," pp. 531–532, 533. Fears surrounding Jewish peddlers resulted in an 1851 California licensing law. See Ann Loftis, *California: Where the Twain Did Meet* (New York: Macmillan, 1973), p. 116. After the Civil War many states enacted laws regulating commercial travelers (traveling salesmen). See Timothy Spear, *100 Years on the Road: The Traveling Salesman in American Culture* (New Haven, Conn.: Yale University Press, 1995), pp. 70–77.

44. Paul E. Johnson, *A Shopkeeper's Millennium: Society and Revivals in Rochester, New York, 1815–1837* (New York: Hill and Wang, 1978); Don H. Doyle, *The Social Order of a Frontier Community: Jacksonville, Illinois, 1825–1870* (Urbana: University of Illinois Press, 1978), pp. 111–112; Jaffee, "Peddlers of Progress," p. 532. In his study of "associational" market values during the antebellum period, Tony Freyer observes that Jews in the community were often equated with outside capitalists. Freyer, *Producers Versus Capitalists,* pp. 75–76.

45. Rumors circulated that Jews committed arson to collect the insurance money. See Cohen, *Encounter With Emancipation,* pp. 25–26; and Dinnerstein, *Anti-Semitism in America,* pp. 36–37, 57. For the prejudices that existed among insurance companies in Britain, see Robin Pearson, "Moral Hazard and the Assessment of Insurance Risk in Eighteenth- and Early-Nineteenth-Century Britain," *Business History Review* 76 (Spring 2002): 1–35.

46. Samuel H. Terry, *The Retailer's Manual* (Newark, N.J.: Jennings Bros., 1869), pp. 159–160.
47. Mostov, "Dun and Bradstreet Reports," pp. 336–337; Griffen and Griffen, *Natives and Newcomers*, p. 104.
48. Mostov, "Dun and Bradstreet Reports," pp. 336–337.
49. Ashkenazi, *The Business of Jews in Louisiana*, pp. 117–118; Tulchinsky, "'Said To Be A Very Honest Jew,'" pp. 206–207.
50. Roger D. Waldinger, *Through the Eye of the Needle: Immigrants and Enterprise in New York's Garment Trades* (New York: New York University Press, 1986), p. 30.
51. Olegario, "'That Mysterious People,'" pp. 183–184, contains examples from the R. G. Dun reports. See also Mostov, "Dun and Bradstreet Reports," p. 349.
52. For an example of a Jewish firm in Springfield, Illinois, whose appraisals improved markedly between 1856 and 1868, see Olegario, "'That Mysterious People,'" pp. 184–185.
53. The treatment of Jews in the German states during the first half of the nineteenth century, when they were culturally and legally regarded as a separate people, was far different. Cohen, *Encounter With Emancipation*, p. 6; Raphael, *Jews and Judaism in a Midwestern Community*, pp. 13–14; Diner, *A Time for Gathering*, pp. 15–16.
54. Mayo, *The Ambivalent Image*, pp. 91, 112–113, 120.
55. Gerber, "Cutting Out Shylock," p. 623; Sachar, *A History of the Jews in America*, p. 53; Tony Fels, "Religious Assimilation in a Fraternal Organization: Jews and Freemasonry in Gilded Age San Francisco," *American Jewish History* 74 (June 1985): 376.
56. Sachar, *A History of the Jews in America*, p. 70; Barkai, *Branching Out*, pp. 105–106; Diner, *A Time for Gathering*, p. 110.
57. Diner, *A Time for Gathering*, p. 3; David A. Gerber, "Introduction," in *Anti-Semitism in American History*, ed. David A. Gerber (Urbana: University of Illinois Press, 1986), p. 18.
58. Raphael, *Jews and Judaism in a Midwestern Community*, pp. 43–44; Clyde Griffen, "Making It in America: Social Mobility in Mid-Nineteenth Century Poughkeepsie," *New York History* 51 (October 1970): 491; Decker, "Jewish Merchants in San Francisco," p. 403; Hertzberg, *Strangers within the Gate City*, pp. 151–152; Cohen, *Encounter With Emancipation*, p. 30.
59. For the reasons behind the intensified anti-Semitism that occurred beginning in the last decades of the nineteenth century, see Dinnerstein, *Anti-Semitism in America*.
60. R. T. Ettinger and D. E. Golieb, *Credits and Collections* (New York: Prentice-Hall, 1917), pp. 166–167.
61. Gerber, "Cutting Out Shylock."

5. Growth, Competition, Legitimacy

1. Edwin T. Freedley, *A Practical Treatise on Business* (Philadelphia: Lippincott, Grambo, 1853 [1852]), p. 129.

2. Roy A. Foulke, *The Sinews of American Commerce* (New York: Dun and Bradstreet, 1941), pp. 157–159. For a description of credit terms for different lines of goods at the beginning of the twentieth century, see Peter P. Wahlstad, *Credit and the Credit Man* (New York: Alexander Hamilton Institute, 1917), chapter 10.

3. Bill R. Moeckel, *The Development of the Wholesaler in the United States, 1860–1900* (Garland Publishing, 1986), p. 150; National Wholesale Druggists Association, *A History of the National Wholesale Druggists Association* (New York: National Wholesale Druggists Association, 1924), p. 50; Proceedings of the Annual Convention of the National Association of Credit Men (hereafter NACM), 1897, typewritten document, scrapbook ledger, NACM Archives, Columbia, Md. (hereafter cited as NACM Archive).

4. Moeckel, *The Development of the Wholesaler,* pp. 147–148. For cash discounts, see Herman E. Krooss and Martin R. Blyn, *A History of Financial Intermediaries* (New York: Random House, 1971), p. 72; and J. H. Tregoe, *Credit and Its Management* (New York: Harper and Brothers, 1930), p. 32.

5. The greater reliance on single-name paper led to a decline in "real bills," the traditional IOUs that buyers gave to sellers, which the latter could discount at a bank. Because single-name paper was not backed by a commercial transaction but purely by the borrower's reputation, it drastically curtailed the ability of banks to assess their customers' creditworthiness. This assessment now devolved increasingly upon the note brokers. Naomi R. Lamoreaux, *Insider Lending: Banks, Personal Connections, and Economic Development in Industrial New England* (Cambridge: Cambridge University Press, 1994), pp. 89–90.

6. William H. Maher, *On the Road to Riches: Practical Hints for Clerks and Young Business Men* (Chicago: J. Fred Waggoner, 1878), p. 200. Book credit lost some of its perceived riskiness when the first finance company specializing in accounts receivable was organized in Chicago in 1904. After nearly a year of operation, the company was incorporated as the Mercantile Credit Company of Chicago. Earlier finance companies had purchased installment accounts for items such as pianos and farm equipment. Foulke, *The Sinews of American Commerce,* pp. 196–197.

7. Susan Strasser, *Satisfaction Guaranteed: The Making of the Mass Market* (New York: Pantheon Books, 1989), pp. 61–62.

8. Roger L. Ransom and Richard Sutch, *One Kind of Freedom: The Economic Consequences of Emancipation* (Cambridge: Cambridge University Press, 1977), p. 121.

9. Moeckel, *The Development of the Wholesaler,* p. 12; Paul B. Trescott, *Financ-*

ing American Enterprise: The Story of Commercial Banking (New York: Harper and Row, 1963), p. 64; U.S. Bureau of the Census, *Historical Statistics of the United States, Colonial Times to 1957* (Washington, D.C.: Government Printing Office, 1960), chapters P, Q, R, and X. The index rose again after 1896; it was at 150 by 1913. Gilbert C. Fite and Jim E. Reese, *An Economic History of the United States*, 3rd ed. (Boston: Houghton Mifflin, 1973), pp. 302–303. Exceptions to the downward trend in prices occurred in 1871–1872 and again in 1878–1882. After 1886 fluctuations in prices were no longer violent, and prices began to rise in 1896. Moeckel, *The Development of the Wholesaler*, pp. 61–62, 191.

10. Moeckel, *The Development of the Wholesaler*, pp. 34–35, 38, 67, 70–71, 74, 94–104, 118, 181. See also Walter Friedman, *Birth of a Salesman: The Transformation of Selling in America* (Cambridge: Harvard University Press, 2004), pp. 58–59.

11. Maher, *On the Road to Riches*, p. 150.

12. Foulke, *The Sinews of American Commerce*, pp. 158–159.

13. Fite and Reese, *An Economic History of the United States*, p. 321. By about 1860, wholesaling and retailing became separate functions. Moeckel, *The Development of the Wholesaler*, p. 3.

14. Harold Barger, *Distribution's Place in the American Economy Since 1869* (Princeton, N.J.: Princeton University Press, 1955), table B-4, p. 131; Frank G. Coolsen, *Marketing Thought in the United States in the Late Nineteenth Century* (Lubbock: Texas Tech Press, 1960), p. 17, note 23. The census of 1890 was the first to distinguish between wholesale and retail merchants, but no breakdown by cities is furnished in the tables of occupations until the census of 1900. Moeckel, *The Development of the Wholesaler*, pp. 66–67.

15. Peter R. Earling, *Whom to Trust: A Practical Treatise on Mercantile Credit* (Chicago: Rand, McNally, 1890), p. 118.

16. Ransom and Sutch demonstrate that these storekeepers took on the credit role previously filled by cotton factors. The storekeepers' presence limited the spread of rural banks in that region. Ransom and Sutch, *One Kind of Freedom*, p. 122 and chapter 7.

17. Strasser, *Satisfaction Guaranteed*, chapter 5.

18. Ralph M. Hower, *History of Macy's of New York, 1858–1919: Chapters in the Evolution of the Department Store* (Cambridge, Mass.: Harvard University Press, 1946), p. 96. See also William Leach, *Land of Desire: Merchants, Power, and the Rise of a New American Culture* (New York: Pantheon Books, 1993).

19. George B. Hotchkiss, *Milestones of Marketing* (New York: MacMillan, 1938), pp. 191–196. Historians disagree about which retailer can claim to be the first true department store. Hower states that the New York City firms of Lord and Taylor and R. H. Macy and Company became the first American department stores in the 1870s. Hower, *History of Macy's*, pp. 144–145.

20. Wayland A. Tonning, "The Beginnings of the Money-Back Guarantee and the One-Price Policy in Champaign-Urbana, Illinois, 1833–1880," *Business History Review* 30 (June 1956): 202–204.

21. Moeckel, *The Development of the Wholesaler,* pp. 133–141, 213–221. See also Glenn Porter and Harold Livesay, *Merchants and Manufacturers: Studies in the Changing Structure of Nineteenth-Century Marketing* (Baltimore, Md.: Johns Hopkins University Press, 1971) and Strasser, *Satisfaction Guaranteed,* chapter 5.

22. Friedman, *Birth of a Salesman,* pp. 86–87.

23. Moeckel, *The Development of the Wholesaler,* pp. 223, 229.

24. James W. Kimball, *The Dry-Goods Jobbers* (Boston: Commercial Agency, n.d. [1865–1880?]), pp. 13,16.

25. Maher, *On the Road to Riches,* pp. 191, 196–199.

26. Proceedings of the Annual Convention of the NACM, Kansas City, June 1897, typewritten document, scrapbook ledger, NACM Archives.

27. Earling, *Whom to Trust,* pp. 124–125, 209. In 1912 the NACM's Committee on Credit Department Methods urged creditors to be less indulgent of debtors who abused credit terms. Report of Committee on Credit Department Methods (pamphlet), in Proceedings of the Annual Convention of the NACM, 1912, NACM Archives.

28. Wayland A. Tonning, "Department Stores in Down State Illinois, 1889–1943," *Business History Review* 29 (December 1955): 341–342.

29. Strasser, *Satisfaction Guaranteed,* pp. 76–77; Moeckel, *The Development of the Wholesaler,* p. 150.

30. Earling, *Whom to Trust,* pp. 101–102.

31. Strasser, *Satisfaction Guaranteed,* pp. 227, 239, 241–242.

32. T. J. Zimmerman, "Commercial Agency Ratings and Methods," in *Credits, Collections, and Finance: Organizing the Work, Correct Policies and Methods; Five Credit and Collection Systems* (Chicago: A. W. Shaw, 1914), pp. 37–38.

33. Dun, Barlow & Co., circular, February 7, 1874, Dun and Bradstreet Collection in folder marked "Forms, Circulars, Letters" Baker Library, Harvard Business School (hereafter cited as Dun and Bradstreet Collection). See also Zimmerman, "Commercial Agency Ratings and Methods," p. 40.

34. Alfred M. Lee, *Daily Newspaper in America: The Evolution of a Social Instrument* (New York: MacMillan, 1937), pp. 63–65.

35. Lewis Atherton, *Main Street on the Middle Border* (New York: Quadrangle / New York Times Book Company, 1975 [1954]), pp. 165, 167.

36. [E. St. E. Lewis], ed. *The Credit Man and His Work* (Detroit, Mich.: Book-Keeper Publishing, 1904), p. 191.

37. Charles F. Clark, quoted in Foulke, *The Sinews of American Commerce,* p. 349.

38. Currently, accounts receivable make up from 20 to 60 percent of a company's assets. Ian Edmonds, "Winds of Change," *Business Credit,* May 1998, p. 60.

39. Peter Earling warned that "in these cases you are trusting, not alone to the

man's honor, but also to the good will and friendly feeling of the mortgagee toward his and your debtor." Earling, *Whom to Trust*, p. 154.

40. Ibid., pp. 40, 175–177.

41. Blank form, Bradstreet Mercantile Agency, Portland, Oregon, office, 1890s, in possession of the author.

42. William Y. Chinn, *The Mercantile Agencies against Commerce* (Chicago: Charles H. Kerr, 1896), pp. 255–256.

43. Earling, *Whom to Trust*, p. 24. See also Foulke, *The Sinews of American Commerce*, p. 337.

44. Gary Previts and Barbara Merino, *A History of Accounting in America: An Historical Interpretation of the Cultural Significance of Accounting* (New York: John Wiley and Sons, 1979), pp. 81, 88–89.

45. Samuel H. Terry, *The Retailer's Manual* (Newark, N.J.: Jennings Bros., 1869), p. 92.

46. Ibid., pp. 94–95, 251, 256.

47. Gerald Carson, *The Old Country Store* (New York: Oxford University Press, 1954), p. 107.

48. Terry, *The Retailer's Manual*, pp. 37–39, 106.

49. Even today, many small private businesses decline to provide financial information to credit-reporting firms. The problem is especially acute in fragmented industries such as construction, in which small private firms dominate. Journals serving credit professionals often comment on this problem. See, for example, "Is Customer Bankruptcy a Surprise? Comments from a *Business Credit* Roundtable," *Business Credit*, October 1998, pp. 36, 38; "Credit Managers Talk Technology: Q&A from a *Business Credit* Roundtable," *Business Credit*, January 1999, pp. 54–57.

50. Foulke, *The Sinews of American Commerce*, pp. 335–336; Dun, Barlow & Co., *Report of Important Cases against the Mercantile Agency* (New York: Dun, Barlow, 1877), p. 74.

51. Zimmerman, "Commercial Agency Ratings and Methods," pp. 37–39.

52. Dun, Barlow & Co., *Report of Important Cases against the Mercantile Agency*, p. 112. See also the testimony of W. T. Pridham, a reporter for the Buffalo, New York, office, p. 111, and that of Henry E. Moffatt, city reporter for John McKillop and Company, a competitor firm, pp. 116–117. Moffatt's testimony implies that the practices of the two agencies were similar, indicating that Paul's description of the procedures he followed were typical in the industry. The report of this case consisted of the judge's notes, in which he summarized and paraphrased the witnesses' statements.

53. Clark W. Bryan, *Credit: Its Meaning and Moment* (New York: Bradstreet Press, 1883), p. 14.

54. Dun, Barlow & Co., *Report of Important Cases against the Mercantile Agency*, pp. 83–90. Emphasis added.

55. Ibid., pp. 83–90.

56. Ibid.

57. Earling, *Whom To Trust*, p. 117.

58. R. G. Dun & Co., advertisement [1871 or 1872?], Dun and Bradstreet Collection, in folder marked "Sales Contracts." Both R. G. Dun and Bradstreet continued to insist on the superiority of discursive reports rather than tabulated ones until well into the twentieth century. See, for example, National Association of Credit Men, Report on the Mercantile Agency and Credit Co-operation Committee (pamphlet), in Minutes of the Thirteenth Annual Convention, 1908, NACM Archives. On the importance of character traits over capital rating, see [The Credit Bureau], *Credit Guide: Standard on Third, Wall and State Streets*, vol. 5 (Philadelphia: Credit Bureau, 1879). The firm soon dissolved and continued as Brock's Register of Desirable Customers and Depositors.

59. Letter from Charles Clark to the NACM, June 3, 1899, Proceedings of the Annual Convention of the NACM, 1899, scrapbook ledger, NACM Archives.

60. Advertisement in R. G. Dun and Co., *The Mercantile Agency United States Business Directory for 1867* (New York, 1867). See also the arguments made by R. G. Dun's counsel in *Gibson v. R. G. Dun*, in Dun, Barlow & Co., *Report of Important Cases Against the Mercantile Agency*, pp. 84–85. British creditors were urged by the National Association of Trade Protection Societies to make a similar distinction between character and capital. Previous failure did not automatically brand an individual as a bad credit risk. Margo Finn, *The Character of Credit: Personal Debt in English Culture, 1740–1914* (Cambridge: Cambridge University Press, 2003), pp. 300, 304–305.

61. [The Credit Bureau], *Credit Guide: Standard on Third, Wall and State Streets*, vol. 5, no page indicated.

62. Judy Hilkey, *Character Is Capital: Success Manuals and Manhood in Gilded Age America* (Chapel Hill: University of North Carolina Press, 1997), p. 27.

63. Karen Halttunen, *Confidence Men and Painted Women; A Study of Middle-Class Culture in America, 1830–1870* (New Haven, Conn.: Yale University Press, 1982), pp. 203–205.

64. Hilkey, *Character Is Capital*, p. 127.

65. Maher, *On the Road to Riches*, p. 125.

66. Earling, *Whom To Trust*, pp. 42–53. See also Dorr A. Kimball, "The Credit Department of Modern Business," in *Lectures on Commerce, Delivered Before the College of Commerce and Administration of the University of Chicago*, ed. Henry R. Hatfield (Chicago: University of Chicago Press, 1904), pp. 222–223; B. H. Blanton, *Credit, Its Principles and Practice* (New York: Ronald Press, 1915), p. 46.

67. Thomas F. Meagher, *The Commercial Agency "System" of the United States and Canada Exposed: Is the Secret Inquisition a Curse or a Benefit?* (New York, 1876), pp. 12–13.

68. Earling, *Whom To Trust*, p. 51.

69. Ibid., pp. 104, 153–156, emphasis added. British legislation exhibited a sim-

ilar tendency to favor debtors, leading the National Association of Trade Protection Societies to claim that "character is now much more regarded by prudent traders than legal facilities for the recovery of debts." National Association of Trade Protection Societies, annual report, 1868, quoted in Finn, *The Character of Credit*, p. 299. The problem of state exemption laws continued to frustrate creditors. In 1917 the NACM's Committee on Amendments to Exemption Laws described them as "so rooted and grounded within some of the states that desirable changes . . . are seemingly unattainable." Proceedings of the Annual Convention of the NACM, 1917, in *Bulletin of the NACM* (August 1917).

70. Moeckel, *The Development of the Wholesaler,* p. 157.
71. Earling, *Whom To Trust,* pp. 143–146.
72. James E. Hagerty, *Mercantile Credit* (New York: Henry Holt, 1913), p. 60. See also James G. Cannon's remarks, Minutes of the first Annual Convention of the NACM (pamphlet), Toledo, Ohio, June 23, 1896, scrapbook ledger, NACM Archives.
73. R. G. Dun & Co., circular, March 16, 1866, in Owen Sheffield, "The Mercantile Agency . . . A Private History," 4 vols. (Dun and Bradstreet, unpublished manuscript, 1965), Dun and Bradstreet Collection, IV-8, pp. 3–4.
74. James D. Norris, *R. G. Dun & Co., 1841–1900: The Development of Credit-Reporting in the Nineteenth Century* (Westport, Conn.: Greenwood Press, 1978), pp. 93–94; David G. Burley, " 'Good for all he would ask': Credit and Debt in the Transition to Industrial Capitalism—The Case of Mid-Nineteenth Century Brantford, Ontario," *Histoire Sociale—Social History* 20, no. 39 (May 1987): 79–99. Credit manuals and the agencies themselves continued to insist on the importance of character traits. See Chapter 6.
75. R. G. Dun & Co., circular, Hartford office, December 1871, Dun and Bradstreet Collection, in folder marked "Notification Sheets (Changes)."
76. *The New England Business Directory and Gazetteer,* no. 12 (Boston: Sampson, Davenport, 1885). See also *The Commercial Agency Reports on the Wool and Cotton Dealers and Manufacturers in the United States and Canada* (New York: Commercial Agency, 1884).
77. Chinn, *The Mercantile Agencies against Commerce,* pp. 50–51.
78. Norris, *R. G. Dun & Co.,* pp. 113–115, 122.
79. Ibid., pp. 112, 121.
80. Foulke, *The Sinews of American Commerce,* p. 298. See also James H. Madison, "The Evolution of Commercial Credit Reporting Agencies in Nineteenth Century America," *Business History Review* 48 (Summer 1974): 164–186, especially 182–185.
81. Norris, *R. G. Dun & Co.,* pp. 67–68, 115–120.
82. Edward N. Vose, *Seventy-Five Years of the Mercantile Agency: R. G. Dun & Co., 1841–1916* (New York: R. G. Dun, 1916), p. 108.
83. Sheffield, "The Mercantile Agency," vol. 1, sec. 2, p. 23. Afterwards, the firm appears to have returned to a policy of self-sufficiency for all branches.

See Proceedings of the Annual Convention of the NACM, Detroit, Michigan, June 22–24, 1898, in scrapbook ledger, NACM Archives.

84. Foulke, *The Sinews of American Commerce,* p. 336; Proceedings of the Convention of the NACM, Detroit, Michigan, June 22–24.

85. Quoted in Foulke, *The Sinews of American Commerce,* p. 336.

86. Foulke, *The Sinews of American Commerce,* p. 318.

87. Norris, *R. G. Dun & Co.,* pp. 43, 106, 108, 115, 157, 163; Foulke, *The Sinews of American Commerce,* p. 295; Bryan, *Credit: Its Meaning and Moment,* p. 26. See also Proceedings of the Annual Convention of the NACM, 1897.

88. Ransom and Sutch calculated that R. G. Dun covered some 90 percent of all stores in the cotton South during the 1870s and 1880s. Ransom and Sutch, *One Kind of Freedom,* pp. 132, 313–314.

89. John M. Keese, J. M. Bradstreet & Son, circular [1871?] Dun and Bradstreet Collection, in folder marked "Bradstreet Co.; Contracts, Letters, Miscellaneous."

90. John McKillop & Co., circular, Philadelphia, March 1874, Dun and Bradstreet Collection, in folder marked "Tappan Family."

91. Letter from Charles Clark to National Association of Credit Men, June 3, 1899, in Proceedings of the Annual Convention of the National Association of Credit Men, 1899, scrapbook ledger, NACM Archives.

92. R. G. Dun & Co., circular, November 1875, Dun and Bradstreet Collection, in folder marked "Forms, Circulars, Letters."

93. Information on the 1874 edition comes from Norris, *R. G. Dun & Co.,* p. 111. In an 1873 circular, R. G. Dun claimed that the reference book contained "nearly 700,000 names." Dun, Barlow & Co., circular, New York, March 1873, Dun and Bradstreet Collection, in folder marked "Forms, Circulars, Letters."

94. R. G. Dun & Co., circular, New York, July 2, 1873.

95. Proceedings of the Annual Convention of the NACM, 1897.

96. Dun, Barlow & Co., circular, New York, December 1871, Dun and Bradstreet Collection, in folder marked "Forms, Circulars, Letters."

97. *Chicago Times,* reprinted by R. G. Dun & Co., c. 1870s, Dun and Bradstreet Collection, in folder marked "Forms, Circulars, Letters."

98. Norris, *R. G. Dun & Co.,* p. 189, note 68. See also Vose, *Seventy-Five Years of the Mercantile Agency,* p. 96, and James H. Madison, "The Evolution of Commercial Credit Reporting Agencies in Nineteenth-Century America," *Business History Review* 48 (Summer 1974): 175.

99. Norris, *R. G. Dun & Co.,* p. 144; Previts and Merino, *A History of Accounting in the United States,* p. 134; Foulke, *The Sinews of American Commerce,* p. 374; JoAnne Yates, *Control Through Communication: The Rise of System in American Management* (Baltimore, Md.: Johns Hopkins Press, 1989), pp. 39–45.

100. R. G. Dun & Co., manual, quoted in Vose, *Seventy-Five Years of the Mercantile Agency,* p. 126.

101. Norris, *R. G. Dun & Co.*, pp. 140–141.

102. Chinn, *The Mercantile Agencies against Commerce*, pp. 50–51.

103. Foulke, *The Sinews of American Commerce*, p. 315.

104. Norris, *R. G. Dun & Co.*, pp. 111, 113.

105. R. G. Dun & Co., advertisement for reference book [1871 or 1872?], Dun and Bradstreet Collection, in folder marked "Sales Contracts"; Bryan, *Credit: Its Meaning and Moment*, pp. 30–31.

106. *Chicago Times*, reprinted by R. G. Dun & Co.; Bryan, *Credit: Its Meaning and Moment*, pp. 21–23.

107. Norris, *R. G. Dun & Co.*, pp. 111–113.

108. Foulke, *The Sinews of American Commerce*, pp. 323–326.

109. Dun, Barlow & Co., circular, New York, Jan. 29, 1875, Dun and Bradstreet Collection, in folder marked "Failures." The compilations did not include railroad or bank failures. See also Norris, *R. G. Dun & Co.*, p. 90.

110. Dun, Barlow & Co., circular, n.d., Dun and Bradstreet Collection, in folder marked "Failures."

111. Dun, Barlow & Co., circular, New York, March 6, 1873, Dun and Bradstreet Collection, in folder marked "Forms, Circulars, Letters"; R. G. Dun & Co., circular, no date, Dun and Bradstreet Collection, in Folder marked "Forms, Circulars, Letters."

112. Norris, *R. G. Dun & Co.*, p. 129.

113. Bryan, *Credit: Its Meaning and Moment*, p. 20.

114. *Bradstreet's Book of Commercial Ratings of Bankers, Merchants, Manufacturers, etc., in the United States and the Dominion of Canada*, vol. 36 (New York: Bradstreet Co., 1875); [The Credit Bureau], *Credit Guide: Standard on Third, Wall and State Streets*, vol. 5 (1879), no page indicated.

115. *Chicago Times*, reprinted by R. G. Dun & Co.

116. Ransom and Sutch, *One Kind of Freedom*, p. 313.

117. Maher, *On the Road to Riches*, pp. 226–228.

118. *Chicago Times*, reprinted by R. G. Dun & Co.

119. Frederick B. Goddard, *Giving and Getting Credit: A Book for Business Men* (New York: F. Tennyson Neely, 1896), pp. 134–135.

120. Proceedings of the Annual Convention of the NACM, Detroit, Michigan, June 22–24, 1898.

121. J. M. Bradstreet & Son, circular, Richmond, October 2, 1873, Dun and Bradstreet Collection, in folder marked "Bradstreet Co.; Contracts, Letters, Miscellaneous."

122. [Dun, Barlow & Co.], *Reports of the Four Leading Cases Against the Mercantile Agency for Slander and Libel* (New York: Dun, Barlow, 1873), p. 260.

123. *Dry Goods Bulletin*, April 15, 1879.

124. *Toronto Mail*, December 9, 1975, quoted in Meagher, *The Commercial Agency "System,"* pp. 157–158. For a more ambivalent appraisal of the agencies by another Toronto journal, see the *Monetary Times*, October 24, 1867.

The *Times* also criticized the agencies as "an organized system of espionage and inquisition" but acknowledged that "to refuse to legalize them may be restricting injuriously the right of enquiring into the character and standing of the customer asking for credit in his business transactions."

125. Bryan, *Credit: Its Meaning and Moment,* p. 13.

126. Earling, *Whom To Trust,* pp. 300–302. The uniquely American nature of the institution continued to fascinate credit practitioners and scholars. Surveying the field in 1913, marketing professor James Hagerty observed that in Europe the kind of investigations conducted by American credit-reporting agencies were monopolized by the state. Private agencies existed, but their information was not as complete. He added that the right of private agencies in Europe to consult government records was restricted, whereas in the United States, "records have always been open to the inspection of the public within reasonable limits." James E. Hagerty, *Mercantile Credit,* p. 140.

127. Norris, *R. G. Dun & Co.,* p. 126.

128. Meagher, *The Commercial Agency "System,"* p. 169.

129. Ibid., pp. 56, 60, 71–72, 110–111, 114–115, 117, and chapter 12 generally.

130. Ibid., chapters 16, 18.

131. Chinn, *The Mercantile Agencies against Commerce,* pp. 111–112, 147, 157.

132. Ibid., pp. 123–128, 135.

133. Ibid., pp. 201–202.

134. Earling, *Whom To Trust,* pp. 32–33.

135. Joseph W. Errant, *The Law Relating to Mercantile Agencies, Being the Johnson Prize Essay of the Union College of Law for the Year 1886* (Philadelphia: T. and J. W. Johnson, 1889), pp. 24–26.

136. In 1870 Dun's counsel, Charles O'Conor, estimated that some twenty suits had been brought against R. G. Dun. [Dun, Barlow & Co.], *Reports of the Four Leading Cases Against the Mercantile Agency,* pp. 189–190.

137. Quoted in Errant, *The Law Relating to Mercantile Agencies,* pp. 38–39. British mutual protection societies faced similar litigation. In the case of *Macintosh v. Dun* (Privy Council, 1908), the London Association for the Protection of Trade argued that "as a Mutual Association, our members were entitled to require from us communications containing information, circulated *bona fide* and without malice, concerning the financial position and credit reliability of any firm that they were interested in and that so long as our members regarded the Communications as confidential neither they nor ourselves were liable to an action for libel. This was a definite claim clear cut and easily understood but one that we regarded as vital to our future." Quoted in C. McNeil Greig, *The Growth of Credit Information: A History of UAPT-Infolink plc.* (Oxford: Blackwell Publishers, 1992), p. 133.

138. See Errant, *The Law Relating to Mercantile Agencies.*

139. [Dun, Barlow & Co.], *Reports of the Four Leading Cases Against the Mercantile Agency,* p. 302.

140. Errant, *The Law Relating to Mercantile Agencies,* pp. 28–30, 40.
141. See, for example, R. G. Dun & Co., contract dated 1870s, Dun and Brad-street Collection, in folder marked "Sales Contracts."
142. See, for example, *M'Cready's Credit Register for Retail Dealers and Country Store Merchants,* 2nd New England ed. (Boston: Alfred Mudge and Son, 1884), p. iii.
143. Dun, Barlow & Co., circular, New York, July 21, 1874, Dun and Bradstreet Collection, in folder marked "Forms, Circulars, Letters." See also Letter, M. P. Stacey of Philadelphia office to Dun, Barlow & Co., circulated by Dun, Barlow & Co., July 24, 1874, Dun and Bradstreet Collection, in folder marked "Forms, Circulars, Letters."
144. R. G. Dun & Co., circular, Hartford office, December 1871.
145. Dun, Barlow & Co., circular, March 5, 1881, Dun and Bradstreet Collection, in folder marked "Notification Sheets."
146. "Report of the Mercantile Agency and Credit Co-operation Committee" (pamphlet), in Minutes of the Thirteenth Annual Convention of the NACM, Denver, June 23–26, 1908, scrapbook ledger, NACM Archives.
147. Goddard, *Giving and Getting Credit,* 131–132.

6. From Competition to Cooperation

1. Alfred D. Chandler, *The Visible Hand: The Managerial Revolution in American Business* (Cambridge, Mass.: Harvard University Press, 1977); Glenn Porter and Harold Livesay, *Merchants and Manufacturers: Studies in the Changing Structure of Nineteenth-Century Marketing* (Baltimore, Md.: Johns Hopkins University Press, 1971). See also Robert H. Wiebe, *The Search for Order, 1877–1920* (New York: Hill and Wang, 1967); Martin J. Sklar, *The Corporate Reconstruction of American Capitalism, 1890–1916: The Market, the Law, and Politics* (Cambridge: Cambridge University Press, 1988), pp. 20–33.
2. Nathan O. Hatch, ed., *The Professions in American History* (Notre Dame, Ind.: University of Notre Dame Press, 1988), p. 6.
3. Gary J. Previts and Barbara D. Merino, *A History of Accounting in America: An Historical Interpretation of the Cultural Significance of Accounting* (New York: Wiley, 1979), pp. 135, 138–139, 177, 188, 229.
4. In its circular of July 1915, the Federal Reserve Board defined a trade acceptance as "a bill of exchange drawn to order having a definite maturity and payable in dollars in the United States, the obligation to pay which has been accepted by an acknowledgment, written or stamped, and signed, across the face of the instrument, by the company, firm, corporation or person upon whom it is drawn." The acceptor of the draft or bill agreed to pay at maturity without any qualifying conditions. Charles A. Mayer, *Mercantile Credits and Collections* (New York: Macmillan, 1919), pp. 89–91. Although the

trade acceptance was used extensively in foreign export trade, the vast majority of domestic commercial credit in the United States continued to be carried in the form of open book accounts. "The Use of Credit in Export Trade, Address by Dr. E. E. Pratt," Proceedings of the Annual Convention of the National Association oi Credit Man (hereafter NACM), *Bulletin of the NACM* 17 (August 1917): 711–719. The *Bulletin* became the *Credit Monthly* in April 1920.

5. Roy A. Foulke, *The Sinews of American Commerc* (New York: Dun and Bradstreet, 1941), p. 316. The new brokerages securitized the accounts receivable of businesses and traded the securities on the market. Banks that may have been reluctant to loan money directly on accounts receivable became more willing to do so when they were securitized by these brokerages. L. Galloway and R. S. Butler, *Advertising, Selling and Credits,* 3rd ed. (New York: Alexander Hamilton Institute, 1912), pp. 514–515.

6. [E. St. E. Lewis], ed., *The Credit Man and His Work* (Detroit, Mich.: Book-Keeper Publishing, 1904), p. 296.

7. Editors of the Modern Business Series, *Credit and the Credit Man, Modern Business,* vol. 8 (New York: Alexander Hamilton Institute, 1919), pp. 168–169.

8. Edward M. Skinner, "Essentials in Credit Management," in *Credits, Collections, and Finance: Organizing the Work, Correct Policies and Methods; Five Credit and Collection Systems* (Chicago: A. W. Shaw, 1914), p. 14. For a history of credit analysis considered as part of the marketing function, see Robert Bartels, *The History of Marketing Thought,* 2nd ed. (Columbus, Ohio: Grid, 1976).

9. Minutes of the First National Convention of Credit Men, Toledo, Ohio, June 23, 1896, scrapbook ledger, National Association of Credit Men Archives, Columbia, Md. (hereafter cited as NACM Archives); George R. Barclay, "Address," in *Proceedings of the Twenty-Fifth Annual Convention of the National Association of Credit Men, Held at Atlantic City, N.J., June 1–5, 1920* (Park Row, N.Y.: NACM, 1920), p. 31.

10. Minutes of the Meeting of the Board of Administration of the NACM, September 20, 1897, New York City, scrapbook ledger, NACM Archives; William A. Prendergast, *Credit and Its Uses* (New York: D. Appleton—Century, 1906), pp. 334–335; R. T. Ettinger and D. E. Golieb, *Credits and Collections* (New York: Prentice-Hall, 1917), p. 376; "Strength through the Years: 100 Years of NACM History" (NACM, 1996).

11. NACM, *Laws Regulating the Sale of Stocks of Goods in Bulk,* 4th ed. (New York: National Association of Credit Men [1906?]); Proceedings at the Second Annual Convention of the NACM, Kansas City, June 9–11, 1897, scrapbook ledger, NACM Archives; Minutes of the Board of Administration of the NACM, 1899, scrapbook ledger, NACM Archives; Minutes of the Annual Meeting of the Board of Directors of NACM, Saint Louis, Mo., De-

cember 10, 1900, scrapbook ledger [no title on ledger], NACM Archives; President's Annual Address, 1901, Minutes of the Executive Committee of the NACM, 1897–1902, scrapbook ledger, NACM Archives; Minutes of the Meeting of the Board of Directors of NACM, Chicago, November 24, 1902, scrapbook ledger, NACM Archives; Barclay, "Address," p. 32.

12. Minutes of the First National Convention of Credit Men, June 23, 1896; Peter R. Earling, *Whom To Trust: A Practical Treatise on Mercantile Credits* (Chicago: Rand, McNally, 1890).

13. Walter A. Friedman, *Birth of a Salesman: The Transformation of Selling in America* (Cambridge, Mass.: Harvard University Press, 2004), pp. 159–160.

14. "Report of Committee on Credit Education and Management" (pamphlet), in Proceedings of the Nineteenth Annual Convention of the NACM, Rochester, N.Y., June 23–26, 1914, scrapbook ledger, NACM Archives.

15. Hatch, *The Professions in American History*, p. 2. See also Burton J. Bledstein, *The Culture of Professionalism: The Middle Class and the Development of Higher Education in America* (New York: Norton, 1976).

16. Prendergast, *Credit and Its Uses*, pp. 334–335, emphasis added.

17. James E. Hagerty, *Mercantile Credit* (New York: Henry Holt, 1913), pp. 106–107.

18. Prendergast, *Credit and Its Uses*, pp. 108–109.

19. See B. H. Blanton, *Credit, Its Principles and Practice* (New York: Ronald Press, 1915); William Prendergast, "Address," in *Proceedings of the Twenty-Fifth Annual Convention of the National Association of Credit Men Held at Atlantic City, N.J., June 1–5, 1920* (Park Row, N.Y.: 1920), p. 27.

20. Proceedings of the Second Annual Convention of the NACM, Kansas City, June 9–11, 1897; Reports of President and Secretary, Proceedings of the Convention of the NACM, Detroit, Michigan, June 22–24, 1898, scrapbook ledger, NACM Archives; Minutes of the Board of Administration of the NACM, 1899 [erroneously marked 1897], scrapbook ledger, NACM Archives; Minutes of the Annual Meeting of the Board of Directors of NACM, December, 1900.

21. Previts and Merino, *A History of Accounting in America*, pp. 116, 184–186.

22. Minutes of the Meeting of the Board of Administration of the NACM, Kansas City, June 1897, scrapbook ledger, NACM Archives.

23. Blanton, *Credit, Its Principles and Practice*, p. 92; Herman Flatau, "Financial Statements, Their Form and Analysis," in M. Martin Kallman, Alfred K. Care, et al., *Mercantile Credits: A Series of Practical Lectures* (New York: Ronald Press, 1914), pp. 82–84; Ettinger and Golieb, *Credits and Collections*, pp. 202–203. The NACM urged credit reporting agencies to retain the stamped envelopes containing financial statements, as proof that they were sent through the mail. "Report of the Mercantile Agency Committee" (pamphlet), in Proceedings of the Seventeenth Annual Convention of the NACM, Boston, Mass., June 18–21, 1912, scrapbook ledger, NACM Archives.

24. James O. Horrigan, ed., *Financial Ratio Analysis: An Historical Perspective* (New York: Arno Press, 1978), p. 285.
25. Previts and Merino, *A History of Accounting in America,* p. 230.
26. Minutes of the Board of Administration of the NACM, 1899.
27. Naomi R. Lamoreaux, *Insider Lending: Banks, Personal Connections, and Economic Development in Industrial New England* (Cambridge: Cambridge University Press, 1994), p. 103. According to banker Alexander Wall, the 50 percent rule evolved out of long usage rather than "any analytical study." Alexander Wall, "New System for Analysis of Financial Statements," *Credit Monthly* 22 (November 1920), pp. 9–12, 20.
28. Sister Isadore Brown, "The Historical Development of the Use of Ratios in Financial Statement Analysis to 1933," The Catholic University of America, Studies in Economics, Abstract Studies, vol. 2, Washington, D.C., 1955, pp. 11–12, reprinted in Horrigan, *Financial Ratio Analysis; Bulletin of the NACM* 2 (May 5, 1902): 32. Later in the twentieth century, ratios would be used to compare a company's statistics over time and with those of other firms in its industry. During this earlier period, however, businesses typically kept statements for only one year before discarding them.
29. Flatau, "Financial Statements, Their Form and Analysis," pp. 65–66. See also [E. St. E. Lewis], *The Credit Man and His Work,* p. 206; Editors of the Modern Business Series, *Credit and the Credit Man,* pp. 100–101; Hagerty, *Mercantile Credit,* p. 104.
30. Blank form, Bradstreet Mercantile Agency, Portland, Oregon, office, 1890s, in possession of the author.
31. Request for financial statement, endorsed by NACM, reprinted in Peter P. Wahlstad, *Credit and the Credit Man* (New York: Alexander Hamilton Institute, 1917), p. 79.
32. "Letter from Charles Clark to the National Association of Credit Men, June 3, 1899," Proceedings of the Fourth Annual Convention of the NACM, Buffalo, New York, June 6–8, 1899, scrapbook ledger, NACM Archives.
33. Hagerty, *Mercantile Credit,* p. 106.
34. W. C. Mushet, "Audits and Investigations," in M. Martin Kallman, Alfred K. Care, et al., *Mercantile Credits: A Series of Practical Lectures* (New York: Ronald Press, 1914), p. 121.
35. Howard R. Huse, "Wholesale Credits and Collections," in *Credits, Collections and Finance* (Chicago: A. W. Shaw, 1914), p. 73. See also Flatau, "Financial Statements, Their Form and Analysis," p. 76.
36. Wahlstad, *Credit and the Credit Man,* pp. 202–203.
37. Emphasis in original. Robert H. Montgomery, *The Fallibility of Unverified Financial Statements: An Address Before the National Association of Credit Men at the Annual Convention, Cincinnati, June 19, 1913* (New York: Lybrand, Ross Bros. [1913?]), p. 8.
38. "Report of Credit Department Methods Committee," in Proceedings of the

Annual Convention of the NACM, 1901 and 1912, scrapbook ledgers, NACM Archives.

39. "R. G. Dun's Reply, Report of the Mercantile Agency and Credit Co-operation Committee" (pamphlet), Minutes of the Thirteenth Annual Convention of the NACM, Denver, June 23–26, 1908, scrapbook ledger, NACM Archives. Full reports did, however, indicate when a business owner refused to provide a statement. See "Report of the Mercantile and Credit Co-operation Committee" (pamphlet), in Minutes of the Fifteenth Annual Convention of the NACM, New Orleans, May 17–19, 1910, scrapbook ledger, NACM Archives.

40. Skinner, "Essentials in Credit Management," pp. 16–17; Prendergast, *Credit and Its Uses,* p. 203; "Report of the Committee on Credit Co-operation" (pamphlet) in Proceedings of the Seventeenth Annual Convention of the NACM, June 18–21, 1912.

41. Wahlstad, *Credit and the Credit Man,* pp. 117–118, 131–132.

42. See, for example, Huse, "Wholesale Credits and Collections," p. 67; Skinner, "Essentials in Credit Management," pp. 16–17; Wahlstad, *Credit and the Credit Man,* p. 96.

43. Wahlstad, *Credit and the Credit Man,* pp. 91–93; Ettinger and Golieb, *Credits and Collections,* pp. 159, 166–167.

44. See, for example, Skinner, "Essentials in Credit Management," pp. 16–17; Frederick B. Goddard, *Giving and Getting Credit: A Book for Business Men* (New York: F. Tennyson Neely, 1896), p. 20; Wahlstad, *Credit and the Credit Man,* p. 97; [E. St. E. Lewis], *The Credit Man and His Work,* p. 201. One credit man compared American banks to those in France, which carried much fuller files that "could almost be compared to the records in a foreign detective office." Blanton, *Credit, Its Principles and Practice,* p. 72.

45. Hagerty, *Mercantile Credit,* pp. 104, 139, 142, 167–168; Ettinger and Golieb, *Credits and Collections,* pp. 175–176.

46. J. Smith Homans and J. Smith Homans Jr., *A Cyclopedia of Commerce and Commercial Navigation,* 2nd ed., vol. 2 (New York: Harper and Brothers, 1859), pp. 1344–1345. See also William H. Maher, *On the Road to Riches: Practical Hints for Clerks and Young Business Men* (Chicago: J. Fred Waggoner, 1878), pp. 119–120.

47. Joseph W. Errant, *The Law Relating to Mercantile Agencies, Being the Johnson Prize Essay of the Union College of Law for the Year 1886* (Philadelphia: T. and J. W. Johnson, 1889), p. 39.

48. Friedman, *Birth of a Salesman,* p. 66.

49. Huse, "Wholesale Credits and Collections," pp. 67–68. See also Ettinger and Golieb, *Credits and Collections,* pp. 159, 166–167.

50. Harry Futterman, "Credit and the Alien Melting Pot," *Credit Monthly* 22 (September 1920): 17.

51. Proceedings at the Second Annual Convention of the NACM, June 9–11,

1897; *Membership List of the NACM as of July 1, 1898* (published member-ship directory), NACM Archive; President's Annual Address, 1901; Report of the Secretary, 1901, Minutes of the Executive Committee of the NACM, 1897–1902, scrapbook ledger NACM Archives.

52. Minutes of the Meeting of the Board of Administration of the NACM, September 20, 1897; Proceedings of the Convention of the NACM, June 22–24, 1898.

53. Minutes of the Board of Administration of the NACM, 1899.

54. Minutes of the Meeting of the Board of Directors of the NACM, November 24, 1902.

55. Minutes of the Executive Committee of the NACM, 1899.

56. "Speech of W. N. Finley," Proceedings at the Second Annual Convention, 1897.

57. Ibid.; Minutes of the Executive Committee of the NACM, 1897–1902.

58. Margo Finn, *The Character of Credit: Personal Debt in English Culture, 1740–1914* (Cambridge: Cambridge University Press, 2003), pp. 294–297, 314–315.

59. Hagerty, *Mercantile Credit*, p. 140.

60. These trade protection societies have not been well researched. See "Credit Reporting Unions: Report of United States Consul J. C. Monaghan," Proceedings of the Second Annual Convention of the NACM, June 9–11, 1897.

61. Minutes of the First National Convention of Credit Men, 1896; Bill R. Moeckel, *The Development of the Wholesaler in the United States, 1860–1900* (New York: Garland Publishing, 1986), p. 146; Meeting of the Board of Directors of NACM, 1900; Proceedings of the Annual Convention of the NACM, *Bulletin of the NACM* 4 (July 1, 1904): 72; Proceedings of the Annual Convention of the NACM, *Bulletin of the NACM* 17 (August 1917): 759–769; Editors of the Modern Business Series, *Credit and the Credit Man*, pp. 111, 204; Marcus M. Marks, *Credit Cooperation: An Address Delivered at a Dinner of the New York Credit Men's Association, April 25th, 1901* (New York: Powers Press [1901?]). (Marks was President of the National Association of Clothiers.)

62. *Bulletin of the NACM* 5 (July 15, 1905): 84; Wahlstad, *Credit and the Credit Man*, pp. 105–115, 131–132. A few attempts were made to organize retailers' interchanges for the sharing of consumer credit information. This type of information became more widely available after World War II. Maher, *On the Road to Riches*, p. 229; [E. St. E. Lewis], *The Credit Man and His Work*, pp. 209, 212–213; *Bulletin of the NACM* 5 (July 15, 1905): 85.

63. Galloway and Butler, *Advertising, Selling and Credits*, pp. 557–558. See also Wahlstad, *Credit and the Credit Man*, pp. 124–125.

64. See, for example, Minutes of the Executive Committee of the NACM, 1899.

65. Annual Report of the Secretary, Minutes of the Executive Committee of the NACM, 1897–1902.

66. *Bulletin of the NACM* 2 (July 5, 1902): 36.

67. *Bulletin of the NACM* 2 (November 5, 1902): 20–23.

68. Ibid., 37–40.

69. Reports of the President and Secretary, Proceedings of the Convention of the NACM, June 22–24, 1898; "Report of the Mercantile Agency and Credit Co-operation Committee" (pamphlets) in Minutes of the Annual Convention of the NACM, 1908 and 1910, scrapbook ledgers, NACM Archives.

70. Minutes of the Executive Committee of the NACM, 1899; Meeting of the Board of Directors of NACM, 1902. Complaints about abuse of the interchange system continued for many years. See, for example, "Report of Committee of Credit Cooperation" and "The Interchange of Ledger Information: Its Uses and Abuses, Address by Vernon Hall," Proceedings of the Annual Convention of the NACM, *Bulletin of the NACM* 17 (August 1917): 582–594.

71. Minutes of the Meeting of the Board of Directors of NACM, November 24, 1902.

72. Minutes of the Meeting of the Executive Committee of the NACM, 1899, scrapbook ledger, NACM Archives.

73. Minutes of the Meeting of the Board of Directors of the NACM, November 24, 1902.

74. [E. St. E. Lewis], *The Credit Man and His Work,* p. 191.

75. *Bulletin of the NACM* 2 (April 5, 1902): 7–9.; Ettinger and Golieb, *Credits and Collections,* p. 137; Wahlstad, *Credit and the Credit Man,* p. 128.

76. "Report of the Committee on The Improvement of Commercial Agency Service," Proceedings at the Second Annual Convention of the NACM, June 9–11, 1897; *Bulletin of the NACM* 2 (March 5, 1902): 20–26; Editors of the Modern Business Series, *Credit and the Credit Man,* p. 134.

77. Wahlstadt, *Credit and the Credit Man,* pp. 125–127.

78. Blanton, *Credit, Its Principles and Practice,* pp. 99–100.

79. Editors of the Modern Business Series, *Credit and the Credit Man,* pp. 134–135.

80. *Bulletin of the NACM* 2 (March 5, 1902): 20–26; *Bulletin of the NACM* 2 (November 5, 1902): 37–40.

81. "Report of the Committee on Improvement of Mercantile Agency Service," Proceedings of the Convention of the NACM, June 22–24, 1898; *Bulletin of the NACM* 2 (March 5, 1902): 20–26.

82. *Bulletin of the NACM* 2 (April 5, 1902): 7–9.

83. *Bulletin of the NACM* 2 (May 5, 1902): 12–13.

84. *Bulletin of the NACM* 2 (April 5, 1902): 7–9.

85. Meeting of Board of Directors, Chicago, November 25, 1901, scrapbook ledger, NACM Archives.

86. Wahlstad, *Credit and the Credit Man,* pp. 124–125, 128–131. Recent research suggests that reporting both positive and negative information is opti-

mal. See John M. Barron and Michael Staten, "The Value of Comprehensive Credit Reports: Lessons from the U.S. Experience," in *Credit Reporting Systems and the International Economy,* ed. Margaret J. Miller, (Cambridge, Mass.: MIT Press, 2003), pp. 273–310.

87. Editors of the Modern Business Series, *Credit and the Credit Man,* pp. 129, 131.
88. *Bulletin of the NACM* 4 (July 1, 1904): 67–77.
89. "Report of the Mercantile Agency and Credit Co-operation Committee" (pamphlets) in Minutes of the Annual Convention of NACM, 1908 and 1910.
90. "The Use of Credit in Export Trade," Proceedings of the Annual Convention of the NACM, *Bulletin of the NACM* 18 (July 1918): 732.
91. L. R. Browne, "Making the World Safe for the Credit Man," *Credit Monthly* 22 (April 1920): 23–24.
92. Ibid.
93. "The National Association of Credit Men, A Builder of Conscience and Commerce," *Credit Monthly* 22 (April 1920): 24b.
94. E. B. Moran, "The Credit Interchange Bureaus: How They will Operate to Give Nation-Wide Clearance," *Credit Monthly* 22 (May 1920): 31–32. See also "Strength through the Years: 100 Years of NACM History."
95. "Report of Credit Department Methods Committee," Proceedings of the Sixth Annual Convention, Cleveland, Ohio, June 12–13, 1901, scrapbook ledger, NACM Archives.
96. Prendergast, *Credit and Its Uses,* p. 206.
97. Mayer, *Mercantile Credits and Collections,* pp. 57–58.
98. Foulke, *The Sinews of American Commerce,* p. 295.
99. Wahlstad, *Credit and the Credit Man,* pp. 98–99.
100. *Bulletin of the NACM* 5 (July 15, 1905): 55.
101. [E. St. E. Lewis], *The Credit Man and His Work,* pp. 196–197. Until about 1910, the agencies also continued to send weekly lists of changes to subscribers.
102. Wahlstad, *Credit and the Credit Man,* pp. 98–100.
103. "Report of the Mercantile Agency and Credit Co-operation Committee" (pamphlets), Minutes of the Annual Convention of the NACM, 1908 and 1912. See also Blanton, *Credit, Its Principles and Practice,* p. 82; Hagerty, *Mercantile Credit,* 156–157.
104. Proceedings of the Convention of the NACM, June 22–24, 1898.
105. See, for example, Hagerty, *Mercantile Credit,* p. 63; Blanton, *Credit, Its Principles and Practice,* pp. 84–85; Wahlstad, *Credit and the Credit Man,* pp. 100–104; T. J. Zimmerman, "Commercial Agency Ratings and Methods," *Credits, Collections, and Finance: Organizing the Work, Correct Policies and Methods; Five Credit and Collection Systems* (Chicago: A. W. Shaw, 1914), p. 32; *Bulletin of the NACM* 2 (May 5, 1902): 31–36.
106. Flatau, "Financial Statements, Their Form and Analysis," pp. 65–66.
107. [E. St. E. Lewis], *The Credit Man and His Work,* pp. 199, 207.

108. Proceedings of the Convention of the NACM, June 22–24, 1898. See also Hagerty, *Mercantile Credit,* 156–157; *Bulletin of the NACM* 2 (May 5, 1902): 31–36; *Bulletin of the NACM* 2 (November 5, 1902): 37.

109. *Bulletin of the NACM* 5 (July 15, 1905): 58–59; Minutes of the Meeting of the Board of Directors of the NACM, Chicago, October 23, 1905, scrapbook ledger, NACM Archives.

110. Proceedings of the Convention of the NACM, June 22–24, 1898.

111. Minutes of the Meeting of the Executive Committee of the NACM, 1899.

112. "Report of the Mercantile Agency Committee" (pamphlet), Proceedings of the Seventeenth Annual Convention of the NACM, June 18–21, 1912.

113. "Report of the Committee on the Improvement of Commercial Agency Service," Proceedings of the Second Annual Convention of the NACM, June 9–11, 1897. See also Minutes of the Meeting of the Executive Committee of the NACM, 1899; Minutes of the Annual Meeting of the Board of Directors of the NACM, December 10, 1900; *Bulletin of the NACM* 2 (July 5, 1902): 28–35.

114. Proceedings at the Second Annual Convention of the NACM, June 9–11, 1897. NACM president William Prendergast later agreed that there were "a great many from whom it would be a waste of time to solicit statements, and idle to consider them if obtained, such as people of small means, saloon keepers, newsdealers, milliners, and others, whose unfamiliarity with business methods is self-evident." Prendergast, *Credit and Its Uses,* p. 199.

115. Proceedings of the Convention of the NACM, June 22–24, 1898. See also Hagerty, *Mercantile Credit,* 139.

116. "Proposed address to the Commercial Agencies," Proceedings at the Second Annual Convention of the NACM, June 9–11, 1897; Blanton, *Credit, Its Principles and Practice,* pp. 84–85; Ettinger and Golieb, *Credits and Collections,* pp. 186–187.

117. "Report of Committee on Mercantile Agencies and Credit Co-operation" (pamphlet), in Minutes of the Fifteenth Annual Convention of the NACM, May 17–19, 1910.

118. Proceedings at the Second Annual Convention of the NACM, June 9–11, 1897.

119. Minutes of the Meeting of the Executive Committee of the NACM, 1899; Proceedings of the Annual Convention of the NACM, *Bulletin of the NACM* 18 (July 1918): 638–639.

120. *Bulletin of the NACM* 5 (July 15, 1905): 56.

121. Proceedings at the Second Annual Convention of the NACM, June 9–11, 1897.

122. *Bulletin of the NACM* 2 (November 5, 1902): 37–38; *Bulletin of the NACM* 5 (July 15, 1905): 56–57; Galloway and Butler, *Advertising, Selling and Credits,* pp. 557–558; [E. St. E. Lewis], *The Credit Man and His Work,* pp. 205, 218–219.

123. *Bulletin of the NACM* 5 (July 15, 1905): 58.

124. "Report of Committee on Mercantile Agencies and Credit Co-operation" (pamphlet), Minutes of the Fifteenth Annual Convention of the NACM, May 17–19, 1910.

125. Proceedings of the Convention of the NACM, June 22–24, 1898; Minutes of Meeting of the Board of Directors of the NACM, November 24, 1902.

126. Minutes of the Meeting of the Executive Committee of the NACM, 1899; Meeting of the Board of Directors of the NACM, 1900 and 1902.

127. Proceedings of the Convention of the NACM, June 22–24, 1898.

128. Bulletin of the NACM 2 (July 5, 1902): 29.

129. Proceedings of the Second Annual Convention of the NACM, June 9–11, 1897.

130. James W. Kimball, The Dry-Goods Jobbers (Boston: Commercial Agency [1865–1880?], p. 26.

131. Ettinger and Golieb, Credits and Collections, pp. 331–332.

132. Kimball, The Dry-Goods Jobbers, p. 26.

133. In England, only bankruptcy could guarantee that all creditors were treated equitably. However, to avoid the expense of bankruptcy proceedings, creditors and debtors often resorted to "compositions," a forerunner of the American adjustment bureau. Compositions were generally seen as more efficient than bankruptcy proceedings, provided the debtor acted in good faith and all creditors cooperated, which was not always the case. Julian Hoppit, Risk and Failure in English Business, 1700–1800 (Cambridge: Cambridge University Press, 1987), p. 30.

134. "The Workings of the Portland Merchants' Protective Union," Proceedings of the Sixth Annual Convention of the NACM, Cleveland, Ohio, June 12–13, 1901, scrapbook ledger, NACM Archives.

135. Proceedings of the Annual Convention of the NACM, Bulletin of the NACM 8 (July 15, 1908): 400; "Report of the Adjustment Bureau Committee" (pamphlet), Minutes of the Thirteenth Annual Convention of the NACM, June 23–26, 1908.

136. F. C. DeLano, "Amicable Adjustment with Insolvent Debtors," in M. Martin Kallman, Alfred K. Care, et al., Mercantile Credits: A Series of Practical Lectures (New York: Ronald Press, 1914), p. 197; "The Workings of the Portland Merchants' Protective Union"; "Report of the Adjustment Bureau" (pamphlet), Proceedings of the Seventeenth Annual Convention of NACM, June 18–21, 1912, and "Value of Adjustment Bureaus, Address by F. B. McComas," Proceedings of the Seventeenth Annual Convention of NACM, June 18–21, 1912.

137. See, for example, Proceedings of the Annual Convention of the NACM, Bulletin of the NACM 17 (August 1917): 679–687.

138. Proceedings of the Annual Convention of the NACM, Bulletin of the NACM 8 (July 15, 1908), p. 400; "Report of the Adjustment Bureau Committee" (pamphlet), Minutes of the Thirteenth Annual Convention of the NACM, June 23–26, 1908.

139. Proceedings of the Twenty-Fourth Annual Convention of the NACM, Detroit, Michigan, June 10–13, 1919, scrapbook ledger, NACM Archives.

140. Minutes of the Meeting of the Board of Directors of NACM, Saint Louis, Mo., June 11, 1903, scrapbook ledger, NACM Archives.

141. Proceedings of the Convention of the NACM, June 22–24, 1898. See also Minutes of the Meeting of the Board of Directors of the NACM, November 24, 1902.

142. Blanton, *Credit, Its Principles and Practice,* pp. 184–185.

143. Minutes of the Meeting of the Board of Administration of the NACM, September 20, 1897.

144. In 1904 the total funds of the local associations were designated as the "national" fund. Minutes of the Meeting of the Executive Committee of the NACM, 1899; Meeting of the Board of Directors of NACM, 1902 and 1904.

145. "Report of the Investigation and Prosecution Committee" (pamphlet), Minutes of the Thirteenth Annual Convention of the NACM, June 23–26, 1908.

146. Montgomery, *The Fallibility of Unverified Financial Statements,* p. 5.

147. M. Martin Kallman, "System and Efficiency in the Credit Department," in M. Martin Kallman, Alfred K. Care, et al. *Mercantile Credits: A Series of Practical Lectures* (New York: Ronald Press, 1914), p. 18. There are numerous instances where character was emphasized above capital and business ability. See, for example, Prendergast, *Credit and Its Uses,* pp. 221–224; T. J. Zimmerman, "The Function and Work of the Commercial Agency," in *Credits and Collections: The Factors Involved and the Methods Pursued in Credit Operations,* ed. T. J. Zimmerman (Chicago: System Co., 1904, reprinted 1910), p. 48; President's Annual Address, Minutes of the Executive Committee of the NACM, 1897–1902; Dorr A. Kimball, "The Credit Department of Modern Business," in *Lectures on Commerce Delivered Before the College of Commerce and Administration of the University of Chicago,* ed. Henry R. Hatfield (Chicago: University of Chicago Press, 1904), p. 222; Ettinger and Golieb, *Credits and Collections,* pp. 92–95, 249–250; Skinner, "Essentials in Credit Management," pp. 14–15; David R. Forgan, President, National City Bank of Chicago, and Vice President, Chicago Clearing House, in Edward M. Skinner, *Credits, Collections and Finance: Organizing the Work, Correct Policies and Methods; Five Credit and Collection Systems* (Chicago: A. W. Shaw, 1914), p. 65; Blanton, *Credit, Its Principles and Practice,* p. 46; *Bulletin of the NACM* 2 (May 5, 1902): 32, 35–36.

148. Hagerty, *Mercantile Credit,* pp. 59–60.

149. Ettinger and Golieb, *Credits and Collections,* p. 308.

150. Reprinted in Wahlstad, *Credit and the Credit Man,* p. 79.

Epilogue

1. National Association of Credit Management (hereafter NACM), www.nacm .org (2001). Of course, trade creditors often rely on bank loans as the basis for their own credit granting. Large manufacturers and wholesalers, for example, can borrow from banks at an advantageous rate to finance sales and credit. The precise historical relationship between bank credit and mercantile credit has not been systematically studied. See Carl Rieser, "The Great Credit Pump," *Fortune* (February 1963): 122–124, 148–157.

2. U.S. Federal Reserve Board, *Flow of Funds Accounts of the United States* (Washington, D.C., 2006), tables L. 102, D. 3.

3. Official statistics do not treat credit-reporting agencies as a separate category, so it is difficult to find a total industry figure. Industry analysts agreed, however, that Dun and Bradstreet accounted for a large majority of the total industry. In September 2000, Dun and Bradstreet spun off its Moody's credit-rating subsidiary into a separate publicly traded company. Its 2000 annual report restated the revenues of previous years to make them compatible.

4. www.dnb.com (2000); The World Bank, *World Development Report 2002: Building Institutions for Markets* (New York: Oxford University Press, 2002), p. 58.

5. Dun & Bradstreet, annual report, 1997, frontispiece.

6. According to J. H. Tregoe, secretary-treasurer of the NACM during the early 1920s, women credit practitioners had become "an established institution" by 1920. See J. H. Tregoe, "Women Who Check Credits," *Credit Monthly* 22, no. 5 (June 1920): 17–19.

7. NACM, "Strength Through the Years: 100 Years of NACM History, 1896–1996"; and NACM, "Strength in Numbers" (brochure no date), NACM Archives, Columbia, Md.

8. Much of this section, particularly the recent information on Dun and Bradstreet, is based on Jarl K. Kallberg and Gregory F. Udell, "Private Business Information Exchange in the United States," in *Credit Reporting Systems and the International Economy,* ed. Margaret J. Miller (Cambridge, Mass.: MIT Press, 2003).

9. Ibid.

10. This is in contrast to the bond-rating institutions, Moody's and Standard & Poor, which have far greater power to influence the allocation of credit. See Timothy J. Sinclair, "Reinventing Global Authority: Embedded Knowledge Networks and the New Global Finance," *Environment and Planning C: Government and Policy 2000* 18: 487–502; and "Evaluating the Bond-Rating Agencies," *Financial Times,* May 27, 1997.

11. See, for example, the directories of credit-reporting firms produced by private information providers, Creditworthy and Creditsafe (U.K.). No study has yet determined how market share is divided among the large international firms and smaller, locally owned and managed agencies.

12. Joyce R. Ochs and Kenneth L. Parkinson, "Using Credit Screening to Manage Credit Risk," *Business Credit* (March 1998): 22, 24–27; Jeff Brill, "The Importance of Credit Scoring Models in Improving Cash Flow and Collections," *Business Credit* (January 1998): 16–17; Michael G. Ash, "Analyzing Credit Information: What You See Isn't Always What You Get," *Business Credit* (March 1996): 7–8.
13. See, for example, "Online Credit-Rating Reports Are Not Always Credible," *Los Angeles Times*, August 19, 1998, sec. D, p. 6.
14. Until the explosion of bank credit cards, retailers provided the vast majority of consumer credit. See Lendol Calder, *Financing the American Dream: A Cultural History of Consumer Credit* (Princeton, N.J.: Princeton University Press, 1999); Martha L. Olney, *Buy Now, Pay Later: Advertising, Durables, and Consumer Credit in the 1920s* (Chapel Hill: University of North Carolina Press, 1991); Robert M. Hunt, "The Development and Regulation of Consumer Credit Reporting in America" (working paper no. 02–21, Federal Reserve Board of Philadelphia, November 2002). For an early manual on how to set up a consumer credit bureau, see C. O. Hanes, *The Retail Credit and Adjustment Bureaus: Their Organization and Conduct* (Columbia, Mo.: C. O. Hanes, 1915). Hanes was secretary of the Retail Merchants' Association.
15. NACM, newsletter, n.d., at www.nacm.org (2000).
16. Ibid.
17. "Tagging Deadbeats is Big Business," *Crain's Chicago Business*, November 18, 1996, p. 15; John M. Barron and Michael Staten, "The Value of Comprehensive Credit Reports: Lessons from the U.S. Experience," in *Credit Reporting Systems and the International Economy*, ed. Margaret J. Miller (Cambridge, Mass.: MIT Press, 2003), pp. 273, 289–299; Raphael W. Bostic and Paul S. Calem, "Privacy Restrictions and the Use of Data at Credit Registries," in *Credit Reporting Systems and the International Economy*, ed. Margaret J. Miller (Cambridge, Mass.: MIT Press, 2003), p. 313; Rafael del Villar, Alejandro Diaz de Leon, and Johanna Gil Hubert, "Regulation of Personal Data Protection and of Credit Reporting Firms: A Comparison of Selected Countries of Latin America, the United States, and the European Union," in *Credit Reporting Systems and the International Economy*, ed. Margaret J. Miller (Cambridge, Mass.: MIT Press, 2003), pp. 411, 425.
18. Evidence from forty industrial and developing countries indicates that when a country's legal system becomes better developed, the reliance on trade credit relative to other kinds of credit decreases. The World Bank, *World Development Report 2002*, p. 58.
19. This section relies heavily on Margaret J. Miller, "Foreword," "Introduction" and "Credit Reporting Systems around the Globe: The State of the Art in Public Credit Registries and Private Credit Reporting Firms" in *Credit Reporting Systems and the International Economy*, ed. Margaret J. Miller (Cambridge, Mass.: MIT Press, 2003), pp. vii–ix, 1–79.

20. Information on credit-reporting firms outside the United States is available at www.creditworthy.com.

21. Tullio Jappelli and Marco Pagano, "Public Credit Information: A European Perspective," in *Credit Reporting Systems and the International Economy*, ed. Margaret J. Miller (Cambridge, Mass.: MIT Press, 2003), pp. 93–97, 102.

22. "Asian Firms Seek Stamp of Approval from D&B," *Journal of Commerce*, December 17, 1998, p. 2A.

23. Response by a manager of a credit-reporting firm in China to a survey conducted by the author, September–October, 2000.

24. In the United States, Experian and Equifax primarily serve the consumer credit sector. It is not clear how direct a role the parent companies played in monitoring the quality of the information provided by their foreign subsidiaries and partners.

25. "Savvy Exporters Do Credit Checks," *Journal of Commerce*, May 3, 2000, p. 10.

26. Based on information on the Web sites of international credit reporting agencies linked to Creditworthy.com, www.creditworthy.com (2002).

27. The Web sites of Latin American credit agencies, accessible through www.creditworthy.com, warn about the restrictions on bank data.

28. Comments from a manager of a credit-reporting firm in Kenya, in response to a survey conducted by the author, September–October 2000.

29. Miller, "Credit Reporting Systems around the Globe," pp. 49–51.

Index

Adams, Charles Francis, 96
Adjustment bureaus, 196–197
Alexander Hamilton Institute, 177
ALIAC, 207
American Association of Public
  Accountants, 174, 182
American Bankers Association, 179
American Business Information Association,
  207
American Collection Agency, 63
American Institute of Accountants, 83
American Legal Association, 50
American Temperance Society, 103
American Trade Acceptance Council, 175
Amistad, 40, 45
Ashkenazi, Elliot, 125
Associated Trades Credit Exchange, 184
Atherton, Lewis, 49, 86, 106, 117
Attorneys, 22, 30, 31; as credit
  correspondents, 49–52, 85, 137, 145–
  146, 183

Baldwin, Roger Sherman, 54
Balleisen, Edward, 30, 32
Baltimore & Ohio (B&O), 83
Bank of England, 13, 19, 120
Bankruptcy, 95, 96–97, 124–125, 127,
  137, 196–198, 199–200, 231n58,
  231n61, 262n133. *See also* Failure
Banks, 16, 19, 24, 26, 27, 46, 55, 77, 82,
  99, 180, 181, 182, 183, 202, 203, 206,
  208, 216n58, 217n83, 244n5, 245n16,
  254n5, 257n44, 264n1
Baring Brothers (House of Barings), 25,
  37–38, 39, 70, 72, 76, 77

Beardsley v. Tappan, 58, 67, 71, 72, 73,
  108, 170
Bills of exchange, 9, 15, 17, 18–19, 20, 21,
  214n35
Birney, James G., 54
Black businesses, 2, 113, 115, 234n124,
  237n143, 237n144, 237n145.
Blackstone, William, 231n58
Boosterism, 28, 86, 105, 127, 128
Bradstreet agency, 3, 11, 157, 158;
  reference books, 3, 11–12, 65–68, 86,
  162, 164, 191; inclusiveness of coverage,
  65, 78, 158–159, 160–161; instructions
  to correspondents, 146, 160; financial
  information request form, 148–150,
  180–181; expansion of products and ser-
  vices, 163; and National Association of
  Credit Men, 176, 181, 182, 191–196
Bradstreet, John M., 65, 139, 158
Bradstreet, Milton, 65, 139, 158
Brock and Company, 166
Bulletin of the NACM, 178, 180, 188, 192,
  198
Bureau of Corporations, 179
Business Credit, 12, 204
Business education, 107

Cannon, James Graham, 180
Carnegie, Andrew, 107
Carson, Pirie, Scott, and Company 145
Chandler, Alfred, 178
Character, 1–2, 7, 36, 66–67, 81, 82,
  89–92, 114, 141, 153–156, 182, 199,
  248n60, 248–249n69
Chesapeake planters, 22–23